The Wilderness Within

Reflections on Leisure and Life

———————————

Third Edition

Daniel L. Dustin, PhD

Sagamore Publishing
Champaign, IL 61820

©2006 Sagamore Publishing L.L.C.
All rights reserved

Production Manager: Janet Wahlfeldt
Cover design: Janet Wahlfeldt
Cover photo: Elizabeth Carmel
www.ElizabethCarmel.com
Pen and ink drawings: Kathleen Dustin (Half Dome and Burton
Tower), Susan Driver (Boca Grande lighthouse)

ISBN: 1-57167-561-2
Library of Congress Catalog Card Number: 2006921450

Sagamore Publishing L.L.C.
804 N. Neil
Champaign, IL 61820

www.sagamorepub.com

Printed in the United States

10 9 8 7 6 5 4 3 2 1

For Carol

Contents

Acknowledgments

I would like to thank Sagamore Publishing for making this third edition of *The Wilderness Within* possible. Five essays from previous editions are reprinted here with permission from the following sources: San Diego State University's Institute for Leisure Behavior ("The World According to Gorp"), the Intermountain Leisure Symposium ("In Search of Rescue," "The Myth of Comfort," and "Inside, Outside, Upside Down: The Grand Canyon as a Learning Laboratory"), and the U.S. Forest Service ("Gardening as a Subversive Activity"). Two new essays are reprinted with permission from the University of Northern Iowa ("Is This Heaven?") and the U.S. Forest Service ("Mapping the Geography of Hope.")

Many people have influenced my thinking about wilderness, recreation, and leisure over the years. Among them are people I know only through the literature: Henry David Thoreau, George Perkins Marsh, John Muir, Robert Service, Bob Marshall, Aldo Leopold, Sigurd Olson, John McPhee, Wallace Stegner, Joseph Sax, and Garrett Hardin. Others I have had the pleasure to meet: Willi Unsoeld, Rick Ridgeway, Edward Abbey, David Brower, Roderick Nash, Lee Stetson, and Barry Lopez. Still others I count as my mentors, friends, and colleagues: Bev and Susan Driver, Ross Tocher, John Schultz, Leo McAvoy, Tom More, Larry Merriam, Tim Knopp, Rich Knopf, Rich Schreyer, Doug Wellman, Dan Williams, Janna Rankin, Arthur Frakt, Gene Lamke, Larry Beck, and Andrea Philips. I would like to think there is a little bit of all these people in what follows.

I also owe much to Emilyn Sheffield, Dana Zweibohmer, Tom Goodale, Geof Godbey, Jack Harper, Ingrid Schneider, my sons Andy and Adam, and my wife, Kathleen, for their friendship and support during the years that provided the grist for the 11 new essays in this edition.

Finally, I want to acknowledge the memory of my parents, Lucille and Derby, for whatever they did in my upbringing that allows me to look critically at myself without falling apart. Perhaps it was their modeling that we are never finished products, that there is always room for improvement, that we can and should strive to become more than we presently are. Perhaps it was also their modeling to forgive and forget.

Preface

In his wonderful little book, *A Guide for the Perplexed*, E. F. Schumacher organizes the ways we come to know the world around us into Four Fields of Knowledge. The First Field consists of our own feelings, which cannot be experienced directly by anyone but us. The Second Field consists of the feelings of others, feelings that we cannot experience directly. The Third Field consists of our own appearance, an appearance visible to everyone but ourselves. Finally, the Fourth Field consists of the appearances of others, appearances visible to all but those who display them.

While wisdom about the world is derived from learning in all Four Fields of Knowledge, Schumacher reasons that knowledge about the First Field, or self-knowledge, is a precondition to everything else. How can we empathize with the feelings of others (Field Two) if we have not examined our own feelings? How can we interpret how others see us (Field Three) if we have no sense of ourselves? And how can we begin to understand the larger exterior world (Field Four) until we come to grips with our own interior one?

The essays in this book are explorations in the First Field of Knowledge. They are about me from my perspective. Most of them are about journeys I've taken to places "out there," the exterior world of mountains, forests, deserts, and tundra. But in a more important sense they are about journeys I've taken "in here," in my interior world, a world invisible to you. Indeed, the fact that you cannot see what is going on inside my head is what compels me to write in the first place. I want to share with you what it is like to be me. But I also write from the conviction that in coming to know me better you will come to know yourself better as well.

I have added several new essays to this third edition. They represent my Florida years in the same way previous editions represent my California years. They are a mixture of adventure-based outdoor recreation themes and themes that flow out of everyday pastimes: visiting with friends, playing games, enjoying good food, listening to music, appreciating the landscape, connecting with family, and engaging in self-reflection. The new essays reflect what I have been thinking and learning as I have journeyed farther along my life's path.

Leisure is at the heart of what makes life worthwhile. When we are free to choose what we want to do, when we exercise that choice, and when we recognize that in doing so we are making the meaning of our lives, then, and only then, are we really living.

I should not talk so much about myself
if there were anybody else whom I knew as well.
Unfortunately, I am confined to this theme
by the narrowness of my experience.
—Thoreau

Part One—The California Years

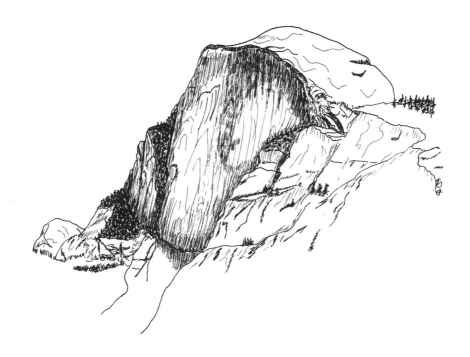

Chapter 1

IN SEARCH OF RESCUE

I have a close friend, a researcher with the United States Forest Service, who wondered out loud to me recently if we had not been condemned by our education to a life of unhappiness. I, too, wonder about that. We are both graduates of the University of Michigan, a campus that was a center of political protest during the 1960s in the name of peace, civil rights, and other social causes. Psychologically, we came of age at a time when it appeared as though the world's problems could be resolved by a global coming together and a reaffirmation of that which makes us humane beings. Our slogans reflected our idealism: "we shall overcome" and "give peace a chance." It was as though we were intoxicated with the prospects for humanity if only we could persuade those less enlightened than us to join in the march.

The years since Ann Arbor have had a sobering effect on both of us. Our continuing education has taught us that things are much more complicated than we ever imagined and that they are likely to become even more so. Those lofty prospects for humanity that we sang and chanted about so fervently back in the 1960s have given way to a new realism. Our attention now has turned to the management of complexity and coping, both at home and abroad, with irreconcilable differences.

For both of us, then, it is as if our education has played a cruel trick on us. Psychologically, we have been nurtured to hope for, perhaps even to expect, social unity, a consensus of some sort about what it means to live a good life. But our intellects have taken us down a different path. The resulting divergence between what we long for and what our ongoing education tells us is possible has precipitated this malaise, or what my friend has termed this inevitable unhappiness.

I begin with this personal reflection not because I think our situation is unique, but rather because I think it typifies the mindset of many Americans. For lack of a better term, and with apologies to Henry Winkler and company, I call it the "Happy Days" syndrome. We long for a future just like the past, but present realities make it impossible. We strive for clarity of purpose, commonly held values, and security for our children. But we must deal with contradictory purposes, conflicting values, and an age of immense insecurity when the fate of our children rests in the perspiring hands of nervous world leaders, all of whom have access to their own "buttons." Indeed, it is comforting to drift back to those images of malt shops, Fats Domino, and slow dancing.

Sooner or later, however, unless we want to live a life of perpetual escapism, we must come back to the present world, the world unfolding before us at this very moment, the world of contradictions, conflicts, and insecurity. For this is the world in which we must ultimately make our way. And it is in this world that we must somehow make our happy days, if indeed we are to have them.

Perhaps the best way to prepare ourselves for these uncertain times is by considering the possibility that it has never been otherwise. Is it not a fact that all we really have, and have ever had for that matter, is the precarious present moment, the moment that comes and goes even as I write about it? Is it not also a fact that what we call "memories" are really present recollections of past events, and that what we call "anticipation" is really a present imaging of what we expect a future event will be? Does it not then follow that despite our language, which suggests a past and a future, there is really nothing but the present unfolding of experience, that everything else is an illusion?

Is it not also reasonable, therefore, to suggest that living, by its very nature, is impermanent, unstable, and insecure? Attempts to make life more permanent, more stable, and more secure, are thus not only futile, they work against the human condition itself. Yet we try. It is as though we want to hold onto something that cannot be held. Just as running water, when cupped in the hands, stops running, so life, when held in check, loses its essence. To be alive is to be in motion, to be on the go, to be vulnerable. The wonder is not that this is so; the wonder is that, knowing this, we fight so hard against it. We try our hardest to insulate ourselves against life's insecurities. We take out insurance. We hedge our bets. We file lawsuits. Many of us even go so far as to not get involved, to sit on the sidelines, because the prospect of being hurt or failing is more terrifying than the prospect of not playing the game at all.

Why we choose to be this way I do not know. Perhaps it has something to do with our unspoken anxiety about death. In the absence of a deep and abiding faith that promises life everlasting, it is not surprising that so many of us do everything in our power to forestall that final breath. If we can't be saved by divine intervention, then we'll give most anything else a try; from vitamin supplements to artificial hearts. Some of us even give up smoking.

While I gather a certain amount of anxiety about death is healthy for the soul, it is the extremes to which people go to avoid that which is ultimately unavoidable that concern me. I am concerned because a preoccupation with the future and what might happen and what might go wrong gets in the way of being open to the present moment. It precludes living in the here and now. And that, if my earlier argument holds any water, means not really living at all.

There is, I believe, a lesson in this for us. It has been stated best by Alan Watts as the "Backwards Law"[1], or the law of reversed effort. Put simply, to live life fully is to let go of life completely. The Backwards Law reminds us that to cling to life in an effort to preserve it is to snuff it out. Hold your breath and you lose it. Take the risk out of life and you take the life out of life.

This lesson, although clear, is incredibly hard to benefit from. Its message runs counter to almost all of our accepted strategies for living. We have been brought up to believe that we should hold on tightly to those things we cherish most. This results in a possessive quality that permeates not only our attitudes toward our own lives but also our attitudes toward relationships with other people. A popular bumper sticker says it best: "If you love something, let it go. If it doesn't come back, hunt it down and kill it."

If we are to have any chance at happiness in this uncertain world, we must learn to embrace its insecurities, to give in to change, to celebrate the present moment. To do otherwise is to do battle with ourselves. We are as a wave moving forward to a distant shore. No matter how turbulent the sea, no matter how strong the urge to return to port, there is no turning back. Our happiness rests in our recognition of this fact of life and in our subsequent determination to enjoy the ride.

The notion, then, that we human beings have a "right to risk" is misleading. We have no choice in the matter. There is nothing but risk. What we do have a choice about is the way we deal with life's risks. We can delude ourselves, hide behind our fears, and pretend it just isn't so. Or we can confront the risks, announce our fears, and give it a go.

I prefer the latter choice. Moreover, I prefer to exercise it most in wilderness. To me, wilderness is the logical place, the ideal place, to marvel at life's unfolding, to live at life's edge. It is in wilderness that we can best discard the protective armor that shields us from life itself. It is in wilderness that we can best get down to earth, that we can best open up and receive the world around us. It is in wilderness that we can best rejoice in the here and now.

But the way wilderness is managed these days tends to undermine this opportunity. Wilderness is subdivided into zones, and wilderness recreationists are required to file backcountry trip itineraries indicating where they will be on any given day. Then, should something go wrong, they are searched for and, on occasion, rescued. These measures are taken in part to protect wilderness itself. But they are taken to protect wilderness recreationists as well. Wilderness managers, too, have been brought up to believe that we should hold on tightly to those things we cherish most. And wilderness recreationists are the beneficiaries of that upbringing. Or are they?

Remember the Backwards Law. To live life fully is to let go of life completely. Attempts to make wilderness less wild, to protect wilderness recreationists from the consequences of their mistakes or the quirks of nature, however humanitarian on the surface, work against living life fully. What remains is essentially illusory. Left unchecked, this kind of wilderness promises to end up strikingly similar to that portrayed by William Leitch in "Backpacking in 2078"[2]: electronic devices implanted in wild animals for shocking purposes should they impose a threat to people, and tracking devices attached to people for rescue purposes should they impose a threat to themselves. It will be wilderness where recreationists will likely be turned every which way but loose.

I ask you to consider a clear alternative to Leitch's future scenario, a scenario where all illusions would be stripped away to leave nothing save the individual and the present moment. We'll call it with horrifying clarity "no-rescue" wilderness,[3] and we'll place it far away in Alaska. Then we'll insist that people who choose to go there must assume all the risks, indeed embrace all the risks, and insist further that a government that would shelter them from themselves would be barred from doing so.

No-rescue wilderness would not be for everyone. It would not be for those who are busily trying to insulate themselves against life's bad bounces. Nor would it be for those who are reluctant to get involved in the game while the outcome is still in doubt. No, it would be for a different sort. No-rescue wilderness would be for people who want to breathe deeply of the precarious, precious present, for those who want to dance on the edge of life. It would be for strong people who recognize their weaknesses and weak people who recognize their strengths. It would be a place to savor the tenuous, fragile, temporary, changing, and fluid nature of life itself, a place to square off with reality.

Wilderness managers, while sympathetic to the spirit of this idea, have pointed out a myriad of problems that make it unworkable. Chief among them is the fact that most people would not want it that way. They would welcome a little help from a friend. Moreover, there are all those other issues—legal liability, ethical considerations, and the potential litter at the base of the cliff. Wilderness managers are concerned about what might happen, about what might go wrong in the future. And so it goes.

To say that this no-rescue wilderness proposal has not been well received would be an understatement. Some say it's ahead of its time. Others say it's behind its time. Of course, you and I know better, since there is no time other than the present. It's now or never, and it will always be that way. Such is the nature of our journey.

I don't know what else to say to convince you of my sincerity or my seriousness in this matter. So I'll leave you with the "George Gray" epitaph from Edgar Lee Masters' *Spoon River Anthology*. May it not at the end of your life befit you as well:

I have studied many times
The marble which was chiseled for me—
A boat with a furled sail at rest in a harbor.
In truth it pictures not my destination
But my life.

For love was offered me and I shrank from its
    disillusionment.
Sorrow knocked at my door, but I was afraid;
Ambition called to me; but I dreaded the chances.
Yet all the while I hungered for meaning in my
    life.

And now I know that we must lift the sail
And catch the winds of destiny
Wherever they drive the boat.
To put meaning in one's life may end in
    madness,
But life without meaning is the torture
Of restlessness and vague desire—
It is a boat longing for the sea and yet afraid.[4]

Chapter 2

THE WORLD ACCORDING
TO GORP

Henry David Thoreau said, "the mass of men lead lives of quiet desperation."[1] It's amazing. He didn't even know me. Recently, I was promoted into an office without windows. Can you imagine that? I teach about the outdoors. I write about the outdoors. I love the outdoors. But in my day-to-day existence I have only an Ansel Adams print, a Sierra Club calendar, and my sister's artwork on barrel stays to remind me of who I am and what I care about.

So I find it necessary from time to time to make a pilgrimage, to go back to the source of my concern and caring. This time it is California's John Muir Trail, a 210-mile thread along the backbone of the High Sierras connecting the summit of Mt. Whitney in the south with Yosemite Valley in the north. Of course, since I only decided to take this journey at the last minute, I am told I must start 30 miles south of Mt. Whitney. "It's the busy season," the permit ranger says matter-of-factly. "Space in the wilderness is hard to come by."

I take a fishing pole, a pipe, two hardcover books, a notebook, a small tent, and food for 18 days. I soon realize it's too much for my Camp Trails pack. Something has got to go. I take out several meals. Then I'm off.

I'm taking this walk alone. There is no one to catch up to or slow down for. I also have no one to share this with, or to praise or blame for the way I feel. I have to be responsible for myself. This could be revealing.

At first, it's hard to concentrate on anything other than the weight of my pack. The first several miles are uncomfortable. My heart is pounding. I experience shortness of breath. There is no turning back, though. I'm on a mission.

I stop for the day in mid afternoon and stretch out on my sleeping bag. The next thing I know it is three hours later. Apparently, I'm exhausted after six or seven miles on the trail. I consider the possibility that I've bitten off more than I can chew. "Ah, but a man's reach should exceed his grasp, or what's a heaven for?" I fall asleep trying to remember who said that.

Things start to fall into place the second day. I feel strong most of the walk, although my feet begin to throb as the day wears on. I still don't cover much ground. At the rate I'm going, it should take about 40 days to complete the trip.

In the evening I puff on my pipe. I'm trying to be a mountain man. The only problem is that the pipe goes out every 30 seconds. At this rate, I'll be out of matches in a week. Mountain men's pipes shouldn't go out on them.

My first dilemma concerns water. If you believe all the literature the rangers give you, giardia is on the rampage. "Boil your water for at least five minutes," they say. At that rate, I'd be out of fuel in a week, too. No matches, no fuel. Touché. Finally, I decide if you can't drink this water, you might as well pack it in. Nuclear threat indeed! What kind of future do we have if we can't drink the water?

This country is absolutely beautiful. I'd like to bring everybody I know out here. It sure has an effect on me. But, of course, if everybody took me up on my offer, it wouldn't be the same. And I know this isn't everyone's idea of a good time. Then again, "good time" seems to trivialize what I'm having. It's more than that. Most of the time I'm huffing and puffing. It has the flavor of a struggle more than a "good time." It's work.

Ah, but the hurting feels so good! I think this all must have something to do with the difference between comfort and pleasure. I live a comfortable existence. But it is hardly pleasurable. It's the change of pace, the novelty of all this that makes it so pleasurable. Even as I walk it's hard work. But when I stop to rest or drink or munch on gorp, I undergo a transformation. I am able to look around and absorb the beauty. Amidst the struggle of the hike there are time-outs when I am especially aware of the trees, the flowers, the streams, the sky, and the wildlife. But it is only when I pause in the walk that I seem to be really sensitive to these things.

The wilderness is my well of souls. I'm stripped down to the weight on my back. There is nothing much left but me and my wits. Everything is laid open for me and the wilderness to see. I am not cushioned by the civilized world. There is no one to make excuses for me. There is no system to blame things on. My assets stand out. My liabilities announce themselves. Strengths I was unaware of surface at opportune times. Weaknesses have their moments, too. But there's no denying them or hiding from them or running away from them. I am stuck with myself.

I like going up better than coming down; especially the passes. Their negotiation demands honest work. If you stick to it, if you persevere, you make it eventually. There are no tricks or gimmicks. It's just one step after another. Coming down is a different story. Gravity teases you. If you aren't careful, you begin to think you can fly down. But then the rocks trip you, or you twist an ankle or stub a toe. I think going up is for those who like the struggle. Coming down is for those who are looking for the easy way out.

It is 5:30 in the morning. I am awakened by the sound of a bear rummaging through my backpack, which is leaning against the base of a nearby tree. I fumble for my glasses and zip open the tent fly in time to see a large black bear shinnying up the trunk toward the limb where my food supply is counterbalanced in two stuff sacks. "Show some compassion!" I shout. "I'm going all the way to Yosemite!" Unmoved, the bear goes about its business. "You're just like all the others!" I chortle. "You don't care about me as a person! You only care about what you can get from me!" Empty-pawed, the bear drops down to the ground and lopes away to find better pickings. After five days in the wilderness, I'm having a one-sided conversation with an animal. Clearly, I'm beginning to feel at home.

As I start up the trail, I hear a helicopter overhead. Thinking that perhaps the President is in need of a new National Park Service director, I decide to stick around and see if it's coming for me. The helicopter is set down about 100 yards from where I camped, and a crewman runs across the meadow to another tent. Always concerned about my fellow backpackers, and wary of the possibility of a high-tech heist, I take off my pack and go to investigate. In a few minutes, I find myself at the foot of a stretcher assisting in the evacuation of a woman who is having a gall bladder attack. I can't believe it—Dan Dustin, a chief proponent of no-rescue wilderness, aiding and abetting a search and rescue operation. No photographs, please. I consider dropping my end of the stretcher once or twice as a sign of protest.

There are lots of people on the trail today. If I were Edward Abbey, I'd call this the "John Muir Freeway." But I don't resent the others being here. They've certainly earned their way into this wilderness. More power to them. Who was it that said "the woods are overrun and sons-a-bitches like me are half the problem"?

I'm paying attention to things here that I never pay attention to at home. My life has been reduced to decisions about making sure I have enough water to drink, figuring out how far I want to walk each day, deciding where I want to camp, choosing what I want to eat, and rationing matches for my pipe. Everything is very basic and routine. Things I pay attention to at home aren't important here—the mortgage, the mail, the Middle East. Again, it seems to be the contrast, the change of pace, that makes it all so engaging.

I thought for a while this morning that my body was going to give out on me, to go on strike. It turned out to be a work slow-down. I think the problem is the freeze-dried food. It's getting to me. Thoughts of fresh fruit and vegetables are working their way into my head—sweet corn (it's August for God's sake) and tomatoes and melons. I'd better stop. I'll be suicidal. I have to go at least another week before I can entertain these thoughts.

I want to bring my sons, Andy and Adam, here someday. If I could just tear them away from video games. I don't know how to generate a love for the outdoors in them. I don't want to push them. Perhaps I'll do what my dad did. He taught me to fish early in life, and then he took me to the edge of the Bob Marshall Wilderness in Montana and turned me loose. The rest, as they say, is history.

I'm camping tonight in Evolution Basin. I'm looking up at Mt. Darwin, Mt. Huxley, and several other peaks named after prominent evolutionary thinkers. How strange. I am not a particularly religious person, but I find it hard to believe that all this beauty, all this perfection, is the result of some cosmic quirk, some earthly indigestion that fractured the strata to create the Sierra Nevada. I find it hard to believe that this wasn't premeditated by a Great Premeditator, whoever she, he, or it might be. To think otherwise is to acknowledge that great beauty can be created as easily by Bill Russell bouncing basketballs dipped in paint on a canvas as a da Vinci agonizing over a Mona Lisa. Evolution perhaps, but I can't help but continue to wonder whose idea was that?

I went almost 20 miles today. My head felt good, my back felt good, my legs felt good, and my feet felt good. I was moving. At about the nine-mile mark, I saw a blur of fur. It could have been a deer or a bear or a chipmunk. I don't know. I was in overdrive. I'm just thankful the good Lord gave me the strength and the ability, and that I was able to put it all together out there today. I'm not taking anything away from the wilderness. It put up one heck of a scrap. It was just my day. One more thing: "Hi, mom!"

Why am I doing this? Why does anyone get out of bed in the morning? To go to work to earn money to survive. But do I have to do this to survive? Well, certainly not in any physical sense. The value of this, it seems to me, must be in my mind. This experience enhances my quality of life by giving me a different perspective from which to ponder the same questions I ponder in my everyday life. Who am I? What am I doing here? How do I fit in? What should I be doing with my life? But why is wilderness so special for this kind of reflection? Why not a park bench? Why not a slot machine stool in Las Vegas? I don't have an answer.

Is wilderness friendly, hostile, or indifferent? I think it must be indifferent. Other than the bears and fat marmots who want my food, I don't think the wilderness gives one damn about what happens to me. But why, if that's the case, should I care so much about it? Oh, the pain of unrequited love!

I'm beginning to think this is all symbolic. I'm beginning to think wilderness is a metaphor. We make of it, like everything else in life, what we will. For some, wilderness is a place to search for good wood; for others, good fishing. For me, wilderness is a place to search for answers that elude me in the rest of my life.

There is a sense of immortality here. I think the rivers will flow forever. I think the trees will grow forever. I think the mountain passes will have their ups and downs forever. There are never ending patterns here. There are never ending cycles. The wilderness endures. And, like everything else that has stood the test of time, it has lessons to teach. For those who take the time to watch and listen, wilderness offers wisdom.

There is also peace and quiet. Just me and my thoughts and a little breeze to keep me company. And now the sun is going down. The sky is a brilliant combination of yellow and blue and white. Mt. Ritter and Mt. Banner dominate the horizon 30 miles to the north in the Ansel Adams Wilderness. It's so beautiful I want to cry. For a few moments everything I see is perfect. Somehow it gives me hope that there can be perfect moments in other dimensions of life as well—between people, between nations. Tonight, the wilderness is setting an example.

It's dark now. I feel isolated and alone. But soon there is a jet overhead, a moving light among the stars. It's so easy to imagine the plane is heading for San Francisco and the flight attendant is having a last call, since "we'll soon be landing." Civilization is so near and yet so far.

And, oh, the mysteries overhead! Just when I think I'm approaching a measure of understanding of the meaning of wilderness in my life, I look up and realize that to solve the mystery of the wilderness would be only a beginning, a first step in making sense out of all the rest. I can't believe how little I know.

I'm about ready for this walk to end. I want to see my children; I miss them dearly. I'm glad I've done this, though. I'm glad I've taken the time to be on my own for a while. I'm 38 years old. Bob Marshall died when he was 38. You never really know how much time you have to do the things you want to do. Like the band Chicago said, "Does anybody really know what time it is?"

There is something special about a journey, an odyssey, a pilgrimage that challenges you, that tests your limits. And then the realization that you're going to make it, that even though you've bitten off more than you can chew, you're going to be able to chew it after all. It's an affirmation of your ability to break barriers, to forge ahead, to grow. It's an affirmation of your potential as a human being.

Maybe that's what is so special about wilderness to me. It offers the kind of challenge that is increasingly rare, a paring down to the essentials, a stripping away of the civilized veneer that shields us all so that we can once again experience the basic nature of our existence. This kind of outing allows us to appreciate what we have accomplished as a species; the building of a comfortable, stable, and predictable life. Hopefully, wilderness will always exist as a barometer, as a gauge against which we can place these human achievements in their proper perspective.

But there's more to it than that. Although I have not yet been able to describe it, or define it, or even come close to putting my finger on it, wilderness is much more than a stage for my little soliloquy. There is something else going on. There is a strong sense of affinity here. There is a strong sense of bonding. I do believe I am part of the wilderness. I do believe I belong here. But I can't tell you why. I don't know if this feeling of kinship is rooted in my psychic history or in my imagination. But I do know I feel it. As I begin the last day of my walk, there is a tune I can't get out of my head. It is "Amazing Grace," and with it come visions of a movie by the same name I saw some time ago in the Lodgepole Visitor Center in Sequoia National Park. I think that tune and its associated images of giant sequoias, sparkling water, sunlight, and the High Sierra express the essence of wilderness for me. How ironic that sight and sound should be the vehicles for my understanding. I am a writer. But words fail me in this matter. Wilderness remains a mystery to my intellect, if not to my heart.

How, then, do I feel as I take the last steps of my journey? I am at the same time happy and sad. I am happy because I will soon be among friends again. I am, after all, gregarious, a social being. But I am also sad because I'm leaving behind another kind of friend, an environment that has served as a mirror unto myself. The Sierra Nevada is called the Range of Light. It certainly has enhanced my vision. It has forced me to take a closer look at myself. And for that I will be forever grateful.

I am also humbled by this walk. I feel as though I've been permitted to get through it all unscathed, that there has been a benevolent force at work. I can't explain it, but I do feel it. There were so many times when I could have, when I should have taken a tumble. But I didn't. I feel as though I've been cradled. And now I feel as though I am being delivered. By whom or what, I have no idea.

Finally, I feel confident and optimistic. I'm looking forward to the future. I'm rejuvenated. As I charge down into Yosemite Valley, a young day-hiker asks me how it's going. After 18 days, after 10 passes, after 240 miles of ups and downs, I hear myself say, "Okay." But that's only on the outside. On the inside, it's another story. On the inside, Mark Twain is doing all the talking for me. "Whoo-oop! I'm the old original iron-jawed, brass-mounted, copper-bellied corpse-maker from the wilds of Arkansaw! Look at me! I'm the man they call Sudden Death and General Desolation! Sired by a hurricane, dam'd by an earthquake, half-brother to the cholera, nearly related to the smallpox on the mother's side! Look at me! I take nineteen alligators and a bar'l of whiskey for breakfast when I'm in robust health, and a bushel of rattlesnakes and a dead body when I'm ailing. I split the everlasting rocks with my glance, and I squelch the thunder when I speak! Whoo-oop! Stand back and give me room according to my strength! Blood's my natural drink, and the wails of the dying is music to my ear. Cast your eye on me, gentlemen, and lay low and hold your breath, for I'm 'bout to turn myself loose!"[2]

Chapter 3

THE MYTH OF COMFORT

I was recently invited to debate the idea of no-rescue wilderness with several search and rescue professionals. I shuddered. After all, until now my writing about the idea of no-rescue wilderness had been just that—writing. But now there would be people present who put their lives on the line for others. Would they find me contemptible for what I had to say? Would they want to clean my clock? I fought off the urge to take out some insurance.

Instead, I went looking for another kind of help. I traveled to New England. Maybe if I walked in the footsteps of Thoreau I would somehow sense what needed to be said. Just as the cold is transmitted through the soles of one's feet to chill the entire body, perhaps the law of conduction would channel the essence of Thoreau up from the soil to inspire my entire being. It was worth a try. Unfortunately, it didn't work. The only thing to wind its way upward through the soles of my feet was the heat of an unusually warm New England day.

Disappointed in my footgear, I headed back to San Diego. On the way, however, the Boeing 767 touched down briefly in St. Louis, Missouri. It was 103 degrees outside. The steward offered his condolences to those exiting the plane, and then he turned his attention to the remaining San Diego-bound passengers nestled snugly in the air-conditioned seats. Our dinner choices would be chicken, beef, or shrimp creole. Fancying myself as a risk-taker, I opted for the last one. Then, as we winged our way westward, I thought of Joseph Sax[1] and how just as the automobile insulates people from really experiencing the national parks so did this new jet insulate me from really experiencing a 103-degree day in St. Louis, Missouri. I chuckled smugly to myself as I bit into the shrimp.

Yech! The rubbery excuse for seafood jolted me. Then, déjà vu—something out of the past, something I'd read. What was it?

Something about a man biting into what was supposed to be a sausage only to find it filled with fish. What was it he had said of his experience? Something like, "it gave me the feeling that I'd bitten into the modern world and discovered what it is really made of . . . everything slick and streamlined, everything made out of something else."[2]

And that, in turn, reminded me of a piece I had just read in *Newsweek*. By next year, "visitors to the Grand Canyon will not even need to venture into the park to 'experience' its splendors. At a $5 million complex going up less than a mile from the park boundary, they can view a 30-minute film of the canyon's four seasons in a 100-foot-high theater. Next door, 32 tourists at a time can brave a five-minute simulated raft ride through four feet of artificially swooshed waters, riding rafts just like the ones real river runners use. 'We'll show visitors what they can't see by standing on the rim and looking in,' says . . . a spokesman for FORMA Properties, which is planning similar thrill centers outside Yosemite and Yellowstone."[3]

What was that book, anyway? And who wrote it? Then it hit me! I remembered. The book was called *Coming Up For Air*. And the author—and, just as suddenly, I knew exactly what needed to be said.

You see, in 1949 that same British author penned another work of fiction in which he predicted the failure of a society characterized by warmth, comfort, and the absence of strain. That society failed because however appetizing on the surface, once bitten into it was inherently distasteful to a human being. The author, of course, was George Orwell. And the book was *Nineteen Eighty Four*.[4]

No, I am not suggesting that the kind of life portrayed in Orwell's fiction mirrors the world we live in today (tempting as it is). But I do wish to direct your attention briefly to one of the principal themes of Orwell's book—the myth of comfort.

It was Orwell's contention that while human beings pursue comfort in the name of pleasure, having attained it for any length of time they actually find it painful. Guy Murchie underscores this point in his book *The Seven Mysteries of Life* when he adds, "of course there must be millions of people, particularly in Earth's more materialistic and complacent societies, who reject the need for . . . any kind of serious struggle in life. . . . Many of them no doubt would love . . . conscious life to be really just a bed of roses—roses without thorns of course—and they imagine they would be happy to loll in thornless roses forever if they actually got the chance. But any sensible person could tell you that . . . it is certain (assuming they possessed a streak of humanity) that the lolling would get so deadly dull within a week that they would yearn for something to break the monotony: anything, even if it hurt."[5]

That which makes life interesting to human beings are the contrasts, the conflicts encountered. That which makes life challenging to human beings are the problems to be solved. That which makes life enjoyable to human beings are the struggles after all. Remove the contrasts and conflicts, remove the problems—indeed, remove the struggles—and you remove the sources of life's interest, challenge, and joy. You find comfort turned into discomfort. You find pleasure turned into pain.

Murchie tells us that, ". . . the human soul thrives on a challenge or a problem and, once it is stretched by struggling with any sort of adversity, it can never shrink all the way back to its original dimensions. And so it grows bigger."[6] Eliminate the adversity, eliminate the risk, and while in the name of comfort you may save the body, you sacrifice the soul. George Orwell understood this. It is no accident, then, that "the worst punishment in 1984 is to be compelled to live."[7]

If you are committed to comfort, if you are committed to the belief that the only good recreation is safe recreation, if you are committed to protecting recreationists from themselves, you must therefore consider the possibility that you are impeding the growth of the human spirit. You must consider the possibility that you are doing a disservice to humanity, however good your intentions.

Moreover, I urge you to reconsider what seems to be the corrupt nature of the ideal of comfort itself. Orwell has illustrated dramatically for us how uncomfortable a comfortable society can be. Life, it seems, is more characteristically governed by what Murchie calls the "polarity principle." I know of no better expression of this principle than the thoughts of Willi Unsoeld and Tom Hornbein on the summit of Mt. Everest. Having reached the pinnacle, having conquered the mountain, "Willi and Tom did not try to talk. They were full of understanding beyond understanding. They turned off the oxygen and stood looking down on the world. Within the beauty of the moment they felt loneliness. Within the roar of the wind they felt silence. Within the glory they felt fear, not for their lives, but for the unknowns that weighed down on them. Within the triumph, they felt disappointment that this, only this, was Everest, the summit of their dreams. They knew that there were higher summits still if they could only see them."[8] Just as the answer to every question includes a new question, just as the solution to every problem includes a new problem, just as the conquest of every mountain includes a new mountain to be climbed, so must we realize that safeguarding recreationists includes new dangers, while allowing them to experience danger includes new life.

What, then, do I want? I want recreation land managing agencies to reassess their commitment to the goal of providing a system of safe recreation opportunities. I want them to work proactively to expand opportunities for choice. I want them to promote independent functioning in the citizens they serve. Finally, to that end, I want them to sanction the right to risk in wilderness in its ultimate sense. I want these things not in the name of comfort, which is a myth, but in the name of struggle, which is the stuff of life itself.

Fortunately, we do not live in an Orwellian society. On the contrary, if you put much stock in *Megatrends*, our culture is moving in the opposite direction; from institutional help to self-help, from representative democracy to participatory democracy, from either/ or options to multiple options.[9] Are recreation land managing agencies to be dragged along reluctantly in this current of societal change? Or are they to lead the way?

If, as Naisbitt argues, Americans are beginning to disengage from their institutional dependencies and are relearning the ability to grow on their own, then I believe our government has an obligation to provide them with the room. We cannot guarantee human growth. That is a matter of individual responsibility. But we can guarantee the environment to nourish it. And if we are to extend true freedom to the citizenry, we must respect their right to succeed and fail. Such freedom is, indeed, a risky proposition. But I, for one, would not have it any other way.

Chapter 4

THE WILDERNESS WITHIN: REFLECTIONS ON A 100-MILE RUN[1]

❝ Climb the mountains and get their good tidings. Nature's peace will flow into you as sunshine flows into trees. The winds will blow their own freshness into you, and the storms their energy, while cares will drop off like autumn leaves.❞[2] All right, John Muir! Show me the way.

I can't believe I'm actually doing this. I can't believe it's finally happening. I've invested so many hours, so many days, so many weeks, so many months into this moment. I've invested so many miles. Now I'm on my way. I'm running across the Sierra Nevada.

I started out at the base of Sequoia National Park's General Sherman Tree. That was no coincidence. The General Sherman Tree is the largest living thing on Earth. Later on, when I run out of fuel, when my glycogen gauge reads "zero," when I begin to experience the pain of burning muscle, I'll draw on the strength of that colossal soulmate, and I'll persevere. You've heard of carbohydrate loading. Well, I inspiration loaded.

In my fanny pack I have a polypropylene shirt, a small water bottle, a Baby Ruth candy bar, a packet of Gatorade, a flashlight, Vaseline, aspirin, and Kleenex. All the comforts of home.

I'm running these first six miles on the highway through the Giant Forest. At Crescent Meadow, a place John Muir called the "gem" of the Sierra, I'll pick up the High Sierra Trail and head east 71 miles to the summit of Mt. Whitney. Then I'll do the last 23 miles to Lone Pine by way of Whitney Portal. If all goes according to plan, I'll finish the run in 24 hours. If all doesn't, perhaps the run will finish me.

I'm here because "I [wish] to live deliberately, to front only the essential facts of life, and see if I [can] not learn what it [has] to teach, and not, when I [come] to die, discover that I [have] not lived. . . . I [want] to live deep and suck out all the marrow of life, to live so sturdily and Spartan-like as to put to rout all that [is] not life, to cut a broad swath and shave close, to drive life into a corner, and reduce it to its lowest terms."[3] Thank you, Henry David Thoreau.

I'm running because I have to. There is so much to work through. There is so much to learn. If I were to walk, I would not be able to get where I want to go. I would come up short. But running makes it possible to get there from here. Aristotle said it best when he defined motion as "the mode in which the future belongs to the present . . . the joint presence of potentiality and actuality." By running, I can get to that place I would not otherwise know. I can transcend barriers that have held me back so far. I can break new ground.

Besides, I need to practice. I'm the real-world equivalent of the pilot, Orr, in the novel *Catch-22*.[4] Remember him? Everybody thought he was crazy for crash-landing his plane in the Mediterranean all the time; crazy, that is, until they heard he had crash-landed safely in Sweden, free at last from the madness of a world at war. Well, I'm getting accustomed to running across national parks now so that when they hike those entrance fees I'll still be able to get my fill.

> *This land is your land, this land is my land,*
> *From California to the New York islands.*
> *From the Redwood Forests to the Gulf Stream waters,*
> *This land was made for [those who pay]!*

I can feel the extraneous matter peeling away. Just like these exfoliated domes. As I "settle [myself] and work and wedge [my] feet downward through the mud and slush of opinion, and prejudice, and tradition, and delusion, and appearance, that alluvia which covers the globe, through Paris and London, through New York and Boston and Concord, through Church and State, through poetry and philosophy and religion, till [I] come to a hard bottom and rocks in place, which [I] can call reality, and say, This is . . . "[5]

Kaweah Gap is. Twenty miles east of Crescent Meadow, it is 10,700 feet of reality, of hard bottom and rocks in place. The problem with reality, of course, is you have to deal with it. (Well, at least some folks do.) But this is what I wanted, my world reduced to its simplest terms, my challenge laid out before me in the clearest language, mile after mile. Simply a test of me. A matter of looking the dragon in the eye and mustering the courage to move ahead, one foot in front of the other, a straightforward and honest task, an opportunity to be seized.

I take water whenever I find it. It is my lifeblood. I can feel its regenerative power as it flows through my body. Like a wilted flower, I perk up when I splash myself, when I water myself. There is no more beautiful sound when you're thirsty than that of an unexpected stream up ahead. There is no more beautiful sight than that of cascading water high above the trail coming down to greet you. Nature's drinking fountains. A run like this, at the minimum, is an important reminder of water's primacy in the order of things.

See these? The Australian Olympic coach, Percy Cerutty, calls them "forelegs." When things are clicking, when all four limbs are in synch, we revert back to an earlier time. "Running well, we affirm our kinship with other mammals. Our senses become sharper, our motives purer. Gray areas disappear. Life rushes out to meet us in bright primary colors. We run for our lives. If only we could remember: the terror of flight, the triumph of pursuit, the ache of distance, the fulfillment of approach."[6]

When I started this run, I felt kinship with the deer. I pranced the first several miles. At Bearpaw Meadow, I romped through a gauntlet of wet ferns, each of them slapping me gently on the behind, each of them urging me on. Going up Kaweah Gap brought out the badger in me, the hardheaded tenacious side. Now, working my way up to the Chagoopa Plateau, it's other critters. Most recently the fool's hen.

Any time you're in something for the long haul, there are moments when your vision fails you, when you forget what it is that attracted you to the challenge in the first place. Whether it's a job, a relationship, or a long distance run, these are the dangerous moments. If you don't regain your perspective, if you don't come back to your senses, you risk cashing it all in for some short-term relief. Then you regret it:

When you're lost in the wild, and you're scared as a child,
    And Death looks you bang in the eye,
And you're sore as a boil, it's according to Hoyle
    To cock your revolver and die.
But the Code of a Man says: 'Fight all you can,'
    And self-dissolution is barred.
In hunger and woe, oh, it's easy to blow . . .

It's the hell-served-for-breakfast that's hard.
   'You're sick of the game!' Well, now, that's a shame.
You're young and you're brave and you're bright.
   'You've had a raw deal!' I know—but don't squeal,
Buck up, do your damnedest, and fight.
   It's the plugging away that will win you the day,
So don't be a piker old pard! Just draw on your grit; it's so easy to
    quit:
It's the keeping-your-chin-up that's hard.

It's easy to cry that you're beaten—and die;
   It's easy to crawfish and crawl;
But to fight and to fight when hope's out of sight
   Why, that's the best game of them all!
And though you come out of each grueling bout,
   All broken and beaten and scarred,
Just have one more try—it's dead easy to die,
   It's the keeping-on-living that's hard.[7]

Ah, Robert Service. You wouldn't think I'd be inspired by his poetry. He wasn't like John Muir or Bob Marshall or other wilderness visionaries. Service was cut from a different cloth. He was a bank teller who dreamed of doing larger-than-life kinds of things, too. But he fell short. He once tried to hike from New York City to New Orleans, but he cashed it all in for a train ticket. Disappointed in himself, Service headed for the Yukon and a fresh start. Once there, he settled for writing about characters who were larger than life. But he, himself, was limited.

I'm beginning to realize I'm more of the ilk of Robert Service than that of either John Muir or Bob Marshall. Maybe that's why I like his poetry. At least he could laugh at himself. As the miles wear on, my limitations are becoming more and more evident, too. I think I knew that would be the case before I started. I think that's why I chose a route without a train station.

The midway point in the run does not bring the uplift in spirit I anticipated. Instead of feeling good about the fact that the majority of the miles are now behind me, I am depressed by the fact that I have a similar amount yet to go. Instead of feeling good about the fact that the next 10 miles are on a relatively flat stretch along the Kern River, I am depressed by the fact that I must resist the temptation of the Kern River Hot Springs if I am to go on.

Instead of rejoicing in the fact that I am well on my way to reaching the goal I set for myself, I am mad at myself for having set such a ridiculous goal in the first place. Clearly, I have an attitude problem.

This journey is not exactly unfolding the way I thought it would. I expected it to be a celebration, a dance with the wilderness. But it's beginning to take an ominous turn. Instead of probing outward for connectedness, my psyche is focused inward. It is time for self-scrutiny, for self-doubt. Nightfall doesn't help matters.

What's going on here? Is this a midlife crisis? Fighting your newly sensed mortality? Trying to trim the waistline? Rewinding the old ticker? Impressing the ladies? Bought any Grecian Formula 16 lately? Just who are you kidding, anyway? It's after midnight, for God's sake! You ought to be home in San Diego in bed, falling asleep to *The Tonight Show*. You ought to be acting your age.

Whether you make it or not, the fact of the matter is running 100 miles across a mountain range doesn't prove a thing. If you succeed, it's only because your fear of failure overpowered your good sense to treat your body with respect. Finishing the run would be nothing more than Tarzan beating his chest. Big deal. It's macho. It's hollow. It's hype.

You're a "nature faker," Dustin. Wilderness is not meant to be run through. You don't run through museums, do you? You are a defiler of wilderness. You are committing sacrilege for the sake of self-aggrandizement. Stop it now. If not for yourself, then for Sigurd Olson and Aldo Leopold and all those others who actually care about wilderness.

Just what are you trying to prove, anyway? Do you honestly think that by pulling this off you can purge all the mistakes you've made in your life? That's it, isn't it? This is an act of exorcism. You think that this accomplishment will wipe the slate clean, that you will be remembered for this one feat, that everyone will forget all the other blunders. You are divorced, Dustin. You have hurt people. You are flawed. Learn to live with it.

The real long distance runners are all around you. They're your parents, who have persevered through 50 years of ups and downs to sustain their marriage. They're your neighbors, who show their children unconditional love. They're your own sons, who think the world of you despite your selfishness. They are the ones who understand the meaning of endurance. They are the ones you could stand to learn from.

You are so shallow. You see this run as some sort of cleansing, as an act of purification, as a way of expunging your accumulated shame. Do you really think you can sweat away all the wrongdoing, that you can huff and puff away the unwanted past? Do you really think that at the end of all this you will be redeemed, that you will walk more upright, that you will be a better person?

Come on. Nothing will change. Nothing. You will come out of this the same stumbler, the same bumbler, you were to begin with. You'll be exhausted, sore, and hungry. But a warm bath, some food in your stomach, and a good night's sleep will bring you back to normal. You will be your old inadequate self again. You'll need to prove yourself once more. You'll be back to square one. Ah, the circle of life. You will have run 100 miles for nothing.

Why not put an end to this silliness and invest your energy in something useful? Be a Big Brother. Volunteer in a soup kitchen. Anything but this pitiful self-flagellation. This isn't worth the price of admission, let alone a Golden Eagle Passport. How many people would be foolish enough to pay five dollars to run across the Sierra Nevada, anyway?

I'm being too hard on myself. I have to lighten up, regain my perspective, gather my wits about me. I've got to remember why I wanted to do this in the first place. There must have been a good reason. Think, Dan.

It was to have been an exercise in self-discipline, a year of sacrifice, of 30-, 40-, 50-, 60-, and 70-mile weeks. It was to have been an exercise in delayed gratification. Pay now, play later. Put the body through what it could but would not choose to do of its own accord. It was to have been a test of the wisdom in "The Tortoise and the Hare," an exercise in economy, pace, and self-control. It was to have been a personal validation of the adage "a journey of a 1,000 miles. . . ." It was to have been a lesson that would benefit me throughout my life.

But it was not meant to be an act of machismo. Far from it. The whole point of this, the beauty of it, was that if I could do it, anyone could. It would prove that even Robert Service types could call on other qualities—dedication, commitment, stick-to-itiveness—to overcome their limitations. It would prove that within each of us is the capacity to accomplish more than we thought humanly possible, if only we'd try.

It wasn't meant to be done at the expense of wilderness. On the contrary, it was meant to be done in the company of wilderness. It was meant to be done among friends. What better place? What better acquaintances to share in the quest than those who can relate: the deer to the running, the marmots to scrambling over the rocks, the eagles to the hard-earned views. It was to have been an expression of unity, of oneness with all things.

When running, I become part of all that I run through. I die unto myself:

> The mountain, I become part of it . . .
> The herbs, the fir tree,
> I become part of it,
> The morning mists,
> The clouds, the gathering waters,
> I become part of it.
> The sun that sweeps across the earth,
> I become part of it.
> The wilderness, the dew drops, the pollen . . .
> I become part of it.[8]

We forget the Earth runs, too; continuously, from west to east, just like me. The wilderness runs with it. I am in harmony with nature, not in opposition to it. I am going with the flow. I am giving in to it. This run, when all is said and done, is an act of surrender.

What was it Scott Momaday said? "He was alone and running on. All of his being was concentrated in the sheer motion of running on, and he was past caring about the pain. Pure exhaustion laid hold of his mind, and he could see at last without having to think."[9] By giving in, the pain has lost its sting. What I started out fighting, I now embrace. I no longer feel the knife-like stabs in my legs. I am now one big ache, soon to become numb. As morning comes, I could care less. After 22 hours on the trail, I still must ascend Mt. Whitney.

What was it about that General Sherman Tree? I feel as though I have nothing left. How to say it politely? I am spent. I move on because I don't know what else to do. A creature of habit. I must endure for the sake of the Free World, for America. Anything to force myself to keep moving. Anything to divert attention away from my quadriceps.

I am now kin to the possum belly-up at the side of the road. "Why did the chicken cross the street?" my eight-year-old gleefully asks. "To show the possum it could be done." Where does he get his sense of humor? If something happened to me on this run, he'd turn it into a joke within a week. He did it after the space shuttle *Challenger* accident. He'd do it after mine. It would be all over the playgrounds of Northmont Elementary. "Why did the chicken cross the Sierra Nevada?" Adam Dustin. Wise beyond his years. He knows the show must go on. But I will not be fodder for his comedy act.

I'll show the little bugger.

Storm clouds overhead. Magnificent and terrifying. Magnificent because of their swiftness, their energy, their electricity. Terrifying because I'm exposed. They are waiting for the right instant to unload, to remind all below of the power above. At first, I welcome the drops, a refreshing shower on the switchbacks. But the rain soon turns to hail, and, like my relatives, the rodents, I look for the nearest rock to crawl under. There, in the company of a furry little pika, I burrow in. I wait and watch nature's fireworks. Thunder and lightning.

After 15 or 20 minutes, I peek out to see white fluffy clouds mixed with blue sky. High above me at Trail Crest, I can see snow. Fearing hypothermia, I push on.

Here and now, Dan. Put everything else out of your mind. One step at a time. Don't look up. Don't look down. Concentrate on the next foot placement. Don't even think about how far you have to go. Chip away. Immerse yourself. Savor each moment. Lose yourself in it. Forget who you are. Forget where you are. Find the rhythm. Find the pattern. Your breathing. Your heartbeat. Make a chant out of it. A mantra. There is no beginning. There is no end. There is only now. You are motion. Pure and simple. The embodiment of potentiality and actuality. The future is present. Like a butterfly, you are floating effortlessly, gracefully upward. Believe it. It's true. You are there: 14,594 feet above sea level, atop Mt. Whitney, the highest point in the contiguous 48 states. Go ahead and say it. You've earned the right. "It's all downhill from here."

This was supposed to have been a euphoric moment, a peak experience, the apex of the run. But such is not the case. I consider jumping for its dramatic effect. "He probably thought he could fly," they'd say. "He probably thought he was taking a shortcut to Lone Pine." For all the significance of this event, it leaves something to be desired. It's a bittersweet moment, almost anticlimactic. Or am I just too tired to care?

The problem with a challenge of this magnitude is that it requires so much attention, so much concentration, so much dedication to succeed, that so much else is missed along the way. Anytime you strive to do the extraordinary, you block out other things that also give meaning, purpose, and joy to life. In my case, I have missed much of the beauty of the High Sierra because I have been preoccupied with my next step. Now, as I begin to weigh the costs and benefits of my striving, I am haunted by the question, "Was it worth it?"

They say we should do things in moderation, that we should seek out some sort of balance in life. But if we all adhered to that proposition, who would tackle the really difficult tasks? Who would challenge the outer limits, the frontiers of human accomplishment? If the cause is worthy, we must have people who are willing to extend themselves for the good of the order. We must have people who are willing to live their lives out of balance. We must have people who are willing to say, "It was worth it."

As I start the descent to Whitney Portal, I pass from Sequoia National Park into the John Muir Wilderness, from National Park Service land to Forest Service land, from one land managing agency and philosophy to another. In my present state, however, such distinctions are irrelevant. I don't have a wilderness permit. I don't have anyone's permission. I am alone. I am John Colter running barefoot through six miles of prickly pear to escape the Blackfeet. I am Lewis and Clark running from a grizzly bear. I resurrect the frontier with every stride I take.[10]

I am a dreamer. But don't you see? "All of us are dreamers. Dreams are what started everything. Dreams are the most realistic way of looking at life. Dreamers are not shadowy ephemeral-thinking people. The dreamers are the realists . . ."[11]

Don't you see? "All America lies at the end of the wilderness road, and our past is not a dead past but still lives in us. . . . Our forebears had civilization inside themselves, the wild outside. We live in the civilization they created, but within us the wilderness lingers. What they dreamed, we live; and what they lived, we dream." [12]

Don't you see? The most significant thing about the American wilderness is that it is free. It is that place where we escape the bonds of social convention. It is that place where, unshackled, we recast ourselves each in our own fashion. It is that place where we build anew. The wilderness nurtures character and confidence. It is that place that "provides the ultimate delight because it combines the thrills of jeopardy and beauty. It is the last stand for that glorious adventure into the physically unknown. . . ."[13] The wilderness is all that we have left to discover about ourselves. Don't you see?

They say laughing and crying are similar emotions. I hope so, because I hurt so much that I cry with happiness in this, the last mile. I am, at the same time, so proud of my body for having done what I asked of it and so upset with my mind for having asked it, that I laugh and cry simultaneously. After 28 hours and 45 minutes, I am chock-full of ambivalence, shedding tears of joy and sadness, of relief and remorse, as I finish what I started out to do.

Someday, when I am old and wise, I will look back on this day and smile. I will, no doubt, be in a rocking chair, and I will have that faraway look in my eyes. Perhaps my sons will have told their sons and daughters about grandpa's big run. Perhaps, just perhaps, my grandchildren will want to know more. I don't know what I'll say to them, but I have a hunch I'll begin the story once again with the words of John Muir. "I only went out for a walk, and finally concluded to stay out till sundown, for going out, I found, was really going in."[14]

Chapter 5

INSIDE, OUTSIDE, UPSIDE DOWN: THE GRAND CANYON AS A LEARNING LABORATORY

Kaibab is an American Indian word meaning "mountain lying down." It's a good word, a great word really, for evoking images of the geological masterpiece that is the Grand Canyon. For anyone who has hiked the great chasm's lower reaches knows full well, indeed, feels full well, what the American Indian lexicographer must have had in mind.

First, the Grand Canyon teases you with its awesome vistas. It plays with your sense of space. From the rim, you are treated to incredible views, summit views, and you haven't had to do a thing to earn them. It's so easy. It seems too good to be true.

Then the canyon invites you—no—it entices you to venture below. Propelled by fresh muscles and an eager spirit, and aided by the force of gravity, you charge downward through eons and eons of time and layers and layers of geological history. Then, almost too soon, you are there, right where Major Powell was, languishing on the bank of the Colorado river. You're surprised. You thought it would be harder than this. You smile to yourself. Piece of cake.

Then you look up. Where is the rim, anyway? Towering above you are the walls of the inner gorge. You can't see beyond that. Oh sure, up there somewhere is the Tonto Plateau, and beyond that the rim, civilization, and McDonald's. But at this point it doesn't really matter. At this point you're giving in to the joy of the moment, the warmth of the sun, the sand between your toes, the sounds of the river. At this point you're visualizing Major Powell doing the exact same thing in the exact same spot. This, you think to yourself, is living.

After a while a different impression begins to wash over you. It's a subtle change to be sure, but it's unmistakable in its impact. Gradually, you sense that you're not in a canyon at all, but in the mountains. Everything is up. And everything else is out of sight. Suddenly, you are aware of your joints throbbing. You carry on a debate with yourself. Is gravity really a friend or foe? You realize that, unlike other mountain treks, the descent came first on this one. Now you must ascend. Everything is backward. You must climb to get out, not in. Your summit is at the end, not the middle. Everything is, in the words of storytellers Stan and Jan Berenstain, inside, outside, upside down.

If you have a sense of humor, you chuckle. You know you've been duped by a mountain, a mountain lying down. You're going to have to earn your summit view after all, after 5,000 feet of climbing in the open, in the heat, in the desert-like splendor that is the Grand Canyon. And having made it, having plodded along like a mule, one hoof after another, one slurp of water after another, ever onward and upward until the rim is actually something you're standing on, you look back with incredulity and vow to yourself that you'll never, ever, be duped again.

I have been duped by the Grand Canyon of the Colorado several times. I guess you could say I ask for it. I take students there from San Diego State University.[1] All kinds of students. Good ones and bad ones. Tall ones and short ones. Skinny ones and fat ones. I take them for all kinds of reasons, too. Certainly, I want the students to learn firsthand about the Grand Canyon's geography, geology, and geomorphology. I want them to learn firsthand about its flora and fauna, its past and present patterns of recreational use, its management problems, and its prospects for the future. Certainly, I want to stretch the students' cognitive capacities. I want them to struggle intellectually with the scale, with the size, with the sheer immensity of it all. How did it happen? How could it happen? Who, or what, is responsible for all this, anyway?

But to be honest with you, the main reason I take students to the Grand Canyon is to watch them be duped, too. I want them to be humbled just like I was. I want them to be knocked off their anthropocentric pedestals. I want them to know that there is, indeed, life east of California, and that it is more powerful and majestic than they ever imagined. I want them to consider the possibility, however remote, that Mission Beach, California, is not the center of the universe. But most of all, I want my students to face up to the cold, hard reality that, despite their significance, they are in many respects insignificant to the larger world. I want them to stew over that realization, to wrestle with it, just like I do. I want them to know that, despite what seems to be the weight of the world on their shoulders, despite all their personal problems, predicaments, and pressures, there is a much larger life force that proceeds without them, that is indifferent to their petty concerns. I think that is healthy for students. It forces them to consider their place in the order of things. And for that purpose, I know of no better teacher than the Grand Canyon.

You may find it odd that I single out the instilling of humility in students as the primary academic objective of my wilderness outings. But I do not find it so. On the contrary, to me the value of the lesson is obvious in this age of seemingly unlimited human potentials. It is precisely because we human beings have the capacity and, more telling, the ego to shape this planet's destiny that I seek out humbling experiences, experiences that reveal our frailties, our shortcomings, our limitations as a species. It is precisely because we are running the risk of getting too big for our britches that I look to the Grand Canyon, the High Sierra, and the Rocky Mountains for lessons worth learning. I believe it is essential that we cultivate this humbling awareness of where we fit into the vast scheme of things to offset our increasingly intoxicating feeling of being in control of that scheme. From my experience, backpacking trips contribute to this awareness in ways that traditional classrooms cannot.

Why? I don't know exactly. I suppose it has something to do with the fact that backpacking forces you to leave most of the reminders of human achievement at home: the BMW, the DVD player, the blender. Nothing between you and the earth but Gore-tex. Both of you breathing in and out in cosmic unity. Just you and your flesh and your surroundings: the rock, the dust, the mesquite, and, on the Bright Angel Trail in Grand Canyon National Park, the ever present evidence that mules have been there before you. It is all there for you to deal with directly, in person, as you see fit. In my opinion, it is self-paced instruction at its best.

But it is not only the lessons to be learned in the Grand Canyon that draw me back again and again. It is the way the lessons are presented that appeals to me as well. They are not assigned, announced, or studied for. You cannot cram for them. They simply happen. They sneak up on you when you least expect them; pop life quizzes, so to speak. They are, then, what you might guess I would like to call them—lessons lying down.

Let me recount one such lesson for you. I was hiking out the Bright Angel Trail above Indian Gardens on a particularly hot April day in 1982. The sweat was pouring off my back, my heart was pounding, and my feet were sore. A mule train approached and, as is the custom, I moved to the side of the trail to get out of the way. I bent over to shift the weight of my pack and rest. Then, quite unexpectedly, a stout woman stopped her mule beside me and began to chat. What an incredible place the Grand Canyon was, she mused from her throne atop the animal. What a sight to behold! Wasn't it great that we could get out to explore the Canyon, that we dared to dip down below the rim?

But I wasn't really listening. I was preoccupied. My eyes had somehow fixed on the eyes of her mule, and its on mine. The sweat was rolling off the mule's back, too. My thoughts were weird. Here we were, two beasts of burden, each carrying more than we had bargained for on a scorcher of a day in northern Arizona. A strange sense of camaraderie began to swell up in me. Is this what Thoreau meant when he talked about the miracle of seeing the world through another's eyes? Was I, for an instant, the mule? And was the mule, for an instant, me? Was I actually living life's interconnectedness? Yes, I decided, I was. And that awareness generated a humbling and, at the same time, exalting feeling in me. I was experiencing harmony. Then, having rested long enough, the mule and I parted company, each going about our business, each having a bit of the other locked away inside ourselves. And somehow I felt more hope for the world.

Lessons lying down among mountains lying down. These are the keywords that characterize for me the nature of the learning that takes place on backpacking trips into places like the Grand Canyon. While I recognize that this orientation to learning may make many academicians nervous—where, after all, is the control over what is being taught?—I am confident that what does transpire on these outings is educationally worthwhile in every sense of the word.

Moreover, I am equally confident that it is precisely because of the absence of control over the lessons to be learned on these excursions that they are so important. There is nothing contrived about them. They are not artificial. They happen as life itself unfolds. They are, therefore, rich in substance. They are real. And that is their strength.

But what, then, is the role of the traditional educator in this domain of the hidden teacher? I believe it is quite simply to help students make connections between their experiences and the experiences of those who have preceded them. It is to assist the discoverers in formulating a structure that gives form and meaning to their personal experience. It is the role of coach, critic, and companion.

The college classroom, it seems to me, is a place for celebrating human accomplishments and aspirations. It is a place to profit from others' learning and to add one's own to theirs. People are special there. Nature's university, on the other hand, is a place for celebrating the nonhuman side of life. People are not quite so special there. Rather, it is the unique function of nature's university to cast human accomplishments and aspirations in their proper perspective. In that regard, the Grand Canyon of the Colorado is a master teacher, indeed.

Chapter 6

THE INCIDENT AT "NEW" ARMY PASS

High above me on the switchbacks I can make out 15 ant-like creatures edging their way upward toward New Army Pass. I am puzzled. They are approaching what appears to be a snowfield on a trail that is supposed to be free of snow. Perhaps what I'm seeing is actually above or below the trail? It's difficult to tell from way down here. Fortunately, my coleader, Trish, is with them. Everything should be okay.

We are on a four-day hike that will take us into California's Sequoia National Park via New Army Pass. Eight members of the group are college students enrolled in my summer wilderness course. Another is a fellow professor from a neighboring department. Another is an academic counselor at the university who is accompanied by three of his sons and one of their pals. Finally, Trish and myself round out the group. We are a motley crew.

Yesterday, our first out from the Horseshoe Meadow car campground, was the warm-up. The six-mile hike to Cottonwood Lakes gave me a chance to gauge the backpacking abilities of the group members, to assess their pace, conditioning, and stamina. It also provided us with an opportunity to acclimatize to the higher elevation. Finally, it rekindled memories of my first day's walk five years ago when I began my John Muir trek from the same Horseshoe Meadow Trailhead. Yesterday was topped off by a beautiful campsite on one of the upper lakes in the Cottonwood Lakes chain at the base of New Army Pass.

Now, after a good night's sleep, I have allowed the group members to tackle New Army Pass on their own. The faster walkers are following Trish, who I have instructed to remain in the lead, while the others are proceeding at their own pace. Everyone understands this is not a race. We are here to enjoy the mountains. Should anyone have a problem, they need only stop and wait for me. I am the caboose. We will regroup at the pass before descending into Sequoia National Park and tonight's campsite.

My perplexity over the snowfield soon turns to worry as I see a single file of hikers apparently trudging across it. From my vantage point, I can see nothing below where they are walking but a snow chute and a precipice. It looks dangerous. Surely, I must not be seeing the situation accurately. There must be a trail there. It must be safer than it looks. If not . . . I pick up my pace.

I soon catch up to Kevin who is walking slowly. Kevin is a college athlete, a football player who is 6'2" tall and weighs 260 pounds. He has great physical strength but he has not adjusted well to the altitude. He also has a touch of the flu. I reassure him that everything is fine, that there is no rush. We walk together for a few minutes while I keep glancing up to see if I have misread the situation above us. I see nothing to make me feel better. After several minutes, I tell Kevin to continue at his own speed and rest often. I'm going to forge ahead until I see exactly what's going on higher up. I'll see him shortly. Then I press on.

In a few minutes I reach Veston, the academic counselor, who has stopped to wait for me with the three youngest boys. They have reached the edge of what is, indeed, a snowfield covering the trail for 30 or 40 yards. The white crystalline snow is punctuated only by tracks where the others have already gone. It's just as I feared. The slope is steep and there is nothing to stop a fall. No more than 20 yards below the footprints is a cliff. I can feel my stomach begin to churn.

On the other side of the snowfield, Earl, one of my students, has stayed behind to help "talk" people across the hazard. I overcome the urge to scold him and the others for having crossed the snowfield without waiting for me. Instead, I gather my thoughts. I tell Veston and the three boys to stay put while I check out the situation.

I unbuckle the waist strap on my backpack. Then, stepping in the tracks, I work my way carefully across the snowfield. There is no room for error. I brood all the while about the 11 others who preceded me. What was Trish thinking? Did she understand the risk she was taking? What were my students thinking? What was my colleague thinking? What was Veston's oldest boy thinking? I am haunted by the thought that I have somehow been negligent, that I have allowed people whose safety I am responsible for to take a deadly risk.

I console myself with the knowledge that the others made it across safely. I must concentrate on Veston, Kevin, and the three boys. Once on the other side, I take off my pack and cross back again. Kevin has now reached the edge of the snow-field. I announce that I am going to lead each of them across one by one without packs. I will then make five more round-trips myself to carry the packs. I know the others didn't do it this way, but I am being cautious.

I lead the boys across first. Then I transport their packs. Earl assures me there is no more snow on the trail between us and the pass, so I tell the three boys to go ahead. Then I turn around to go back to escort the other two across. There, in the middle of the snowfield with his pack on, is Kevin. I suppose he felt I shouldn't have to do for him what I did for the youngsters. But now he is stalled in the middle of the crossing.

I tell Kevin to relax and stay put. Then I walk out to him. I instruct him calmly, but firmly, to sit on the up slope. Then I slip the pack off his back. I reassure him that he can make it the rest of the way. "Just take your time, Kevin, and make sure your forward foot is firmly planted before shifting your weight from your back foot. You'll do fine."

As Kevin begins to edge away from me, I slip into his pack and stand up. What happens next is in slow motion. I feel my feet come out from under me as the weight of the pack presses down. I am sliding toward the precipice. I have the presence of mind to roll quickly out of the backpack, and I watch it tumble over the cliff in front of me. Then, out of the corner of my eye, I see a tiny piece of rock outcropping below me several yards and two or three feet to my left. If I can roll while falling, perhaps I have a shot at it. I lunge to my left and then claw at the rock with my right hand while sliding by it on my stomach. My fingernails are torn off in the process, but I manage to grab hold. And there I am, 15 yards below the trail of footprints, five yards above the cliff, hanging on with one hand, bleeding.

Kevin is above me, frozen in his tracks. Veston is beside himself. I can hear the others yelling from still higher up to "hold on!" But I am strangely calm and detached from the scene. It occurs to me that it is June 18th, the day before my oldest son's 13th birthday. He was born on Father's Day. I think to myself that Andy was, and will always be, my greatest Father's Day present. Then I envision what just came very close to being—his birthday without me.

I realize, hanging there by my one hand, that had I buckled the waist strap on Kevin's backpack, I would likely be dead now. I would have never known my son as a 13-year-old. The thought devastates me.

I reassure Veston and Kevin that I'm okay, that I just need a few minutes to compose myself. My emotions are a jumble, ranging from embarrassment at having slipped, to thanksgiving for having survived the mistake, to relief that it was me who had to go through it, to guilt for knowing that had any of the others slipped they likely would have fared much worse than I, since they crossed the snowfield with their packs on and waist straps buckled. I am unnerved, yet I must not show it. There is Veston to consider and whatever is left of Kevin's pack to retrieve. I inch my way back up to the makeshift trail.

After convincing Veston that I am okay, and that without packs we will be able to cross the snowfield safely, I lead him across and return for his pack. I then tell Veston, Kevin, and Earl to proceed up the trail and wait with the others at the pass while I go back down to fetch Kevin's pack. Earl insists on staying put until I return. I don't argue with him.

I walk back down the trail a mile or so and then head across a scree slope to look for Kevin's backpack. All the while I am trying to piece together just what went wrong, trying to understand how I got us into this predicament. The snowfield shouldn't have been there. The backcountry permit ranger in Lone Pine must have given me bad information. Yet that doesn't seem likely. But what else could it be?

After a brief search, I find Kevin's backpack wedged into the base of a large boulder several hundred feet below the snow field. I imagine what it might have looked like had I still been strapped to it. The thought makes me tremble. I gather up everything that has been separated from the pack, including a 35 mm camera that is in pieces, a sleeping bag, and other odds and ends. Then I start back up the trail.

Suddenly, from high above, I see a sleeping bag cascading down the mountain. It unglues me. I fully expect to see a body following it. I have never felt so terrible in my life, so dejected. What mistake in judgment have I made now?

To my great relief, no body is forthcoming. Nothing else tumbles down. But I realize as well that I must now go even farther back down the mountain to retrieve the sleeping bag. We have two more nights out. Whoever it belongs to needs it. So I turn around for the second time.

Eventually, I find the sleeping bag, return with it to the place where I set down Kevin's backpack, put on the backpack, climb back up to the snowfield, cross it one last time, and join Earl, who has been waiting patiently for my return. We make our way together up to the pass and find the others lounging around, wondering just what took me so long? Many of them are oblivious to what I have been through. They are anxious to push on.

The sleeping bag belongs to Veston. In his haste to reach the pass, the bag somehow dislodged from his backpack. Since he only had survival on his mind, he didn't pursue it. He can't believe I went all the way back down the mountain for it. He thanks me profusely.

I am exhausted. I sit by myself for a while to collect my thoughts and rest. I need to put this incident behind me. I have a group to lead and three more days to get through. I talk quietly for a few minutes with Trish about what just transpired. She did not perceive the risk. She felt confident and went for it. What happened to me, anyhow?

The wind whipping through the pass sends shivers up my spine. But I am happy to be cold. I look around at the scene I almost didn't live to see. To the east is the Cottonwood Lakes basin where we camped last night. To the north, just out of sight, is Mt. Whitney. To the west is Sequoia National Park. And to the south, in the distance and just above us, I see the back of a vaguely familiar wooden sign. And in that instant I realize what I have done. That I am looking at the back of the sign means there is another trail coming up from the south side of the mountain. I have unwittingly led my group up and over, not New Army Pass, but Army Pass, an old and little-used pass whose north-facing slope is snow covered late into the summer. The New Army Pass trail, the trail that was cut into the south side of the mountain to create a safer passage, the trail the Lone Pine ranger was referring to, the trail I thought I was on, was built precisely to avoid the kind of accident I just had.

What to say? I was careless. I relied on my foggy memory of the hike five years before to serve as my guide. I screwed up. I was negligent. And 16 lives, including my own literally, hung in the balance.[1]

Chapter 7

THE BARRENLANDS

I am awakened from a deep and pleasant sleep by a gentle tapping on the tent's rain fly. It takes me a few moments to climb out of my stupor, to remember where I am and what I'm doing here. It is July 5, 1990, and I am camped on the north shore of Great Slave Lake in Canada's Northwest Territories. Three days out from Yellowknife, I am one of 14 people paddling three voyageur canoes northeastward 208 miles to the mouth of the Hoarfrost River. There we will portage and paddle the canoes another 70 miles north of Great Slave Lake to Lake Walmsley in the Barrenlands, where we will leave them for Wilderness Inquiry II, a Minneapolis-based nonprofit organization dedicated to the integration of able-bodied people and persons with disabilities on wilderness outings.[1] If all goes according to plan, Wilderness Inquiry II will fly its first group in to Lake Walmsley on July 23rd and us out the same day. But that is a long way and a long time off.

I'm glad I bought a Therm-A-Rest before leaving San Diego. My muscles and joints hurt enough as it is. The Canadian Shield beneath the tent would only add insult to injury. But for the moment I am content. I still have an hour or so before Leo's 5:00 a.m. wake-up call. I can think my thoughts and listen to the raindrops. When I concentrate hard enough, I can almost hear a rhythm to them, a beat, as though they were being orchestrated.

This has the makings of a real adventure. Just three days ago I was sitting in the Wildcat Cafe in Yellowknife with a handful of new acquaintances feasting on pancakes and caribou sausage. My breakfast companions were ardent canoeists and members of the Minnesota Canoe Association. They were regaling me with stories of past trips to the Northwest Territories, the Boundary Waters Canoe Area Wilderness in northern Minnesota, and technique. I made a point of confessing that I knew little of technique, indeed, little of canoeing, and that the only reason I was on this trip was that Leo knew I would work hard and not complain.

A few hours later we were on the water paddling hard and in cadence in front of a BBC television crew, trying to put the skyline of Yellowknife behind us. I shared a bench with Sue, a school teacher from River Falls, Wisconsin. We were seated behind Venice, the 62-year-old President of the Minnesota Canoe Association, who was in the bow. Sue and I were in the milieu position, as the voyageurs called it, a position demanding only steady stroking in unison with Venice. Behind us was the cargo area, and then a bench occupied by Tom, a strong and lanky camp director who was in front of Leo in the stern. Leo was responsible for steerage.

Two of the three canoes had five people in them. In addition to ours, Al's (the trip's coleader with Leo) also had five, and Jim's, a school teacher from Minneapolis, had four. But they were the four biggest people on the trip—Jim, Tony, Bruce, and Dan—each weighing 235 pounds or more.

From the outset, Leo and Al were in charge. They helped build the canoes in the basement of a rundown building in St. Paul. They recruited the crew. They attended to the trip's logistics. They bought 700 pounds of food. They even humored us through the 2,400-mile ride from Minneapolis to Yellowknife; no small accomplishment for 13 people packed liked sardines in a van with gear, canoes, and a trailer in tow. (Larry, the 14 member of our party, flew from San Diego to Yellowknife.) Now, they were in their element; Leo, the former navy navigator, and Al, the former merchant marine, both back home on the water.

Leo set the tone for the expedition. While clearly enjoying himself, he was constantly alert and cautious. As we made our way across the bay that shelters Yellowknife from the open expanse of Great Slave Lake, he kept a dialogue going with Al and Jim. "Stay together!" he said repeatedly. "Keep close enough that we can hear each other talk!" Leo understood the risks. He also understood the responsibility of leadership. The ice had only been off the lake for a week. The water was frigid. A capsized canoe, even with everyone wearing life jackets, could easily result in death from drowning or hypothermia. It was not an undertaking to be treated lightly.

The first few hours were tentative. We had to feel out the canoes. Made of cedar strips with a fiberglass coating, each one was 24.5 feet long. Their seaworthiness had been tested on the Mississippi River in Minneapolis and on Lake Superior near Duluth, but we had to know how they would handle on the open water, in wind and waves with a full contingent of cargo and crew. To everyone's relief, the canoes performed masterfully.

If that could only be said about me. Within an hour of our departure my back ached; my shoulders, biceps, and forearms throbbed; and my rear end moved in and out of numbness. I was going through the motions of paddling, but I wasn't really helping propel the canoe through the water. There was no strength left in my arms. I don't know what I expected of this trip, but it wasn't this. I thought canoeing involved three or four pushes and pulls of the paddle, gliding, and sightseeing. But what we were engaged in was akin to a forced march. We paddled for half an hour, rested five minutes, and paddled again. Sue seemed to be doing much better than I was. She was cheerful and talkative. Maybe it was her paddle. It was curved and made out of lightweight plastic. (Okay, okay. Maybe she was just stronger.)

The sky was a welcome distraction. White clouds floated above us. We paid attention to them. Any changes on the horizon were noted and talked about. Unlike everyday life, the weather here really mattered. We had to be conscious of our distance from land. We couldn't hug the shore because submerged rocks in shallow water might rupture the canoes. But if the weather changed, we had to be able to make it to safety quickly. We had to develop a sense for what could and could not be done. We had to develop an appreciation of the canoes' capabilities. But just as important, we had to develop an appreciation of our own.

The first few days were devoted to feeling out the situation, assessing strengths and weaknesses, hardening soft bodies. In retrospect, the gods were kind to us. Great Slave Lake, the fifth largest freshwater lake in North America, could be tempestuous. But for us it was docile. The breezes were light. The sky was blue. We cut swiftly through the water south and east from Yellowknife and then turned sharply to the northeast. The Hoarfrost River still lay 170 miles in the distance, but we were on our way.

Now, in the wee hours of the third day, I feel better about things. I'm getting stronger. I'm pigging out with the best of them at mealtime, and I'm enjoying the sights while paddling. Maybe Leo didn't make a mistake inviting me after all.

Gradually, an uneasy feeling washes over me, a slowly evolving awareness that things are not what they seem, that my senses are playing a trick. As the light sharpens, I recognize the trickery for what it is. The rhythmic tapping on the tent is not from rain, but from squadron upon squadron of dive-bombing mosquitoes and blackflies.

As I drag myself out of the sleeping bag and grope for my glasses, I wonder what's in store for us. The bugs have been forgiving so far. Is the honeymoon over? Heaven knows we came prepared. I have a headnet, a bug jacket, and two bottles of bug dope laced with deet. But we have yet to experience the onslaught I anticipated. A passage Leo read to us last night from the journal of the British explorer, George Back, who traversed these same waters in the summer of 1835, keeps playing back in my head:

> The laborious duty which had been thus satisfactorily performed, was rendered doubly severe by the combined attack of myriads of sand-flies and mosquitoes, which made our faces steam with blood. There is certainly no form of wretchedness, among those to which the chequered life of a voyageur is exposed, at once so great and so humiliating, as the torture inflicted by these puny blood-suckers. To avoid them is impossible: and as for defending himself, though for a time he may go on crushing by thousands, he cannot long maintain the unequal conflict; so that at last, subdued by pain and fatigue, he throws himself in despair with his face to the earth, and, half suffocated in his blanket, groans away a few hours of sleepless rest.[2]

Through the tent screen I can see Leo and Tom outside hunched over a fire boiling water for coffee. If they are bothered by bugs, they don't show it. They are a hardy twosome. Leo rousts those of us who still need it while Tom tends the fire. We take down tents, roll up sleeping bags, pack duffels, and report to the fire with cups and spoons. Breakfasts rotate between oatmeal, cream of wheat, Red River Cereal, granola and grape nuts with powdered milk and brown sugar, and Al's specialty—pancakes with hot syrup. We have already established a routine. Reveille is 5:00 a.m. Then it's breakfast, break camp, load the canoes, and shove off. We are on the lake by 7:30 a.m. at the latest. There is a military precision to it.

It pays to be on the water early. The mornings are generally calm and we average 10 to 15 miles before lunch. On days when the lake's surface is like glass, Al and Leo push us to make for points of land five, six, or seven miles in the distance. It feels good when we finish these crossings. Each time we cut off one or two miles that we would have had to travel if we had hugged the irregular shoreline. But when we commit to the long stretches there is added earnestness to our paddling. We are letting loose from the protection of land. We attack these stretches vigorously.

Days like this are wonderful. Dipping the paddle deep into the water is like dipping into the sky. The lake's mirror-like surface reflects the clouds, the sky, and the sparkling light in ways that are disorienting. Looking out at Al's and Jim's canoes abreast of us, it is as though they are slicing through air. I can see the sky beneath them. The effect is surreal.

Lost in the rhythm of each stroke and mesmerized by trails of dripping water from my paddle, I lapse into faraway thoughts only to be startled back to reality by the sound of my paddle hitting Venice's or my elbow bumping Sue. I apologize, pick up the cadence, concentrate on what I'm supposed to be doing for a few minutes, and then drift off again. It is remarkable that we are even here; 14 middle aged men and women, a hodgepodge of ordinary people plucked up from everyday life and plopped down in the middle of the Canadian wilderness to fend for ourselves. It is as close as one can come in this day and age to what Aldo Leopold once called a "blank spot" on the map.

In addition to the five-minute rest stops, we make one morning and one afternoon pit stop on shore. Ladies to the right and gents to the left. At noon we take an even longer shore break for lunch, fishing, and a nap. The food packs contain cheese, crackers, peanut butter, jelly, salami, nuts, and trail mix. Afterward, we huddle together like schoolchildren to ration out bags of hard candy.

There is a noticeable drag to the afternoons. The weighty effects of lunch, a nap, the sun beating down on us, and tired muscles from a full morning of work all contribute to a collective sluggishness. Typically, we cover less than 10 miles after lunch. Coupled with our 10- to 15-mile mornings, we are averaging 20 to 25 miles a day. At this rate, we will arrive at the Hoarfrost River on July 12th.

This presumes that the weather will continue to cooperate. Indeed, the only grumbling among the crew so far concerns our frenetic pace. Why not ease up a bit and enjoy ourselves? Leo and Al patiently go over the reasons. We have yet to see Great Slave Lake's bad side. On a body of water this large, high winds and waves could force us to stay put several days. Furthermore, we really have no idea what we will be up against after the Hoarfrost River. Under the circumstances, it is prudent to make the most of the good weather.

So the days unfold. Each afternoon we make one final push for
a distant island or the mainland to camp. Tom goes ashore first to
scout out the site. Is there a good place to land all three canoes?
Are there seven flat areas for the tents? Is there a sheltered spot to
set up the kitchen? When Tom gives the go-ahead, the rest of us
quickly follow. We unload the canoes and carry them out of the
water to high ground. Tom and Leo immediately build a cooking
fire while the rest of us set up camp. Then we report to the kitchen
to pitch in where needed.

I have found my niche on the garlic detail with Tim and Lee
Anne. Garlic flavors all our evening meals, and some of us are born
to peel, cut, and chop. Potatoes, onions, and carrots are also part
of the slaughter. Tony bakes cornbread, brownies, or cakes for dessert, while others resign themselves to the cleanup detail. The meals
are wonderful. The first few days included fresh fruit and vegetables.
Now, we are well into the durables. Each day's main fare—tacos,
burritos, Al's stir-fry, macaroni and cheese, spaghetti, linguini, or
Leo's "kitchen sink" soup—is gratefully devoured. Everyone has
seconds. There is always just enough.

Meals are preceded by, accompanied by, and followed by, coffee. It starts our engines in the morning. It recharges us on cold
and windy lunch breaks. It warms us for bed. The water boils. The
coffee brews. The pot is tapped. Al pours for those of us who swarm
around the fire like beggars with cup in hand waiting for the heat.
When the pot empties, the process starts over. Pot after pot.

Bedtime comes early. Seven or eight hours of paddling a day
take their toll. We've already figured out that by the time we reach
the Hoarfrost, we each will have 250,000 strokes under our belts.
At day's end, we are understandably spent. Darkness, however, never
really comes. We are close to the Arctic Circle, and the summer sky
stays light all night long. I could read at any hour by natural light if
I wanted. In fact, each evening I crawl into my sleeping bag and
begin reading Thomas Kuhn's *The Structure of Scientific Revolu-
tions*, a book I have some interest in. But I only last a page or two
before falling asleep. Leo is getting a kick out of it.

After a week on the lake I am really enjoying myself. The scenery is a combination of crystal clear water, rock outcroppings, high
bluffs, majestic skies, pine trees, and islands. We even see icebergs.
Leo consults his map frequently as he charts our way between the
islands and the mainland. We see bald eagles perched high in the
trees. They wait patiently for us and then, seemingly on cue, soar

away to a distant perch. The dorsal fins of large lake trout knife through the water. The scene is punctuated by the intermittent calls of loons. It is as though the pages of Sigurd Olson's books are coming to life before our eyes.

Now, two days shy of the Hoarfrost River, we stop for lunch on Big Stone Point, a beautiful rock outcropping. As we begin our meal, a red-throated loon buzzes us repeatedly. There is a nest nearby. A quick search reveals the nest and its eggs. We give the loon its space and attend to our meal. It is an idyllic setting. I am flooded with thoughts of how well things are going. The weather is great. We're getting stronger. We're coming together as a group. We are on schedule.

Suddenly, several yards away Venice bends over gasping. For a few moments the rest of us sit still, frozen, not understanding what is happening. Then Leo rushes up to him, grasps him from behind, and pulls up hard once, twice, three times. Chunks of cheese and corn bread come flying out of Venice's mouth.

Venice is okay, but shaken. His ribs are sore. One or more may be broken.[3] Leo goes off by himself. The rest of us exchange uneasy glances and then quietly go about our business of getting back on the water. As we paddle away from Big Stone Point, I look back one last time in disbelief. A few minutes ago we were carefree. Now there is a pall over us. Venice's close call has laid bare something we seldom think about—the precarious nature of our existence. One moment we were full of good cheer. The next moment we were embroiled in a life-or-death crisis. The effect is accentuated by geography. We all know deep down that if Leo's efforts had failed, that would have been it for Venice. There was no opportunity to go for help. There were no telephones, no radios, no emergency vehicles. There was no one but us. The gravity of the situation weighs heavily on me as Big Stone Point disappears behind us and I turn my thoughts to what lies ahead.

The Hoarfrost River is important for several reasons. First, it represents the halfway point of the trip. We are 10 days out from Yellowknife and 10 days away from our scheduled flight back to civilization. Second, it marks the end of our voyage on Great Slave Lake and the beginning of a series of portages to the north. Third, it is the home of bush pilot and sled-dog racer, Dave Olesen, and his wife, Kristen. The Olesens will look after the canoes once we deliver them to Lake Walmsley.

After 10 days on Great Slave Lake and 208 miles of nonstop paddling, Olesen's tiny yellow plane is a sight to behold. We raise our paddles in triumph and shout our arrival. A kennel full of yelping sled-dogs welcome us in turn. Olesen greets us in a low-key manner, with warmth and a smile. He is in his early 30s, tall and wiry, dressed in work clothes. We are free to set up camp on the sand and tour his cabin, kennel, and outbuildings. (Alas, the sauna is not quite finished.) He invites us to make ourselves at home, clean up, and rest for the next phase of our journey.

The stopover at the Olesens' is fascinating. A tour of the homestead reveals the self-sufficient nature of their existence. From generators to medical supplies to foodstuffs, it is clear that Dave and Kristen are prepared to handle just about anything that comes their way. They have a radio and plane at their disposal for emergency use, but any outside assistance is still hours away. They are, for all intents and purposes, on their own.

The romance of it all quickly fades, however. Everything I see reminds me of the extreme northern latitude, a place where it is dark half the year. The climate is inhospitable. Dave and Kristen share the pleasure of each other's company, although how either one of them finds privacy during the long winter months is beyond me. They also have their dogs, honest work, and pristine surroundings, but there are few creature comforts or diversions common to the civilized world. They are living close to the vest. Even now, to make ends meet, Kristen works as a cook in a gold mining camp 200 miles away at Baker Lake. Meanwhile, Dave waits for a barge from Yellowknife bringing the year's supplies, including 10,000 pounds of dog food. Just the thought of having to unload the barge is enough to make me rethink their sanity. Still, I admire them.

A cold bath in the lake, a hearty meal highlighted by potatoes and onions, and a good night's sleep ready me for the day of reckoning. Today, we begin the portages. I have been dreading this day ever since I carried one of the canoes with Leo across his backyard in Forest Lake, Minnesota. I knew then that I would find the portaging difficult. The canoes weigh 200 pounds apiece. Al built two yokes for each of them so that, once hoisted, they could be carried by two people. How they ride remains to be seen.

Our first task, however, is to paddle three final miles to the first portage. "Piece of cake," Larry chuckles. Dave takes Leo's place in our canoe while Leo motors alongside in Dave's boat. Dave will get us off on the right foot. He's blazed the first four portages. After that, we'll be on our own.

As if to show us how lucky we've been, Great Slave Lake whips up a gale as we make our way out from Olesen's cabin. The three miles are the hardest of the trip. We paddle directly into a headwind. The waves are formidable. We lose strength rapidly and take shelter several times to rest, while Leo putters along in the motorboat. Once again, however, the canoes are impressive. They are in no danger of capsizing. Al good-naturedly reminds us that the canoes he built are more durable than the crew.

Once on land we unload the canoes and await Leo's instructions. The first portage is two miles. It is the longest of the 18 we will be tackling. It is well marked with Dave's tree blazes and strategically placed pink ribbons left by a Japanese kayaker who is a few days ahead of us. The route we are attempting has never been done before by white people. Olesen thinks it was traveled by early American Indians in their pursuit of caribou herds from Great Slave Lake to the Barrenlands. But the contemporary route is Pike's Portage several miles to the east. If successful, this route will be a shortcut.

The moment of truth arrives. Leo assigns the biggest people to carry the canoes. That means Dan, Jim, Tony, Tom, and Dave. Leo, Larry, and Al are also involved. Bruce is not involved because of a sore knee. The rest of us are to carry personal packs, food packs, the wanigan (a wooden box containing kitchen equipment that fits into the shell of a canoe), life vests, and paddles. Each canoe will have to be led by one of us because the people carrying the canoes cannot see out from under them. Venice is instructed to carry light gear. All of us, however, will have to make three or four trips back and forth across the portage to move all the equipment forward.

Leo points me to a food pack. It sure beats a canoe, I tell myself. But my mood changes abruptly when I try to pick it up.

The food pack weighs 100 pounds. Leo helps load me and then watches as I double over. I can't believe how heavy it is. I try to be nonchalant, but I am not fooling anyone. I trudge ahead. I am the hunchback of San Diego. Then it begins to rain.

The first day of the portage is the most grueling of my life. I have always prided myself on my endurance, on my physical condition. But this work demands strength, and I must now face up to the fact that I am not very strong. The realization gnaws away at me. It bruises my ego. I don't feel like I'm doing my part. Even though I'm managing the food pack, I'm disappointed that the canoes seem too much for me. I have carried a canoe one quarter-mile stretch with Dan, but another attempt with Leo didn't work well. The yokes didn't ride squarely on either of us. Al quickly took my place; all 5'6" of him. I spell others intermittently under the canoes, and I try to make extra trips to carry other gear. I want to make up in endurance what I lack in strength. But I'm not pleased with myself. Dave Olesen doesn't help matters when I see him put one pack on his back, another on his front, and then toss my food pack back over his head to ride on top of the first one. I'm glad he's going back to his cabin today. I feel emasculated.

Our task over the next few days is to follow a chain of unnamed lakes paralleling the Hoarfrost River. The river itself is not navigable because of rapids near its juncture with Great Slave Lake. This means we have to make several portages ranging from a few yards to a mile or more over uneven terrain. Eventually, we will work our way back to the river and then follow its course northward to Cook Lake and Lake Walmsley.

After the first four portages, we have only the pink ribbons left by the Japanese kayaker to guide us. I feel a sense of kinship with the man even though we have never met. His ribbons are a sign of caring. Perhaps I'll get the chance to make his acquaintance yet.

As we begin each portage, Leo checks his map and compass. He looks for a direct route to the next lake, but he also tries to steer us over high ground. The lower, wetter areas are particularly difficult to negotiate with the canoes because of the unsure footing. We all grab a personal pack, paddles, and life vests and follow. Two or three of the yellow life vests are placed prominently along the way as trail markers. Once the route is established, we quickly go to work portaging the canoes and the rest of the gear.

On the afternoon of the third day, Dave Olesen flies over us. Leo had prearranged a signal in case Venice's condition had deteriorated, but it isn't needed. All is well. Dave circles once and then throws a plastic jar out the window into the lake. We retrieve it and open it. The jar is full of freshly baked brownies and a book of poetry for Leo. With a tip of its wings, the yellow plane disappears into the clouds. Dave will check in on us again in three more days.

It takes five days and a dozen portages to work our way back to the Hoarfrost River. Each day is peppered with wind and rain. On day four, we catch up with the kayaker, Aki, who is wind bound.

He is on a four-month solo journey to the Coppermine River near the Arctic Ocean. Aki is a breed apart. He seems genuinely happy to see us. We share small talk and some meals, but he camps separately and eventually goes his own way.

On the sixth day, as we approach a sandy beach where the Hoarfrost River flows out of Cook Lake, the weather breaks. Al and Leo order a well-deserved rest to dry out and recharge our batteries. Fishing poles are broken out, and before we know it lake trout are being landed left and right. Everybody is catching them. Well, almost everybody. I brought a fly rod on the trip. It was a mistake. Other than one grayling I caught from shore on Great Slave Lake, I have been skunked. Everyone else has spinning rods and lures. They are cleaning up; especially Sue and Dan. Larry offers me his pole. Reluctantly, I accept his offer. I say "reluctantly" because for some reason that I do not understand I am lethargic and uninterested in fishing. I make a few half-hearted casts and then decide to go on a long walk by myself. Later on in the afternoon, we have a lake trout feast, although I'm not particularly interested in eating lake trout, either. Then we shove off into Cook Lake.

Paddling along the western shore of Cook Lake, we leave the tree line behind us and enter the Barrenlands. The terrain looks like pictures I've seen of the Scottish moors. It is rolling, open country, dotted with lakes and little else. This is the tundra. Occasionally, we see sun-bleached antlers on shore reminding us that this is a migration route for caribou herds. There is a forlorn quality to the scenery that is both beautiful and haunting. I have never felt farther away from civilization.

Absorbed once again in the paddling and thinking my faraway thoughts, I am jolted hard back to reality. This time, however, it is a knife-like pain in my left side. The sharpness of it, the stinging sensation, frightens me. I tell Leo something is wrong. I stop paddling. I have to find relief. I lie back and stretch out. It doesn't help. The pain intensifies.

Leo signals the other canoes, and we make for the nearest land. By the time we get there—a small mosquito-infested island—I am in bad shape. I lie on the ground convulsing. I throw up. What's the matter with me? No one knows. Leo and Larry exchange glances. I see the worry in their eyes.

Leo gives the order to make camp on the island. He sets up the pup tent for me and then rigs a tarp across some bushes a few yards away to create a semblance of privacy for the latrine. There is, however, little vanity left in me. I have already tossed my cookies in front of everybody.

My temperature is near normal. Al, Leo, and Larry comfort me. Then they leave me alone in my sleeping bag with a bucket for heaving. I twist, turn, and throw up for hours. In the middle of the night, I stagger outside the tent to empty the bucket and go to the bathroom. The sky is a brilliant red. I look at it in awe, oblivious to the fact that I have no shirt on. I am covered with mosquitoes. "What a cover photo that would be!" I say in my delirium as I stumble back into the tent. Finally, after several hours of misery, I drift off to sleep.

Morning finds me feeling better. Whatever it was now seems to be out of my system. Everyone is relieved. We all speculate as to what had hold of me. Bad water? Bad fish? A chemical reaction to the bug dope getting into my bloodstream through cracked skin? We even consider the possibility that I had a toxic reaction to black-fly bites. No one knows for sure.[4] Leo instructs me to ride in the cargo area of Jim's canoe. I am not to paddle.

At the northeast end of Cook Lake, we must portage around a series of rapids to reach Lake Walmsley. The first portage is about a mile. I feel good enough that I want to carry some of the gear. Leo advises against it, but leaves the decision up to me. In the distance, we see smoke from what must be Aki's latest campfire. As Leo and I walk, we marvel at the setting. It matches our impression of the 19th century American west. We are mountain men on our way to a rendezvous. There are tales to tell.

I make two trips back and forth across the portage before I feel sick again. At lunch I sprawl out on the ground and try not to move. There is still work to be done, but for me the challenge is to hold on. We finally make camp, and Larry quickly puts up my tent. Leo tells me he is thinking about sending me out with Dave Olesen later in the day. I can stay at Olesen's cabin until the 23rd and then fly out with the rest of the group to Yellowknife. The prospect mortifies me.

The next thing I know, the whine of Olesen's plane wakes me from a deep sleep. Everyone is cheering. He's brought oranges and beer and his wife, Kristen, for us to meet. But I am devastated by the thought that his arrival may signal my departure. I don't know what's wrong with me, but I don't want the trip to end this way. I tell Leo and Dave that if I'm a burden to the group, then they can do what they must. But if their concern is for me only, then I want to stick it out. Dave quizzes me about my symptoms and then calms me with his reaction. He is flying back tomorrow to drop Kristen off. She is going to accompany us to Lake Walmsley to photograph our finish. If need be, I can fly out with him then. We can play it by ear. For me, it is the happiest moment of the trip. I thank Dave and then will my Molson Canadian Lager to Leo. I quickly fall back asleep.

July 20th brings the last of the 18 portages. Kristen and Dave join us for the finale. I do little work, but my mood is upbeat. When all three canoes are afloat on Lake Walmsley, Dave takes a few minutes to thank us for our efforts. What we've accomplished, he says, is remarkable. He questions whether a younger and stronger group would have held up as well. He acknowledges the importance of seasoning, maturation, and judgment. He is, in his own way, letting Leo and Al know they did a heck of a job. Finally, Olesen reassures us that the canoes will be put to good use in the Barrenlands and that we are all invited to come back and make use of them ourselves.

On July 21st, we touch ground for good. The canoes have reached their destination. We camp on Maufelly Bay where Dave has a shack he uses in the winter months when he runs his dogs over the snow and ice. For the next two and one-half days, we can relax and unwind. We are off duty.

As for me, the downtime means I can continue to recuperate without feeling guilty about not doing my share of the work. I am much improved over the previous two days, but I feel weak. Nonetheless, I shy away from food. I pass the time reading Olesen's recently published autobiography,[6] and I take particular interest in a chapter where Dave describes an attack of appendicitis he endured while on a dogsled trip in the wilds of Ontario. Leo confesses that the night I got sick he skimmed the same chapter to compare Dave's symptoms with mine. We laugh about it. What a difference a few days make.

Tony soon discovers a wolf den set in the side of a large sand hill and the rest of us while away the hours watching the pups lounge around the den opening. We keep a respectful distance. The adults, however, do not allow themselves to be seen. There is something about the wolves that captivates us. They symbolize the wildness of the Barrenlands. In all likelihood, they have never seen human beings before.

Dan reports that he has seen caribou to the north, and others report Barrenland grizzly bear tracks in the sand. Larry and I take a leisurely day hike to the east just to get a feel for the landscape. It is extraordinarily beautiful in its isolation. It is difficult for me to believe that his country is actually part of the same world I inhabit. It seems ethereal.

On the evening of July 23rd, the whine of a Twin Otter's engine high above us breaks the silence. It is time to go. Larry comes over the ridge, having said farewell to the wolves. The plane circles once and then lands right in front of us. The pilots turn the plane on a dime and taxi up to shore. The cargo hatch opens and we form a conga line to unload the gear. Al and Lee Anne are staying behind to lead this Wilderness Inquiry II group. Dave will join them tomorrow.

I have yet to see anyone other than the pilots. Who are these people, anyway? Then, in the cargo hatch, I see the first figure, the first beneficiary of our three-week effort. A golden retriever peeks out. The guide dog leads its mistress down the steps and across the pontoon to shore. They are followed by two young men, who have cerebral palsy, and a handful of able-bodied others. As quickly as they get off the plane, we give them our headnets, bug jackets, and bottles of bug dope. There is little time for greetings or good-byes. We make quick references to a wolf den, great fishing, and sturdy canoes. Al and Lee Anne have already turned their attention to the new charges. They are in good hands.

The rest of us board the plane and fasten our seat belts. The transition is shockingly abrupt. This can't be happening. The pace of life the last three weeks has been so slow, so deliberate. Every movement has been the result of conscious individual effort. But now the roar of the engine shatters everything. The Twin Otter moves slowly away from shore and then races like an ungainly goose toward the horizon. Gradually, we lift off the surface of Lake Walmsley and begin to rise and rise until, like a dream, the clouds beneath the plane reduce the Barrenlands to a distant memory.

Chapter 8

FLY-FISHING WITH
B. L. DRIVER

The Little Laramie River flows out of the Medicine Bow Mountains to irrigate the ranch land of southeastern Wyoming. Eventually, it spills into the Big Laramie and, in turn, into the North Platte, a river renowned for its role in the westward migration of settlers on the Oregon Trail in the 1840s and 1850s. In addition to being a tributary, the Little Laramie is also home to brown, rainbow, and cutthroat trout. The river meanders over a gravel bottom and alternates between swift moving riffles and slower, deeper pools. If you can get on it, the Little Laramie is a fly fisherman's dream. I say "if you can get on it" because while the river itself is public domain, the river bottom is not. To fish most of the Little Laramie, you have to get somebody's permission. And that takes some doing.

Bev Driver has done it. The mile-long stretch we are going to fish this morning belongs to Mike McGill, a rancher Bev has known for several years. Bev trades honey and garden produce for fishing rights. It is a time-honored Western tradition. In return for his end of the bargain, Bev tells me he has access to a portion of the Little Laramie that is fished by no more than a half dozen other human beings. Upon hearing this, my adrenaline soars. How did I get so lucky?

I first met Bev Driver in the fall of 1972 when I enrolled in graduate school at the University of Michigan. Fresh out of the army, and disillusioned with people, I had decided to devote my life to the protection of wilderness. Michigan's School of Natural Resources seemed like a good place to start. It offered an interdisciplinary program where I could take a lot of different courses from a lot of different professors in a lot of different departments. I liked the thought of that. I also liked the thought of returning to Ann Arbor, a town I was fond of from my undergraduate days, and autumn leaves and football games.

I didn't know it then, but I was enrolling in the program in its heyday. It was headed up by Bev and Ross Tocher, two people whose academic reputations were soaring. Bev was a behavioral psychologist and an analytic thinker. His idea of fun, he once kidded us in class, was to grade papers on Christmas Day. Ross, on the other hand, was a dreamer. He would turn his students on to outdoor recreation, wilderness, sunsets, and the human potential, and Bev would teach those same students how to be good social scientists. I suppose Ross was playing to the right side of our brains and Bev to the left. Whether it was by design or not, they really complemented one another.

Bev and Ross had also just published a seminal paper, entitled "Toward a Behavioral Interpretation of Recreational Engagements, With Implications for Planning,"[1] in which they reconceptualized recreation as an individual psychological state rather than an activity. Their thinking informed their research and their students' thinking, and their students' thinking and research informed the thinking and research of others. In the early 1970s, then, Michigan was an exciting place to be.

But as a master's student, all I knew was that Bev seemed to have little time for me. He was preoccupied with several doctoral students and an ambitious research program. He also taught classes. I remember him telling us in one of them that all he wanted to do was "mess up our heads a little." What he meant, of course, was that he wanted to challenge our thinking, to test our worldviews. But Bev was from the rural south, the Shenandoah Valley of Virginia, and he relished plain talk.

At the end of the academic year, I went to Bev to discuss my future. He said he had a lot on his mind, but if I would walk across campus with him to the Institute for Social Research, he would squeeze me in. I swallowed my pride and went along. I felt like I was being granted an audience with the pope. Bev was about to leave Ann Arbor for a research position with the U.S. Forest Service in Ft. Collins, Colorado, and this was my last chance to talk with him at Michigan. We went upstairs for coffee, and I asked him what he thought about me pursuing a PhD. He mulled it over for a few seconds and then said matter-of-factly that I should get out in the field first to see if I liked it. And that was that. Bev was off to the Rocky Mountain Forest and Range Experiment Station, and a year later, having disregarded his advice, I was off to the University of Minnesota to work on a PhD.

In the years since, I have seen little of B. L. Driver. He has distinguished himself as one of the country's foremost experts on the benefits Americans derive from wild land recreation, published scores of journal articles and scientific papers, designed new research methodology, been elected to the Academy of Leisure Sciences, and been awarded the Theodore and Franklin Roosevelt Award for Excellence in Park and Recreation Research by the National Recreation and Park Association. He is considered by many to be the guru of outdoor recreation research. You will hear nothing to the contrary from me.

I have always seen Bev, however distant, as my stern academic father. I say "stern" not in a negative sense, but in the sense of a person with high standards and high expectations for himself and others. Even though I was only a master's student at Michigan, I was greatly influenced by Bev's presence, by his intellect, and by his allegiance to the scientific method. I suppose I was, and continue to be, somewhat intimidated by the scientist in him. For I, as it turns out, am less of a scientist than an aspirant to philosophy.

Our paths have crossed again because of a mutual friend, Gary Elsner, who is the Assistant Director of Recreation Operations for the U.S. Forest Service. At Gary's request, I was invited to Wyoming to participate in a preliminary discussion concerning a possible program of research to document the spiritual benefits people derive from outdoor recreation engagements.[2] Having concluded that discussion, Bev now thought it a good idea to engage in a little spiritual uplifting of our own.

We are, all things considered, improbable fishing buddies. Bev ties his own flies and builds his own graphite rods. He understands the weighted relationship between the fly rod and the fly line. He knows what knots to use when tying the tippet to the leader and the fly to the tippet. He knows when to fish a dry fly and when to fish a wet fly. He knows what size fly is best under what conditions. He understands hatches and carries a small scoop to sample organisms trout feed on beneath the water's surface. His waders are top of the line. And he reads all the fly-fishing magazines. He is, then, what you might expect him to be—a scientist in a fishing vest.

Not that I am a neophyte. I have fly-fished off and on since I was a teenager, when my father and I took it up on the Sun River in Montana's Bob Marshall Wilderness. But I have not made a science out of fly-fishing. I have approached it more as an art form, relying on my intuition and developing a "feel" for the technique.

On our way to the river, Bev introduces me to Mike, who is working one of his fields. Then they talk garden produce. Afterward, Mike wishes us luck. He doesn't begrudge us our recreation. He tells Bev we can keep any browns we catch, but to release the cutthroats. "How," I ask Bev as we walk away, "can that man get any work done when he lives so close to the river?"

Bev quickly rigs two rods and gives me one with a Muddler Minnow to try for one of the big cutthroats. He ties an Elk Hair Humpy on his, and then it's down to business. We start below a small bridge. I cast across the current and slightly upstream as close to the bridge as possible. My body tingles with excitement as I watch the Muddler ride the current over the length of the hole. If I've presented it right and the trout are feeding, I can expect the splash of a strike at any moment. There is great joy in the anticipation. "It's a wonderful feeling," I tell Bev, "to be fishing again."

"It's all right if you like this sort of thing," he deadpans. "Let's move on. There's better fishing upstream."

Bev goes ahead while I work the hole immediately above the bridge. He soon has his first fish on, a brown trout. He wastes little time in landing, killing, and putting the trout away for safe keeping. He's promised his son, David, fish for supper. David, a recent graduate of the University of Arizona's architecture program, is working on the family cabin back in Centennial, Wyoming. Fish for supper is the least dad can do.

Bev washes the Humpy off in the river, rubs some flotation salve on it, and then air dries it with a few false casts. Then he hands me the rod. "I think you'll find this one more to your liking." Clearly, he wants me to catch fish. I accept his offer. I make a few more false casts and then lay the fly at the upper end of a deep pool 20 yards away. Splash!

"What have you got there?" Bev teases. Then, just as suddenly, the fish is gone. "When you fish with barbless hooks, you can't allow any slack," he says nonchalantly. "You have to keep the pressure on." (Bev releases most of the fish he catches and uses barbless hooks because they are "easier" on the fish.)

Bev soon abandons his own fishing and concentrates on helping me. The first priority is to improve my casting technique. He instructs me to keep my forearm and rod tip on a level plane as I move back and forth with the casting motion. Then he shows me how to take the slack out of the fly line once the fly lights on the water so the line's weight won't drag the fly. Bev knows what he's doing. And he knows how to teach. I am soon catching lots of fish. And with each one he proclaims, "I'm having more fun watching you catch fish than I have catching them myself." It's the same thing my dad used to say to me on the Sun River in Montana.

We fish for two hours before it's time to go. It's a perfect morning, one I'll never forget. White, billowy clouds float over us while beneath our feet the rock bottom shimmers in the clear mountain water. Willows line the shore, and songbirds dart from branch to branch. The colors and sounds are soft and pastoral. It reminds me of an Impressionist painting.

Reveling in the surroundings, it occurs to me that I am, for the first time in my life, truly relaxed in Bev's company. It's a great feeling, one that has been a long time in coming. I also know that Bev is the same person he was almost 20 years ago in Ann Arbor, that my relaxed state says a lot more about me, about the changes I've undergone over the years, than it does about him.

I don't know if Bev still sees me as his student, or if he ever did for that matter, but I do know that I still see him as my mentor. I always want to hear what he has to say, to give it careful consideration. I have reached a point, however, when I can diverge from Bev's thinking without feeling as though I've betrayed him. Indeed, I have arrived at that point, that coming of age, when I am finally thinking for myself.

I remember sitting next to Bev recently at a conference while listening to a panel of scholars reconceptualize recreation in a way that moved away from the individual psychological state to a concern for its social dimensions. It was a way of thinking about recreation I had been sympathetic to for some time. But I could still feel the tug of the orientation instilled in me so long ago at Michigan, an orientation I had accepted and passed on to my students again and again over the years without much critical thought. In the course of the panel's presentation, I could actually feel myself disengaging from that point of view. I was undergoing a metamorphosis of thought. I was becoming my own person.

As I think back on that experience, and as I think back on the experience of fly-fishing with Bev, I imagine that had he been able to see me undergo that transformation, he would have been pleased to see me think for myself in the same way he was pleased when, as a result of his teaching, I was finally catching my own fish.

Chapter 9

COYOTE GULCH
for RICH SCHREYER[1]

We're hightailing it down Hole-In-The-Rock Road on our way to the Red Well Trailhead. Things are looking up. The blizzard in Escalante is behind us, and the sun is breaking through to illuminate a vast expanse of canyon country before us. Leo is delighting in the view, and I'm thanking my lucky stars for the weather change. I was responsible for planning this trip, and I didn't anticipate cold and snow this late in March. "Be prepared, sort of." That's my motto. Leo, on the other hand, is a stickler for details. He leaves little to chance.

We've been looking forward to this outing for a long time. Leo and I have been the best of friends since our graduate school days at the University of Minnesota in the mid 1970s. We both earned PhDs there in education with an emphasis in recreation and park administration. Leo stayed on at Minnesota to teach, while I moved a year later to San Diego State University. We've been writing professionally together ever since and sharing a similar philosophy of life, but other than one overnight backpack in California's Anza Borrego Desert we've taken no long walks together. Coyote Gulch will change that.

Southern Utah has beckoned me for years. When I was a graduate student at the University of Michigan in the early 1970s, Ross Tocher used to pile students into his car and drive nonstop from Ann Arbor to Grand Gulch in southeastern Utah to share his vision of an archeological wilderness, a place where people could experience the American southwest as the Anasazi experienced it a thousand years ago. Ross' enthusiasm fueled mine and that of his other students, particularly Rich Schreyer, who ended up teaching at Utah State University in Logan. Rich always spoke with great fondness of the canyon country, but he carefully avoided specifics. He understood the fragility of it all, especially those places where artifacts from the Anasazi culture could still be seen, picked up, and carried away. Rich didn't want those places to be readily known, and he was doing his part by not naming them.

Leo and I waste little time at the trailhead. We drag the packs out of the van, divvy up four days' food supply, and lock up. Leo lifts my pack and kids me good-naturedly about its weight. "How is it," he wonders, "that your pack is so much lighter than mine? Didn't we divide everything up equally?"

"I don't understand it either," I say sheepishly. "But hadn't we ought to be going?"

The descent into Coyote Gulch is gradual and easy on the feet. We follow a dry wash for two miles until we run into Coyote Creek, a rivulet snaking its way eastward several miles to a confluence with the Escalante River just above Lake Powell. At first, the terrain is open and undulating, but as we work our way into the gulch the walls begin to close in and tower above us. It is as though with each stride we are going farther and farther back into time and deeper and deeper into geological history. We are about to encounter, in the words of novelist Sherwood Anderson, "the bigness outside ourselves."

I have that wonderful feeling backpackers get when the rest of the world melts away. Everyday life is forgotten. Time is here and now. Leo reports a similar transformation, and for him it must be especially sweet, since he's just become the administrative head of his department at Minnesota. It will be good for both of us to put our problems behind us for a few days, to re-create ourselves.

We wade back and forth across Coyote Creek 20 or 30 times. The water is shallow and does not penetrate my Bean Boots. Leo's hiking shoes, on the other hand, are already waterlogged. "If only you had told me we'd be spending most of our time in the stream," he chuckles.

"If only your feet weren't so big, you would be welcome to my boots," I chuckle back.

Seven or eight miles into Coyote Gulch we make our first night's camp on a sandy ledge tucked into the base of the red wall. The setting is delightful. The gurgling of Coyote Creek massages our ears while sheet upon sheet of rich multicolored rock rising all around is music to our eyes. Soaking it all in, Leo marvels at the beauty and wonders how it came to be, while I, for some reason, can only think of chocolate layer cake.

Leo prepares a Mexican meal of burritos, salsa, and chips, while I walk downstream to a bend in the creek where several patches of wet green moss cling to the rock wall. I find the seeps and then place two plastic bottles under the steadiest dripping. As the droplets fall into the bottles, I recall a lesson taught me several years ago by George Peterson, a Forest Service social scientist, on a backpacking trip in the Wind River Mountains of Wyoming. We were discussing the valuation of wild lands and George made the point that water is clearly more valuable than diamonds, more fundamental to life's sustenance. But because of its abundance, we treat water with little respect while treating diamonds as if they were the essence of life itself. Watching the precious liquid splashing into the bottom of the bottles, and knowing it will take all night to fill them, George's point is really hitting home.

The Mexican feast is highlighted by the sharing of our one can of Miller Lite. "Not bad, Leo, if I do say so myself." The satisfaction of a full belly is complemented by the thought that we have just eaten the heaviest food in our packs. The can of refried beans is gone, as is the salsa, as is the beer. We'll be stronger in the morning with lighter packs to carry. Who says I'm not a planner? We catch up on news about each other's family and friends and bask in the glow of the setting sun. Then it's time to hit the sack.

Morning finds us refreshed and eager to go. Today, we'll pass by Jacob Hamblin Arch, Cliff Arch, Coyote Natural Bridge, and eventually Stevens Arch across the Escalante. According to the National Park Service ranger who briefed us in town, if we keep our eyes peeled, we should also be able to see Anasazi pictographs on the canyon wall near Coyote Natural Bridge. The locations of any Anasazi ruins themselves, however, are conveniently overlooked. (Schreyer must have gotten to him.) At any rate, Leo and I are stoked. This is what we came for.

After a quick breakfast and cup of coffee, we break camp and head downstream. The water bottles are full to the brim, and I crow over my procurement. "Dan, the provider. Dan, the outdoorsman. Dan, the man." My ego soon returns to normal, however, when a few hundred yards down the trail, just below Jacob Hamblin Arch, fresh water gushes out of the rock wall in buckets. Leo is kind enough not to rub it in.

Our second day is a tester. The grade is still friendly and the sights spectacular. It's just a lot of walking. Below Coyote Natural Bridge, having failed to locate the Anasazi pictographs, we follow a trail that takes us high up on the red wall. As we leave Coyote Gulch we are treated to breathtaking views of the lower Escalante

River. To the east, Stevens Arch rises high above us. To the south, we can see the upper end of Lake Powell. The sky is blue, the water emerald green, and the rock a chalky red and yellow. When we reach the Escalante, we take off our pants and wade across the frigid, thigh-deep water. We then head up Stevens Canyon, a narrow and difficult side canyon to the Escalante. Its water is punctuated by rifts, folds, brush, and deep pools that must be negotiated carefully. We inch along a mile or so up Stevens Canyon until we find a wide ledge above the streambed. Opposite the ledge is a huge alcove that covers the entire area and gives the feeling of being in an enclosed room. We'll use this spot as a base camp and spend tomorrow exploring the canyon with a day pack. For now, however, it's time to eat and call it a day.

As I lie in my sleeping bag in a sweet state of tiredness, I can see the top of the alcove forming a semicircle against the night sky. As the sky darkens and the stars begin to sparkle, I realize I'm looking up from the same vantage point the Anasazi had hundreds of years ago. I wonder if they were filled with the same impression I am by the alcove's circular outline, that the heavens and Earth must be round?

The morning light stirs Leo, and he, in turn, stirs me. Today we play. We'll scout out Stevens Canyon and explore anything that catches our fancy. We eat a leisurely breakfast and then stuff a day pack with two bottles of water, tortillas, peanut butter and jelly, oranges, and pears. We hide the rest of our gear among nearby boulders and head out. It's going to be a beautiful day for poking around.

We work our way upstream two or three miles before we find what appears to be a possible way up to the top of the red wall. There is no need for discussion. Leo and I both want to climb. We love the scrambling, the picking and choosing of routes, and the reward of the view once on top. It is like a puzzle to be put together one piece at a time. The challenge before us is engaging, absorbing, and total. It has a playful, childlike effect on us. We are gleeful. We are free.

On this climb, the pieces fall together easily until the last obstacle to the top, an eight-foot wall. I check out a narrow ledge that leads to what appears to be a passable route. I call Leo over and he spots for me on the last reach. Leo is more at home in this situation than I. He's an experienced climber. I, on the other hand, am a novice whose enthusiasm for adventure frequently leads me to bite off more than I can chew. Had Leo not been here, this particular stretch would have held more trauma for me than joy. But reassured by his presence, I am soon on top. I offer to reciprocate, but Leo declines. He knows what he's doing.

We explore the top of the plateau for an hour or so and then settle down to enjoy the panorama, eat an orange, and nap. Looking back at the narrow ledge we edged across to reach the top, we can now see the vertical wall beneath it. We look at each other, shake our heads, and laugh.

There is in this moment a wonderful sense of camaraderie between us. Without saying it, we know we are sharing the same feelings—the joy of discovery, the sense of accomplishment, the majesty of our surroundings. We are high up where the wind whistles and eagles fly, looking down with piercing eyes on Stevens Canyon, riveting our attention on any movement that might signify life. It is a heady feeling because our perch among the juniper gives us the sensation of being in control. From this perspective, it is easy to understand why the Anasazi chose to live in alcoves high above the canyon floor.

Finally, it's time to move on. We scramble back down the red wall, pick up our day pack, and head downstream toward base camp. We soon stop to have lunch—peanut butter and jelly spread on tortillas. It's amazing how good they taste. I am flooded with memories of long forgotten childhood lunches. We eat the pears for dessert and then decide to investigate a nearby alcove set high above us in the side of the red wall. A quick 10-minute climb brings us to the mouth of the alcove. And there—to our astonishment—are Anasazi ruins.

"Over here," Leo whispers. I walk carefully across the rock-strewn floor of the alcove to find Leo stooped over the rudiments of a wall around what must have been a sleeping chamber or storage chamber. Petrified corn cobs litter the floor. They were left here 500 years before Columbus "discovered" America. Soon we find pottery shards and an arrowhead. We are stunned by our good fortune.

"Over here," I whisper back. On the rock wall adjacent to the alcove is a pictograph. It is a stick figure in red and white. Who or what it represents is unclear to us, but to think that right here, right in this exact spot where we are standing, another human being stood hundreds of years ago, and painted! To think there was a living, thriving human community here, that its inhabitants looked out upon the same scene we are!

"Over here," Leo whispers. He has found a grinding stone worn smooth by the repeated rubbing of grain against it. And next to the grinding stone is a small circular stone that must have been the tool used to do the work. I pick it up and hold it in my hand. I wonder what it must have been like? I envision the slope below us covered with grasses and people making their way to and from the stream. I imagine children playing games with sticks and adults going about their business. And I imagine a lookout, a guardian with eagle eyes peering down on everything and everyone, vigilant against intruders.

The sense of connectedness to, of bonding with the Anasazi, is incredible. Here we are in the spring of 1991, experiencing their space, their artifacts, their unseen bones. This is what Ross Tocher must have had in mind. This was his dream, that there would be such a place for today's people to get in touch with yesterday's, that there would be a place to savor the feeling of connectedness with those who came before. This is what Rich Schreyer must have meant, too, when he talked about the timelessness of the canyon country that makes events far away appear very close.[2]

Covering our tracks and leaving everything as we found it, Leo and I walk quietly back down Stevens Canyon. We exchange glances. What we have just experienced has touched us both deeply. We have long been advocates for wilderness, for protecting places untrammeled by humankind. But what we have discovered here is something different. We have discovered that people are part of the wilderness as well. Indeed, the Anasazi ruins remind us that human beings are part of the natural order, that we have lived in nature far longer than we have lived in cities and towns. Keeping this thought alive, Leo and I both agree, is important.

Now, of course, my hiking partner wants to check out every alcove in sight. And so we do, although the three or four more we explore on this day do not measure up to the first one. They are, however, each in their own way a mystery and, to us, deserving of attention. At day's end, they lead us to the interesting conclusion that these canyons must be one of the few places on Earth that was more civilized a thousand years ago than it is today.

After a good night's sleep, we head back out Stevens Canyon to the Escalante, ford the river in our underwear, climb back up the red wall, and proceed down again to Coyote Gulch. Our plan for the day is to walk and talk, explore the alcoves bypassed on our way in, and search anew for those pictographs near Coyote Natural

Bridge. It has been a great trip so far and the fact that we've run into only one other person has contributed greatly to our sense of solitude.

As we retrace our footprints, it strikes me that we are not the same two people who made them coming in. The journey has changed us. We are bigger than we were before. We have connected to something larger. Our souls have been stretched. Yet, like our footprints, we look the same.

Suddenly, as we round a bend in a lower stretch of Coyote Creek, I am stopped in my tracks by the sight of a pink balloon wedged into a bush by the side of the trail. In bold, black letters on the balloon are the words MR. FURNITURE: SPRING VALLEY. "I can't believe it," I lament to Leo. "Spring Valley is a suburb of San Diego. It is 670 miles west of here."

Sensing that my wilderness experience has just gone "poof," I consider doing the same to the balloon. Instead, I let the air out of it gradually. I'm going to take the skin back home. I'll give the owners of Mr. Furniture a call and let them know what became of their promotional gimmick. Not that I expect it will change anything.

The rest of the day unfolds pleasantly enough, although we still can't find the pictographs by Coyote Natural Bridge. We decide to stop there for the night, anyway. After setting up camp, Leo goes one way looking for relief while I go in the opposite direction. Finding little in the way of privacy, I begin to climb up toward some large boulders that look like they might provide suitable cover. Once there, I hunker down only to stare in amazement at several large stick figures on the rock wall directly in front of me. I have, it seems, in my own inimitable way, discovered Coyote Natural Bridge's pictographs.

Later in the evening, having thoroughly explored the ruins adjacent to the pictographs, Leo and I reflect on our trip over a cup of coffee. Tomorrow, it's back to our van, our families, and our work. We agree that this get-together has been a wonderful time-out from our ordinary lives. We agree further that much of our joy has been the result of serendipitous occurrences, the discovery of things not sought for. Perhaps it was just as well the ranger did not give us specific directions to the pictographs and ruins. This way, what we did find were our own discoveries. This way, we, too, were explorers. And we both are grateful that there is country like this yet worthy of exploration. We know it doesn't happen by accident. People like Ross Tocher and Rich Schreyer make it so.

Now it's late at night. Stretched out in our sleeping bags, Leo points out Taurus, Orion, and Pleiades in the heavens. "I wonder what the Anasazi called them?" I ask sleepily. "And I wonder what thoughts they inspired?" Leo does not answer. "It wasn't really that long ago," I muse to myself. "A thousand years is but an instant in cosmic time. The night sky is a great leveler."

An owl hoots in a nearby tree. Coyote Creek rushes by. Leo and I are soon fast asleep.

Chapter 10

BACK IN THE USSR[1]

The flight from Helsinki to Leningrad is full of anticipation for me. The last thing I read before leaving home was Zbigniew Brzezinski's *The Grand Failure: The Birth and Death of Communism in the 20th Century*. Last night in the Helsinki airport I saw news reports of 10,000 students demonstrating for democracy in Beijing. Now, on the FINNAIR jet, I am reading an interview with England's Prime Minister Margaret Thatcher who describes the decline of socialist thinking in Great Britain and the inevitability of same in Mikhail Gorbachev's Soviet Union. Were it not for the fact that I am also aware of reports that the Soviet police used poison gas on demonstrators last week in the Georgian capitol of Tbilisi, a city I am scheduled to visit, I would be tempted to conclude that coincident with my arrival in Leningrad is the dawning of a new era in the largest country on the face of the Earth.

I see the differences first from the sky. Accustomed to the checkerboard pattern of America's farmland, the fields below look disorganized. But, of course, there is no need to partition that which only belongs to the state. Descending into Leningrad, I am struck by the abrupt meeting of country and city. High-rise apartment buildings ring the business district of this city of five million, the Soviet Union's second largest, the city christened the "window to the West" by its founder, Peter the Great, in 1703. A few minutes later I am on the ground and quickly through customs. Finally, after five years of preparation, I am behind the Iron Curtain.

I step outside myself briefly and laugh at what I see. There I am with a dinky suitcase, a shoulder bag, and a Boston University Bookstore plastic sack with a game of Monopoly protruding out the top. I have that "lost little boy" look, as though I am about to cry. It's amazing, I conclude to myself. People the world over thirst for freedom, and I am here to experience its opposite. But there's a method to my madness. Just as the spaces between the branches of a tree help give the tree its definition, so will several weeks in the Soviet Union better define for me the United States of America.

My arrival is a surprise to Intourist. After a quick phone call, a good-natured soul named Aleksei gestures to me, and we're off.

"Otkooda vy?" (Where are you from?)

"Ya preeye'khal eez sshah'." (I'm from the United States.)

"Vy gavareete pa-russki!" (You speak Russian!)

"Kak Amerikanets." (Like an American.)

"Nyet, nyet. Vy o'chen kharasho' gavareete pa-russki." (No, no. You speak very good Russian.)

"Spasee'ba bal'shoya." (Thank you very much.)

"So," Aleksei continues in Russian, "you understand that in the Soviet Union there are two currency rates, an official one that you can get at the bank and an unofficial one that you can get on the street? I can give you 15 times the official exchange rate. What do you say?"

"Spasee'ba, nyet." (No thank you.)

"Po'chemoo?" (Why not?)

"Just no thank you, Aleksei."

"Do you understand why I am offering you such a good rate? I need dollars to get a stereo for my children in the Beryozka shop. Rubles are no good there." Beryozka shops, I will soon find out, offer foreigners luxury goods that are unavailable to most Soviet citizens. Only hard currency is honored.

"Ya paneemahyoo, no ya ne kha'choo." (I understand, but I'm not interested.) Aleksei's was a story I would hear a hundred times. Consumer goods are both scarce and of generally poor quality in the Soviet Union. As I will observe over and over again throughout my visit, socialism is plagued by an incentive problem at the production end. So, for the daring, a black market in foreign currency is the only way to get the preferred goods. It will turn out to be one of my more sobering discoveries on this trip that, after 300 years, Peter the Great's grand notion of a "window to the West" is manifested most poignantly today in the form of the Beryozka shop, an outlet for creature comforts that you and I take for granted.

Most visitors to Leningrad hasten to see the Winter Palace, the Hermitage Museum, or the Peter-and-Paul Fortress. But my first priority is in a different direction. I head straight for the Piskarevskoye Kladbee'sche, the memorial cemetery on the outskirts of the city. More than one-half million men, women, and children are buried here in a common grave marked only by the year in which they died. They were casualties of the two-and-one-half year German siege of Leningrad in the Second World War. I am here to pay my respects. Nearby are haunting reminders of other young lives foregone to protect this city that would not surrender. Despite our differences with the Soviet Union, I will never forget that 20 million Soviet people died during the Second World War so that we might remain free. The Soviet people will not forget either.

Later that same day, I chance upon E. R. Sams, a farmer from Pilot Mountain, North Carolina, who is on his way to a reunion in Minsk with Soviet soldiers he knew for only four days in April of 1945 when he was a 20-year-old infantryman with the 69th Infantry Division. They met at Torgau on the Elbe River in what is now East Germany in the closing days of the war. They made a pact that they would work for peace and get together again only for happy occasions. After 45 years, Mr. Sams and his comrades are men of their word. I am proud to have made his acquaintance.

I begin with these two war-related episodes for good reason. Above all else, I have a great deal of respect and admiration for the endurance of the Soviet people. Their history is one of oppression and suffering. They have been attacked repeatedly from both within and without, and yet they have persevered. It would be easy to conclude that they must have some fundamental character flaw that prevents them from taking charge of their own destiny, but that would be unfair. They are, by our standards, a relatively poor and, until quite recently, rural people. Even today it is clear that Soviet investments in heavy industry, defense, and space have come at the expense of the common people. That they push on is testimony to their strength.

But I almost forgot. I am a professor of recreation. It's time to do what I came for, to explore the parks, to poke around, to chat with whomever is willing. Near the Peter-and-Paul Fortress is Lenin Park, a pleasant enough place, full of mothers and grandmothers ("babushkas," as they're called in Russian) and toddlers and babies in prams. Since most urbanites live in apartments, I gather that parks must play a particularly important function in Soviet cities, a refuge, perhaps, from the highly regimented, top-down structuring of life in general.[2] To be sure, I observe lots of reading for pleasure, playing with toddlers, strolling, conversing between sweethearts, and jogging. The setting is reminiscent of the United States back in the 1950s when people seemed to have more time. Scattered throughout the park are statues to motherhood, monuments to the principal child-rearing responsibility carried out by women in the Soviet Union. It is a scene that arouses mixed emotions in me. Children are obviously doted on by their mothers and babushkas. That is good. But where are the fathers? And where are the statues to womanhood?

I approach a young mother with a baby buggy. "Eezveenee'te, pazhah'lsta. Oo vas yehst o'chen kraseevahya do'chka. Mozhna yehyo fotografeerovat'?" (Excuse me, please. You have a very beautiful daughter. May I photograph her?)

"Da, mozhna." The woman seems flattered and, at the same time, ill at ease. There is a reticence to her that tells me not to intrude further. I thank her and move on.

In Pushkin Square, I witness several newlyweds stopping for customary champagne toasts and photographs. It is traditional for the bride and groom to make the rounds to several parks and monuments in their city to pay tribute to cultural heroes, to place flowers by the war dead, and to drink to their dreams of a happy and productive marriage. The ritual strikes me as good because it reinforces human connectedness and acknowledges once more the debt owed those who paid the ultimate price so these new beginnings might be possible. I am also struck by the symbolic significance of these public open spaces to the Soviet way of life.

The next day in a beautiful park called the Summer Garden scores of people are raking leaves, picking up litter, and generally cleaning up. Moved by such civic pride, I ask about its motivation. Low and behold, it's the 22nd of April, Lenin's birthday, and every good Leningrader is expected to pitch in on this "soobbotnik" (volunteer day). Nonetheless, it seems like a good idea to me. The difficulty implementing it in the United States, of course, would be in agreeing on whose birthday it should be done.

At 11:30 p.m., I am dropped off at the train station for an overnight trip to Moscow. It is a scene right out of *Raiders of the Lost Ark*. There are hundreds of people crushed together speaking many different languages. Once aboard, I share a compartment with Yoshinobu Emoto, Deputy Foreign Editor of the Foreign News Department of the *Yomiuri Shimbun*, Tokyo's largest newspaper. He's talkative and we soon find out we have much in common. We're divorced, we're runners, and we love the mountains. I can't believe he's written books about the nomadic tribes of Outer

Mongolia, the people of Tibet, and the tundra. He can't believe
I've run across the Sierra Nevada and that I actually have met Rick
Ridgeway and Barry Lopez. And neither of us can quite believe a
Japanese journalist and an American professor are communicating
with each other in Russian at three o'clock in the morning on an
express train bound for Moscow. If only Yoshinobu didn't smoke.
If only the whole of the Soviet Union didn't smoke. "Bozhe moy!"
(Good God!)

Leningraders told me I would not like Moscow. They were
wrong. Despite its size, which now totals nine million, I ate it up.
Red Square ("krasnaya plo'schad'," as the Soviets call it); St. Basil's
Cathedral; the Kremlin; GUM ("Gasoodarstvenee Ooneeversalnee
Magazeen"), Moscow's main department store; MGU
("Moskovskee Gasoodarstvenee Ooneeverscctet"), Moscow State
University; Gorky Park; "Dom Kneegee" (House of Books); and
"Arbat" Street, Moscow's attempt at an old town, gas lamp quarter. I even spent a morning at "Dyetskee Mir" (Children's World),
the Toys 'R' Us of the Soviet Union. (Later on I will refer to it
cynically as "Toy 'R' Us," because of my inability to find gifts there
for my boys.) You wouldn't have to stay in Dyetskee Mir an entire
morning unless you wanted to buy something. You get the price of
the merchandise at one place, pay for it at another, and pick it up at
a third. Come to think of it, you have to do that with big ticket
items at our Toys 'R' Us, too.

I stood in line 45 minutes to see Lenin's Tomb. They make you
queue up in twos for the procession, and my partner was from
Afghanistan. (No, we did not talk about the Soviet-Afghan war.)
The last time I stood in that long a line was with my sons at the
new Star Tours ride at Disneyland, and, just like at Disneyland, I
found myself saying, "This better be good." After you pass by the
embalmed Lenin, you file out behind the mausoleum past the graves
of Brezhnev, Chernenko, Andropov, the cosmonaut Yuri Gagarin,
and other notables. Stalin is there now, too, since Soviet historians
wrote him out of grace and out of the mausoleum with Lenin.
Nikita Khrushchev is conspicuous by his absence. He's buried across
town at the Novodevichy Convent. One has to wonder, given the
current goings-on in the Soviet Union, just where Gorbachev will
finally come to rest?

I walk this capitol city for three days. On day four, as a validity
check, I take a tour with Larisa, an Intourist guide, and, without
question, a budding feminist. She is a delight. Glasnost, she tells

me, is a big notion. It is the oxygen for perestroika. To prove her point, Larisa takes me by the headquarters of *Izvestia*, one of the two largest newspapers in Moscow (the other being *Pravda*). There is a line of people two blocks long waiting to get a newspaper. If glasnost is the oxygen for perestroika, *Izvestia* and *Pravda* are the containers for that oxygen. Like no other time in history, these newspapers are printing divergent opinions about what should or should not be done about the problems confronting the Soviet Union and the world. They no longer print just the party line. It is a powerful thing to behold: people standing in line for fresh ideas the same way they stand in line for fresh milk or eggs. The very fact that it is necessary to do this, however, differentiates their country from ours.

Larisa and I talk about the terrible Moscow drivers. "It would be better," she says, "if more drivers were women." We talk about day care and equal pay, and we talk about the recent elections in which, Larisa reports with pride, she campaigned and voted for Boris Yeltsin, the liberal Muscovite, who was swept back into power. Larisa thinks things really are going to change. It is difficult budging the entrenched bureaucrats, she admits, but in time. . . . I ask Larisa if Lenin would approve? Yes, she thinks, Lenin would have wanted the people to have a voice by now. There is in this young woman something of a fire. She is taken with a cause.

Later that evening, after supper, I wander into the Yelokhovsky Cathedral where a Russian Orthodox church service is letting out. The interior is beautifully lit with candles, and there are old women everywhere worshipping in a very demonstrative manner. It is moving in terms of the faith being displayed and troubling in terms of the absence of young people. Marx considered religion to be the "opiate of the masses," and religious practice is frowned on in the Soviet Union. They say going to church can hinder one's career. Although there are reports of an easing up in this respect, I have to wonder whether religion will soon die out with the old women attending the service.

Still later that night, I amble across Red Square on my way back to the hotel. It is a beautiful night, almost balmy, and all of the banners are in place for the upcoming May Day celebration. The Soviets are big on slogans, banners, statues, and monuments to their intellectual heroes. They are big on symbols of power. Suddenly, lost in my thoughts, I trip on one of the bricks in front of St. Basil's Cathedral. In that act of tripping, I stumble upon the metaphor of my life. Indeed, I sense that I am in the Emerald City, and all about me are tributes to the all-knowing, all-powerful Oz, a wizard who at this very moment is not more than 100 yards from me, behind a curtain of marble, a mere mortal, a shell of his former self—Vladimir Ilyich Lenin.

Unlike Dorothy, however, two clicks of my heels find me the next day not in Kansas, but at the Yaroslavl Train Station on my way to Siberia. I'm traveling "soft" class, two persons to a compartment. The thing about traveling alone on a train in the Soviet Union is that you never know who they're going to put with you. On a trip of this magnitude, 5,260 miles across two continents over seven long days and nights, your traveling companion is no small concern.

Meet mine. He is Victor Chaschookhin from Pskof, a city near the Baltic Republic of Estonia. Victor is on his way to Vladivostok to visit his son who is in the navy. Victor is friendly enough. He just doesn't talk much. That's okay by me. I'll get a lot of thinking and writing done.

The Great Siberian Railroad is "the experience of a lifetime," according to one book I read. From Moscow to Khabarovsk through seven time zones, it is the equivalent of going from New York City to Los Angeles and back again. There are 50 stops along the way lasting from 2 to 18 minutes each. You jump out and run yourself up and down the platform the way you'd run your family dog on a long car trip back home, and then you scamper to get back on board because the train just leaves. There is no warning, no whistle, nothing. If the conductor on your car doesn't look out for you (in my case a woman named Ludmila) and you are absent-minded, you could be in for trouble. Ludmila had to scold me several times. I took it as a sign of caring.

How best to describe the Trans-Siberian Railroad? It is like backpacking sitting down.[3] It's awkward at first and uncomfortable. You get aches and pains in your backside, the food is marginal, and you toss and turn at night in the narrow berth, which is like a sleeping bag that moves. In the morning, you splash water on your face, get the sleepers out of your eyes, and give thanks one more time that Victor didn't snore. In a day or two you begin to appreciate the little things like Ludmila's glasses of hot tea with sugar and the rhythmic, rocking motion of the train.

Siberia simply overwhelms you with its size. From the Ural Mountains east of Moscow, which separate Europe from Asia as

well as European Russia from Siberia, to the city of Irkutsk by Lake
Baikal, there is nothing but a flat plain lined on each side of the
track by silver birch trees. Three thousand miles of birch trees. It's
amazing. With every bend you expect a different vista to unfold,
but instead you get more of the same. It seems never-ending because it is never-ending. That's what makes it Siberia.

For a diversion you can go to the "stolovaya" (dining car), although what you find there is also unchanging. This is especially so
because inside the train Moscow time is observed. So as you get
farther and farther away from Moscow, it is easier and easier to
become disoriented. One morning I got up with the sun and headed
to the stolovaya for breakfast only to be told by the surly attendant
to come back in six hours.

Another time I entered the dining car when there were three
tables full of people just finishing breakfast. The waitress cleaned
up after them before acknowledging my presence. Fifteen minutes
had gone by. I was alone in the stolovaya with a waitress, a cashier,
a cook, and an administrator. The cash register malfunctioned, and
they all turned their attention to it. One-half hour went by. Three
Soviets entered the car and sat at the table next to me. Nothing
happened. Fifteen more minutes went by. The Soviet passengers
were peeved, too. They yelled at the waitress. She yelled back. I
had been waiting one hour. Finally, the waitress brought the Soviets some soup to quiet them. They pointed out that I had been
waiting even longer. She turned to me defiantly, and I said to her
in my coolest Clint Eastwood manner, "Doomayo, chto menyeh
noozhna escho vremiya." (I think I need a little more time.) Then
I got up and left.

From Irkutsk to Khabarovsk in the Soviet Far East is like the
American west. The Trans-Baikal region near Irkutsk is mountain-
ous with coniferous forests and swift-moving streams. Farther down
the track we touch the northern fringe of the Gobi Desert before
the homestretch run among mixed forests again. By then it is day
seven, and I'm climbing the walls. It is time to pull the ace from
my sleeve, the diversion extraordinaire I've brought to get me
through to Khabarovsk. It is time for Monopoly.[4]

The players are Victor, Ludmila, a South Korean journalist from
Seoul, and me. There are problems at the outset. Victor and I want
the same game piece, the thimble. I could be deferential, but I
choose not to be. I have heard repeatedly on this trip that Americans are soft. It's time to prove otherwise. Victor can have the

thimble only if I can go before him in the course of play. Grudg-ingly, he agrees. Then, after a brief introduction to the concept of private property for Victor and Ludmila's sake, we are ready to begin. Everyone understands that the winner gets to keep the game itself. (This provides the incentive the Soviet system so sorely lacks.)

Victor and I are quickly out of the running. I don't think Victor ever really understood the game. He bought Baltic Avenue for nostalgic reasons, and I, with my public good mentality. . . . But Ludmila and the South Korean go at each other tooth and nail. It's crazy. Here are two people whose countries do not have diplo-matic relations carrying on as if they, too, were not speaking. Fi-nally, it is the wily Ludmila, the veteran of 30 years on the Trans-Siberian Railroad, who prevails. She thanks me repeatedly as I de-part the train in Khabarovsk and promises to give the game to her grandchildren who live far to the west in the Ukrainian Republic of the USSR. I have done my part for America. I have planted the capitalist seed.

All of its discomforts aside, the one thing that must be said of the Trans-Siberian Railroad is that it gives you a taste not only of the enormous size and scale of the Soviet Union, but also of its relatively undeveloped state. You pass hundreds of peasant villages with chocolate-colored houses ("izbas" in Russian) that lead you to believe you are traveling in the early part of the 20th century, if not the 19th. There are no paved roads, no signs of electricity or running water, and almost no cars. By what we're accustomed to, it's unbelievably backward. Mind you, I'm not saying it's worse than our way of life, or even poorer, unless you define wealth in terms of comfort and convenience. But I am saying it's a harder life. To think this is the same Soviet Union that has put men and women into space is incredible. (But, of course, as I say these words, I imagine my counterpart, the Soviet professor of recreation, driv-ing through the south side of Chicago or Watts in Los Angeles or some of the hill country in the Appalachian states saying, "To think this is the same United States that has put men on the moon is incredible.")

Khabarovsk is about as far away from Moscow as you can get in the Soviet Union, and I'm expecting it to be something of a cow-boy town. I'm ready to have someone tell me, "I don't care how they do things in Moscow! This is the way we do them in Khabarovsk!" But I'm disappointed. Khabarovsk is as red as they come, a sign, I suppose, of the iron-like grip of the dictatorship of the proletariat. Many scholars think the only way to hold a country of this size and ethnic diversity together is through a totalitarian regime. If Gorbachev goes much farther with his "democratizatsia," we may soon find out.

I don't quite know how to describe it, but I'm starting to feel a certain heaviness, a psychological weight bearing down on me. It's somewhere between claustrophobia and depression. I think it has to do with the narrowness of this culture, the slim choices, both with respect to food and ideas. I'm getting tired of Lenin this and Lenin that and Marx and Engels. Other people have told me of a general melancholy in the Soviet Union. I wonder if it's catching?

Here I go. Feeling superior. This time the joke's on me. For all the fun I've made of long lines, sparse choices, and shoddy workmanship, I now must entrust my life to the fruits of Soviet labor. It does not help matters that the first planes I see at the Khabarovsk airport with "Aeroflot" on them are pre-World War II biplanes. I am on my way to Irkutsk, the first of five flights I will be taking in the Soviet Union. As the flight attendant makes her preflight announcements, I look the jet over. I count rivets, check for anything that may be loose, and think what may be my last thoughts about those near and dear to me. These pilots have less to live for, I needle myself. Several hours later, safely on the ground in Irkutsk, I marvel at what a jerk I can be.

I think sometimes I think too much. I'm dining alone tonight in the almost empty restaurant of the Intourist Hotel in Irkutsk. In a room that holds 300 people, the waitress seats me by a huge speaker next to the dance floor. I pray the band won't start before I'm through, but it does, and to my surprise the music is neither loud nor unpleasant. In the next two hours I watch the room fill up with happy, smiling faces. Men bring women flowers, and they eat, drink, and laugh together. The Soviet people are enjoying themselves.

Maybe I'm making too much of this socialism thing. Maybe at a very basic level, at the living of one's life level, government is not that big a deal. People focus on their work, their home lives, and their families. Government in the USSR may be something far away and removed just as Washington so often seems in the United States. Maybe at the personal level, what goes on in Moscow doesn't matter that much, either.

Then again, maybe my day at Lake Baikal has done this to me. It's a wonderful place, a gorgeous place, a sparkling, crystal clear, freshwater sea deep in Siberia. Maybe the majesty of this lake has made human problems seem trivial the same way a trip into the Grand Canyon does back home. Maybe it's altered my perspective. Nature has a way of doing that to me.

Then again, maybe it's the vodka I'm having with supper. It's a tasty meal consisting of an exotic salad, shashlik, ice cream ("morozhenoye" in Russian), and—Oh my god, I don't believe it! —the band is playing Stevie Wonder's "I Just Called to Say I Love You." I've been in the Soviet Union three weeks, and it's the first tune I've recognized. Talk about striking a responsive chord! I lean over to the couple seated next to me and tell them I, too, am from Motown. I toast Stevie with one last gulp of Stolichnaya and all seems right with the world. "Byt' v strooyeh!" (Life, be in it!) I shout out to no one in particular as I sashay across the dance floor and out the door.

In Kiev, my spirit continues to soar. Unlike the Siberian cities or Moscow or Leningrad, my arrival in Kiev, the "mother" of Russian cities, is accompanied by the full blossoming of spring. Kiev has been described as a city built in a garden, and, indeed, it has a garden-like atmosphere at this time of year. In my four days here I will walk almost 50 miles. It is a perfect place for someone like me. There are trees everywhere interwoven with human edifices, promenades, and benches. It is a city of parks and open space unlike any other I have visited in my life. Kiev is built for pedestrians as well as automobiles. It is built for enjoyment as well as business. Kiev, in my mind, is what a big city should be if it has to be big.

Kiev is also testimony to the resilience of the Soviet people. It has been fought over, and in, for centuries. It was almost totally destroyed in the Second World War. It is the site of Babi Yar, one of the infamous Jewish concentration camps, and, more recently, it has been associated with Chernobyl to the north. But Kiev endures. Lost in its beauty, I am optimistic about the possibilities for peace in our time. Or, I wonder, am I simply being charmed by a false hope of spring?

On the overnight train from Kiev to Odessa, I debate with myself whether the only difference between our way of life and the Soviets' is a matter of style. We both seem to believe in the production of goods and services as the way to human well-being, but we disagree over the means. By and large, the state owns the means of production in the Soviet Union. By and large, individuals own the means of production in the United States. In the Soviet Union, consequently, the incentive to plan rests with the state, while in our country it rests with the individual. Based on my observations and experiences, coupled with what I've read, it is clear to me that our system is much more effective at developing and delivering the goods. On this point, I concur with many contemporary scholars who have concluded that Marx simply misunderstood human nature. In theory, socialism has a certain intellectual appeal. In practice, it doesn't pan out. So goes the argument of Brzezinski's new book.

Why, then, am I not in a mood to celebrate? It's because this trip has prompted me to take a more critical look at our way of doing things as well. For example, in an article I read recently by Garrett Hardin titled "What Marx Missed,"[5] Hardin says after Marx professed "from each according to his ability, to each according to his needs" he failed to ask "and then what?" But can we not also make this same criticism of capitalism? As far as I can tell, our answer to what comes after the production problem would likely be "more of the same." But is that a viable plan for human fulfillment in a world of limited resources? I think not. Once our creature comforts have been secured, are we not obliged to elevate our aspirations? Wasn't that Maslow's point? But are we really ascending the hierarchy in the United States? Or are we still enamored with consumption and growth? "Growth for growth's sake," Edward Abbey said not too long before he died, "is the ideology of the cancer cell."

I really believe we have come of age in the United States. I know there are some important exceptions, but most of us live a comfortable life. It is now time to get on with it, to exercise our maturity, our wisdom, indeed, our leisure, to promote a way of life that is meaningful and sustainable in global terms. Are we doing this? Or are we now turning abroad to perpetuate the adolescent notion that the good life can best be measured by the increased consumption of things? I do not take it as a particularly good sign that, within the shadow of the Kremlin, the first indication of America's presence in Moscow is the Baskin Robbins logo on the first floor of the Rossia Hotel or that negotiations with McDonald's are proceeding nicely. I know they are part of America and that we're committed to free enterprise, but I also know we have contributions to make that are much more urgently needed in the USSR. The air quality in Leningrad is poor, and the city's water is plagued by giardia. Moscow needs auto emission standards and smog control devices. The Trans-Siberian Railroad could benefit from a sewage disposal system to replace the practice of depositing human waste out onto the track. Certainly, we could be of technical assistance in these matters.

The term "novoye myshleniye" (new thinking) serves as the foundation of Gorbachev's foreign policy. It actually originated back in 1955 in a document remembered as the Russell-Einstein manifesto. "Novoye myshleniye" recognizes that all people share one fragile world and that our common home is in critical danger unless we all learn to develop peaceful, cooperative strategies for dealing with international problems and resolving disputes. The concept appeals to me. It is ecological. It is wise. The question is whether it will ever enjoy the backing of the United States? Or, more specifically, will it ever enjoy the backing of General Dynamics? For what I am talking about in its most fundamental sense is the possibility in our lifetime of converting guns into butter.

To consider seriously the prospect of peaceful coexistence with the Soviet Union is a difficult psychological undertaking. It requires discarding long-held emotional and intellectual baggage. Who among us does not carry images of the young and charming John F. Kennedy representing Camelot juxtaposed against the ruddy-faced, shoe-pounding Nikita Khrushchev representing the Evil Empire? These are powerful images, but they must be erased from our memories. We live in a different world now, a different time, a different day. Different thinking must prevail. Dare I say, "novoye myshleniye?"

But I almost forgot. I am on a sabbatical to study recreation and leisure in the Soviet Union, and Odessa is a city of recreation. It is one of the principal resorts on the north shore of the Black Sea. Along with Yalta, Sevastapol, Sochi, and other coastal cities, it forms the Soviet Riviera. From all points north, Leningraders, Muscovites, and other frozen city dwellers flock to these beaches for sun, mineral waters, and curative baths. The Soviets are big on recreation for its medicinal or health-building powers. It is important to remember that most of the USSR is on a latitude equivalent to that of northern Canada. Warmth is at a premium. In Odessa it is possible to thaw out, recuperate, and recharge one's batteries for the severe Russian winter. It is a place for "r and r," as we used to call it in the army, rest and relaxation, recreation to restore oneself for work.

But is there leisure in the Soviet Union? If leisure is contingent on the freedom to combine the contemplative faculty with action in the public arena to promote the good life, then I have my doubts. Despite the opening up I sense in the Soviet Union, it is clear to me that people are not yet really free here in the way we are in the United States. They are not free to leave their country, to worship as they please, to say whatever they will. They may be free to contemplate, to think their thoughts, but they are not free to translate those thoughts into action like we are in the United States.

Here I go again, feeling superior. Soon after these words come pouring confidently out of my mouth, I find myself seated across the breakfast table from a man who tells me he's from Washington, DC, originally; although, for the last 17 years he has lived in Stockholm, Sweden. A black Vietnam veteran, holder of the Purple Heart, he says he felt compelled to leave the United States in the early 1970s because of his antiwar and civil rights activism. Nothing specific was done to him, he reassures me. He just could not reconcile the fact that after all he'd done for his country, the government still thought it necessary to keep him under surveillance. He now has a Swedish wife and Swedish citizenship. "Blacks [in the United States] are no better off than they were in the 1960s," he sighs. "The situation is not helped any by their generally deteriorating family life." Although he insists he holds no grudges and he talks of frequent trips to visit his parents in Washington, D C, there is something about this man's story that unnerves me. He has forced me to consider the possibility that our society is less free than I want to think it is.

It is probably good that my last two stops on this journey are Tbilisi, the capitol of the Georgian Republic, and Tallinn, the capitol of Estonia. They are very different culturally from the rest of the USSR. Nationalism is strongly felt in both places. If Gorbachev is sincere about developing a more pluralistic society, if he really wants people to have a voice, if he really means it when he talks about democratizing the Soviet way of life, then pay attention to what happens in these two high-spirited, independent-minded republics. The question on everyone's mind is whether the restructuring that must be done to revitalize the economy will undo the political stability of the Soviet Union. Once the Soviet people have tasted something of the freedom we enjoy, will they tolerate any reversion to former ways? The question is up in the air.

For a long time now, the Soviet Union has isolated itself from the rest of the world. That isolation has contributed to an atmosphere of distrust and confrontation. But the USSR is beginning to open up, and, as it turns out, tourism may play the role of peacemaker. What diplomats oftentimes have failed to see, tourists have not. People everywhere have the same concerns for family, friends, and the dignity of work worth doing. There are common bonds that transcend our cultural and linguistic differences. At the most basic level, we are the same. We are one people.

Time is passing quickly now. My trip is almost over. After five years of preparation, after five weeks behind the Iron Curtain, after 15,000 miles by plane, train, boat, bus, car, and foot, after countless conversations with Soviet citizens and many others from abroad, what can be said of all this?

Lake Baikal comes to mind.[6] Like Baikal, which has one-sixth of the world's freshwater, the Soviet Union has one-sixth of the world's land area. Like Baikal, which has over 2,500 different species of marine life, the Soviet Union has 100 different peoples who speak more than 150 different languages and dialects. Like Baikal, whose depth is unfathomable, the Soviet Union is rich beyond belief in natural resources. Like Baikal, whose moods and temperaments defy description, so, too, is the character of the Soviet Union almost impossible to define.

What do I know of this country after five weeks? No more than I know of Lake Baikal after one day. Almost nothing, really. Only that I need to prepare again, that I would like to return someday, that I have my work cut out for me. They say Baikal's water is so pure that a white sheet can be seen clearly in it at a depth of 120 feet. But in the viewing, it is wise to remember that Baikal is over 5,280 feet deep. So it is with the Soviet Union.

In Tallinn, as I board the steamer that will take me across the Gulf of Finland to Helsinki and the Free World, I can't help but think how lucky I am to have been born in the United States of America. I am, for the first time in my life, truly patriotic; not in an "us versus them" sense or in a "we're better than they are" sense, but in the sense of a genuine appreciation for what it means to live in a free, or, perhaps I should say, freer society.

Freedom, I realize now more than ever, brings with it an obligation at the level of the individual that cannot be borne by individuals who are not free to make their own choices, to chart their own lives, to help direct their own nation's destiny. Freedom demands that we personally take responsibility for doing what is right.

My dream for our country is that we will exercise our freedom wisely and carry out its obligations in a way that does justice to all concerned: to our forebears who made freedom possible, to those unfree who look to us for guidance, to our children who will inherit the consequences of our freely chosen acts, to our Mother Earth who is the ultimate source of our freedom, and to each and every one of us who must bear the burden of decisions made.[7]

As the steamer makes its way out into open water, I work my way forward to the bow and put my face into the wind. I take several long, deep breaths of oxygen. Above me, a seagull soars on currents of fresh air. I wonder? Is it just me, or can anyone else on board actually feel the difference?

Chapter 11

SOLDIER LAKE

My son, Adam, is asleep beside me. Where have the years gone? He's so big now. A 12-year-old who can pick me up when he hugs me and who does just that on occasion for the pure joy of it. I wonder what he'll do with his life?

Outside, the wind is coming and going in powerful surges. If it weren't for our body weight, I think the tent would have blown into Soldier Lake by now. With every gust I halfway expect it to collapse on us. How durable can a $25 backpacking tent possibly be?

After three days, Adam and I have abandoned our plan to walk the entire 210 miles of the John Muir Trail. There just didn't seem to be much point in putting either of us through the three week ordeal. Besides, it was largely my idea. I was the one who really felt the need to get away from it all. Adam felt no such compulsion. So now we are focusing on fishing, day-hiking, and enjoying each other's company.

Today, we climbed high above Soldier Lake and then worked our way cross-country to explore the neighboring Rock Creek drainage. We were looking for good fishing but found none. There were lots of fingerlings, but when you set the hook you frequently jerked the fish clear out of the water. Not much sport in that. After lunch, we had to hustle several miles back down to camp to beat the arrival of an afternoon thunderstorm. Adam then proceeded to inhale a dinner of freeze-dried lasagna, catch and release several Golden trout, and cap the day off by challenging me to a dozen hands of gin rummy before dark. By the soundness of his sleep, he had a full day.

Now I'm afraid it's going to be one of those nights. My sleeping bag feels more like a straitjacket than a bed. No matter which way I turn I can't get comfortable. I change position every few minutes but nothing helps. How did Adam do it? Perhaps there is just too much stuff going on inside my head.

Everyone tells me not to take it personally. It's just one of those things. The State of California is in its worst financial crisis since the Great Depression. The California State University System must be pared down accordingly. And San Diego State University, one of 20 campuses within the system, must absorb its fair share of the cuts. According to SDSU's president, nine academic departments have to go. One of them is mine.

Why is it, I wonder, that our Department of Recreation, Parks, and Tourism is such an easy target? What is it about us? We are, to be sure, a small faculty, but we bring in more grant money than any other unit in our college. We have healthy numbers of student majors as well as large enrollments in our general education courses. Our faculty are conscientious about teaching, scholarship, and service. We are, then, by all established measures, pulling our own weight. Why us?

The answer, it is clear to me as I roll over for the umpteenth time, is that eliminating our department is the politically correct thing to do. Most people will accept on face value the president's rationale that a university can continue to exist in economically difficult times without the benefit of an academic program in parks and recreation. Yes, everyone will agree, it's too bad. Yes, they'll say, we had a fine faculty. But when all is said and done, who is really going to bemoan our absence? What mover and shaker—what player—is simply not going to stand for this? And what politician will respond in turn? No one, I sadly conclude, will come to our rescue.

Of more immediate concern is what to tell my boys. While I have failed them in many ways as a father, the one thing I have always felt good about is the example I set regarding my work. While so many people resent or regret what they do for a living, I have taken great delight in my livelihood. I am one of the few people I know who actually looks forward to Monday mornings. In this context, at least, I have been a good role model. And now this.

How could I not take it personally? After 15 years as a tenured professor, what I love to do and look forward to doing has been denied me by one individual who simply pronounced that the area of human service I have dedicated my life to is not central to the mission of San Diego State University. What good is tenure if it is not to protect me from just this kind of person? I have been be-trayed by my own university, the one I have been loyal to all these years. What lesson can I draw from this for my children? What to tell them?

I can hear the chorus building. From every student I've ever taught to every convention delegate I've ever addressed, I can hear them all chanting: "Life is a struggle! Life is a risk! Embrace it! Celebrate it!" Ah, Dustin, if there is a god, it is a god with a sense of humor. You have, have you not, been writing about all these issues, about all these themes related to life's uncertainties, from the certainty of a tenured full professor's perch? You have been feeding at the public trough, secure in the knowledge that tenure, like death and taxes, is forever. You have in your own cerebral way grown fat and complacent.

Well, it's time to pay the piper, to practice what you preach, to put up or shut up. It's time to get lean and mean. Welcome to life's real no-rescue wilderness, a wilderness replete with unemployment lines, inferiority complexes, and inadequate health insurance.

Remember the Backwards Law? And I quote, "to live life fully is to let go of life completely." Try, if you can, to think of tenure, health insurance, and a pension plan as but futile attempts to hold on to what cannot be held. Try, if you can, to live by your own words. "Life, when held in check, loses its essence." Do you find this sentence as profound now as you used to? It's time to cut loose, to see what you're made of, to test your mettle. It's time to see if there's anything more to you than words.

You wonder what Adam is going to do with his life? Never mind Adam. He's on his way to becoming a fisherman. And time is on his side. A more intriguing question is what are you going to do with the rest of your life? What are you on your way to becoming?

Outside the tent, high above Soldier Lake, high above the swirl-ing wind, and high above the mountain peaks that crown the Si-erra Nevada, the night sky is filled with twinkling stars, each one indifferent to my impending joblessness. Meanwhile, I toss and turn and move in and out of various states of consciousness. I take solace in the thoughts that things are bound to look better in the morning light and that my son, Adam, is asleep beside me.

Chapter 12

LEAVE IT TO BEAVER

I like the hustle and bustle of airports. People are everywhere, coming and going, on their way to one meeting or another, about to close a big deal. Nowadays, the most successful people pull suitcases on little wheels with one hand and talk on cell phones with the other. There is an industriousness to their stride. Time is of the essence. Charging up and down the concourses, their careers, and their lives, are going places.

Today I'm on a concourse of my own. I'm at San Diego's Lindbergh Field on my way to Sacramento. My stride, however, leaves something to be desired. I'm in no rush. I have no meeting to attend. I have no deal to close. I'm going to Chico, California, to visit a newly found friend. In 1987, when I first met Emilyn Sheffield, her career was at its low point, while mine was at its high. Now it's the other way around. Emilyn has found "Brigadoon," as she describes Chico, where everything is within walking distance, the turkey sandwiches at Cory's are to die for, and the pace of life is civilized. Emilyn tells me there is even a trout stream meandering through Chico State University's campus. A trout stream. From her description, Chico must be a special place. I could use a dose of that right now. For it occurs to me, as I amble down the concourse, that my career and my life are going nowhere special themselves.

When the president of San Diego State University announced his intention to eliminate my academic department in the spring of 1992, I was beside myself. We had just sailed through an accreditation visit by the National Recreation and Park Association's Council on Accreditation, and we had just been identified in the Journal of Physical Education, Recreation, and Dance as the number one undergraduate program in parks and recreation in the United States in terms of faculty scholarship.

On a personal level, things also were going well. I had just served as President of the Society of Park and Recreation Educators, and I had recently been elected to the Academy of Leisure Sciences, an international scholastic honorary society. I was being invited to give increasing numbers of keynote talks, and my writing, which had always been important to me, was progressing nicely.

The day the word came down, I had just returned from giving a keynote address to a consortium of university faculty and students at the Philmont Scout Ranch near Cimmaron, New Mexico. I was on cloud nine. My speech went well, New Mexico was spectacular, and the rarefied air infused me with renewed enthusiasm for the life I was leading. The future looked bright.

My department chairman walked into my office, asked how my trip went, and then broke the bad news, explaining as best he could what happened. The administration told him the department had to give up half its tenured lines. The most recent hires, including me, had to go. "You might as well eliminate the entire department!" he shot back. The administration agreed.

I couldn't believe what I was hearing. There must be some mistake. Surely, the president or the academic vice president or the dean of the college would come to us and explain how the decision had been made. Surely, they would talk to us face to face about the predicament they were in, about why they were proposing what they were proposing. Surely, they would have the decency to do that. They didn't.

The department self-destructed. One professor took early retirement. Another moved back east to accommodate a spouse's career move. Another took a job in Kansas. Another took a job in Colorado. Another simply quit. A program that had taken 20 years to build came unraveled in a matter of days. It was painful to watch.

Then, in the fall of 1992, five months after the president's announcement, the administration reversed itself. The Department of Recreation, Parks, and Tourism was worth keeping after all. A second look had revealed a fine program with a faculty committed to professional growth, teaching, and service. No need for a bloodletting. No need for anyone to pack.

It was too late. The damage was done. A faculty of 10 was now a faculty of five. The university's position was that nothing bad really happened. No one was let go. Tenure was not violated. A few fidgety professors left of their own accord, but that was their problem. The university itself did nothing wrong.

The rest of us, like wounded deer, now found ourselves in a university that, although it had shot us, was not going to finish the job. I was more offended by that than I was by the threat of elimination. Our "fine" program was, in reality, a mere shadow of its former self. The vote of confidence rang hollow. The hard truth was that the university got what it wanted from us voluntarily. We did to ourselves what they wanted done. They didn't have to soil their hands. From the dean to the academic vice president to the president to the chancellor of the California State University System, I saw no evidence of a backbone. Even when it was clear the president had blundered and should be removed, the chancellor balked. I had seen enough. I no longer wanted to be a professor at San Diego State University. I resigned.

Still, I wanted to remain in San Diego. I had two sons to see through junior and senior high school. I felt bad enough about a divorce from their mother. I was not about to leave them, too. More than they needed me, however, I needed them. They gave my life a sense of meaning and purpose that work no longer did.

I was miserable for several months. When I was a professor, I felt I was part of a larger mission, a larger cause, a larger movement. Now I felt isolated and alone. It was hard to handle. I thought my career was finished, that I was over the hill. It was a sorry feeling. At 46, I was still relatively young. But for some reason, it was hard to look forward, to be optimistic. My best days, I feared, were behind me.

Southwest Airlines doesn't assign seats. It's first come, first served. That's okay by me, because I always get to the airport early. That means I usually get my choice of seats, and that means a window seat. I'm like a little kid when I fly, with my nose stuck to the window trying to identify this or that feature of the landscape beneath the plane. I know the geography of the United States like the back of my hand, and I can often pinpoint where we are on a flight by glancing out the window.

However, on this flight to Sacramento I'm in a fog. Oblivious to my surroundings, I plop down in an aisle seat. How am I ever going to turn things around? Five years is a long time to tread water, to put my career on hold. How am I going to get through this?

The jet takes off over Point Loma and banks to the northwest to parallel the coast to Los Angeles. I brood over my prospects. My friends have already suggested that I have enough of a track record to function on my own as an independent scholar, a "PhD for hire" who works on a contractual basis with whomever is willing to pay for my services. But just what is it that I have to offer? What is it exactly that I do? Who needs me? San Diego State certainly didn't.

The arrival of peanuts and a soft drink interrupts my train of thought. Where are we now? Typically, the flight veers north over Los Angeles and heads up the central valley of California. On a clear day like this the Sierra Nevada will be visible out the right side of the plane. I know the High Sierra from Sequoia National Park north to Yosemite. I've hiked it all. Maybe the gentleman sitting in the window seat next to me would like to benefit from my services, from what it is I do, from what it is I know. Maybe he needs me.

I lean over. And there, looking back at me, to my complete and utter astonishment, is a visage from the distant past, a TV character from my childhood. I'm dumbfounded. This can't be happening. This can't be real. I'm sitting next to the grown-up version of Jerry Mathers, the star of *Leave It To Beaver*. I cannot believe it. Here I am, wallowing in my misery, thinking my best days are behind me, that my career and my life are over, and I'm sitting next to a man whose career peaked in the 1950s when he was a child. Yet here he sits, with his head on straight, a cheerful disposition, and a catering business I will soon find out about.

I introduce myself. We make small talk. I tell him a little bit about my life, and he tells me a little bit about his. He is thoughtful and reflective. Sensitive to my plight, he speaks quietly of the need to let go, to move on, to create new meaning for oneself. For my part, I point out Moro Rock in Sequoia National Park, the Rae Lakes loop in Kings Canyon National Park, and El Capitan and Half Dome in Yosemite National Park. I even point out Hetch Hetchy and begin to recount its history when the pilot interrupts me—mercifully, I suppose, from Mr. Mathers' point of view—to announce our descent into Sacramento. I wind down my lecture.

Bringing my seat back to its upright position, it dawns on me that the brief conversation I just had with Jerry Mathers is significant. Life is full of chapters. The challenge is to appreciate each chapter for itself, to refrain from judging any one chapter until we approach the end of the larger work that is each of our lives. Only then can we really understand how each chapter contributes to the unfolding of the entire story. Only then will we have the proper perspective. There is a need for tolerance, acceptance, patience, humility, humor, and, I think, an abiding faith that things are going to work out in the long run.

As we file off the plane, I say good-bye to Mr. Mathers and thank him for his positive influence on me during my childhood. Then I stroll down the concourse toward the baggage claim area. Ahead of me, with a spring in his step, Jerry Mathers goes about his business. Charging up the concourse in the opposite direction, baby boomers pull suitcases on little wheels and talk on cell phones. Doing double takes, they break out in broad smiles and shout out to no one in particular, "It's the Beaver!"

Chapter 13

BETTING ON BIG BERTHA

When I gave up tenure and walked away from university life, I didn't really think about the ramifications. I was acting on principle. I went from an annual salary of $63,000 to $0. On top of that, I lost my health insurance. Since I was not yet 50, I was not entitled to a retirement income either. I was on my own.

My lack of interest in the "real" world compounded my problems. I knew little about the private sector. I didn't want to look for a job there. I had lived my entire life in classrooms of one kind or another. My world, the world I was at home in, was academe. My life took place largely between my ears.

Neither was I enamored with material things or the wherewithal to acquire them. I was living life as unencumbered as possible. Since I wasn't a spender, I had managed to save some money, which afforded me the time to ponder how I might stay in San Diego and make ends meet without having to venture into the "real" world to get a "real" job.

Peter Witt, a colleague of mine, had just written an essay in a book I edited that struck a responsive chord. Referring to his own academic frustrations, Peter said, "If you can't win with ideas, it is time to move on to a more powerful position."[1]

"Well," I thought to myself, "since I just lost out with ideas, perhaps it is time to move on to a more powerful position." What exactly would that position be? In Peter's case, it was an administrative post high up in his university. In my case, I didn't have a clue. How much power could possibly reside in my one-bedroom apartment?

I thought about trying to write for a living, but the words of another colleague, Tom Goodale, haunted me. In a second book I edited, Tom noted that "among professors who write about parks, recreation and leisure, my guess is that only four earn enough from writing in a year to buy an operable used car. None have shown any inclination to give up their day jobs."[2]

It was about this time that I stumbled on CNBC, the business channel, while fooling around with the TV remote. The ticker moving across the bottom of the screen caught my eye. I was curious. All those symbols marching across the screen seemed to be on a mission. They were going places. Perhaps I could go along, too?

Investing for a living never really occurred to me until that moment. I had been burned once on an oil stock a long time ago, and I could hear my father's admonitions ringing in my ears equating the stock market with Las Vegas. His idea of a good investment was a U.S. Savings Bond. With that mind-set, forged by the Depression, he provided a comfortable living for our family. He slept soundly at night, too. Nevertheless, I stayed tuned to CNBC while I thought about the possibilities. I was going to have a lot of time on my hands. Maybe I could do a quick study of the stock market, make some judicious investments, and monitor the consequences of my decisions from my apartment?

As I mulled it over, the idea took on the appearance of a Faustian bargain. Here I was, with little use for money and little regard for the private sector, thinking about devoting my full attention to making money in the private sector. I would be attempting to make money for the sake of making money. What I was pondering ran counter to just about everything I stood for. I was like the character, George, on the sitcom *Seinfeld* who decided he should do the exact opposite of everything his instincts told him to do. After all, I rationalized, if power is money, and if what I really want to do is move on to a more powerful position, perhaps investing could be a temporary means to a more powerful and ennobling end.

Knowing where to begin was another matter. I soon found out that people listened closely when Peter Lynch, the former Magellan Mutual Fund manager, talked about investing. Although he was semiretired, Mr. Lynch was a frequent guest on CNBC and other financial news programs. He had written a couple of books for the layperson on investing, so I read them.

Mr. Lynch seemed to be making two fundamental points. First, a layperson could be just as astute as a professional when it came to investing. Second, common sense coupled with a lot of leg work would yield the best results. "Invest in what you know," he insisted. "And look close to home."

Emboldened by Mr. Lynch's advice, I took the plunge. I started reading *The Wall Street Journal, Investor's Business Daily, and Barron's*. I signed up for a trial subscription to *Value Line*. I got up every morning at 5:30 to tune in to CNBC. (The market opened at 9:30 a.m. Eastern Standard Time. That's 6:30 a.m. Pacific Time.) I also started looking at San Diego in a very different light. I began to see more than sun and sand. I saw telecommunications, defense, biotechnology, and leisure industries. Finally, I scoured the San Diego *Union* daily for tidbits about local companies that might give me an edge. The game was on.

I started cautiously, testing the waters. I bought a few hundred shares of Chrysler, Southwest Airlines, and Molecular Biosystems, a local biotech company that, according to the San Diego *Union*, was anticipating a positive ruling from a Food and Drug Administration advisory panel on its flagship product, Albunex, an MRI contrasting agent. Then I held my breath.

Letting loose of my money in the stock market made me queasy. I felt like I was walking a tightrope without a net. There was nothing below to protect me from a free fall. If I erred in my judgment, or if the market crashed, there was nothing to hold me up. I was off belay.

At the same time, there was an undeniable excitement to investing. I was risking. Certainly, the prices of my stocks could go down, but they also could go up. If my reasoning was sound, and if I was patient, I would ultimately be rewarded for it. Or so the logic went.

Within a month, Molecular Biosystems shot up from the low $20s to almost $30 a share with the news of a favorable preliminary ruling from the FDA panel. I was ecstatic. The stock quickly started to slide back down, however, before I sold at $25. Instead of feeling good about making a modest profit, I was upset that I didn't sell at the high point. I would not make that mistake again.

Soon thereafter, I sold Chrysler, which I bought at $17, for $27 and felt smug. Within a year, Chrysler was selling at $60.

My education was underway. Investing, I soon realized, was not an exact science. Moreover, investing in biotech companies could be especially hazardous to your financial health. The price of a biotech stock could rise or fall with the latest research report at a conference in Europe. Not only that, most biotechs were not profitable. They were research and development companies. To invest in them would be to gamble on the likelihood of a scientific breakthrough that would eventually lead to a money-making product. It required a long time horizon and an understanding of applied science.

I toyed with the idea of investing in Immune Response Corporation, a San Diego company dedicated to finding a cure for AIDS. It was founded by Jonas Salk, the Nobel-prize winning scientist who developed the polio vaccine in the 1950s. Betting on him seemed like a good gamble. I soon thought better of it and decided that speculating in biotech companies, even those close to home, was not for me.

"Invest in what you know" was also proving to be easier said than done. What I knew was recreation, parks, and leisure studies, but I was reluctant to put my money there. Part of the problem was the nature of many so-called leisure industries. Dominating the category were hotels and casinos. I'd seen enough of Las Vegas to appreciate the investment potential of gaming stocks, but I was uncomfortable with the idea of trying to profit from other people's vices. A brief holding of Circus-Circus stock, which I eventually sold for a profit, confirmed my suspicions. I felt guilty about the gain.

My brief foray into gaming stocks taught me a very important lesson. A conscience could get in the way of making money in the stock market. Successful investors had to get beyond that somehow. Or perhaps, I should say, successful "traders" had to get beyond that somehow. What I was beginning to appreciate was a difference between people who invested for the long haul and people who took advantage of immediate circumstances to make money in the stock market.

I was unsure who I was. I understood the logic of "buy and hold," but because I needed income in the short-term, I was attracted to opportunities that looked like they might pay off sooner rather than later. What that meant was that I had to be opportunistic. When a hurricane hit Florida, I had to anticipate how I could profit from the associated damage. What would people need? New roofs, new carpets, new homes? When the World Trade Center in New York City was bombed in 1993, I had to anticipate the psychological fallout. What would people everywhere start to worry about? Their own security. Well, then, who does business in that industry? Successful traders, I decided, shared many qualities with ambulance chasers. I didn't want to be that kind of person.

Socially responsible investing was also proving to be elusive. Ben and Jerry's Ice Cream aside, sorting out socially responsible from socially irresponsible companies was no mean feat. I had yet to find a company that advertised itself as "socially irresponsible." Although there were mutual funds that specialized in socially responsible investing, the whole point of my experiment was to see if I could succeed on my own. My challenge was to see if I could transfer my skills from the public sector to the private sector and make them work for me. I wanted to see if I could make it on the "outside" on my own terms. If successful, I would give hope to countless other professors who felt trapped in higher education but were unable to free themselves from the shackles of tenure.

One day it occurred to me that there was another, more subtle, explanation for my unwillingness to invest in leisure industries. It was hard for me to take them seriously. Never mind the statistics, which indicated that the amount of money spent on recreation and leisure was staggering. Never mind the reality that tourism was the second largest industry in California. I had just been told by my employer that I was expendable, that my area of expertise was not very important in contemporary life. Under the circumstances, my problem was really one of having little confidence in the significance of what I knew.

The insight jolted me. Who was I going to believe? The university that wanted to jettison my program, or the numbers that indicated the university didn't know what it was doing? Who was I going to place my confidence in? University administrators who knew next to nothing about me, or myself? I began to feel a sea change swelling up inside.

Coincident with my insight, a nascent company was making news in the San Diego *Union*. Callaway Golf had just gone public. The company was the brainchild of Ely Callaway, a former Burlington Industries executive, and more recently the founder of Callaway Vineyards near Temecula, California. Callaway Golf was revolutionizing the golf club industry with its new metal wood, the Big Bertha. "Golf clubs?" I mused. "Hmmm." I recited the mantra. "Invest in what you know." Well, I certainly knew golf. I caddied for several years when I was growing up in Michigan. I played on my high school golf team. I understood the psychology of the game. "And look close to home." Callaway Golf was headquartered in Carlsbad, California, 30 miles north of San Diego. On both counts, the company passed the test.

I hit a golf ball with a Big Bertha. "Ping!" It didn't sound right. I was skeptical. Then I got to thinking about baseball bats. Wooden Louisville Sluggers had given way to metal bats, too. At first, they didn't sound right either. I began to nose around. I asked amateur golfers about the club. I found out how many professional golfers used it on the Nike, PGA, LPGA, and Senior Tours. I visited retailers to get their opinions about it. I looked through the classifieds every Sunday in the San Diego *Union* and discovered that Callaway Golf was not only hiring, it was hiring for shifts around the clock. I drove to Carlsbad at odd times of the day and night (including weekends) to check the factory parking lot. I was doing my leg work.

Above all, I tried to find out more about Ely Callaway. In my mind, he was the key to everything. He was successful at Burlington Industries. He was successful at Callaway Vineyards. Moreover, he had a brashness about him, a confidence I found reassuring. He really believed he was going to revolutionize the golf world. What he felt he had, in effect, was a scientific breakthrough that had culminated in a dynamite, money-making product.

The only difference between the Big Bertha and Albunex was that I knew golf and I knew golfers. The Big Bertha was expensive. I knew that wouldn't matter. If there was one thing I was sure about in life, it was that golfers who would never play on a par with Chi-Chi Rodriguez or Johnny Miller would still want to use their clubs. If there was one thing I felt certain about, it was that golfers, especially amateur golfers, took themselves, and their game, too seriously. An investor could capitalize on that, I thought. I bet the farm.

I held my Callaway Golf stock for a little more than a year. Then, to my delight, I sold it at a large profit. I couldn't believe it. My plan was working. I was earning a living out of my apartment. It was not glamorous work, to be sure. It was tedious and frequently monotonous. I had to get up early every morning. I had to pay attention, it seemed, to virtually everything that was going on in the world, always interpreting events in terms of their possible impact on the prices of my stocks or stocks I was considering. On weekends, I skimmed the financial newspapers, searching for anything that would give me a competitive advantage. I was always on the prowl for a new opportunity. I was always looking for a trend that might lead to some measure of predictability that I could profit from.

I also felt a certain pride in transferring my analytic skills, which I applied formerly to questions of outdoor recreation planning and policy, interpretive techniques, and environmental ethics, to the appraisal of potential investments. Investing was turning out to be not so much a matter of intellect as a matter of having the stomach for it. Stocks had, on average, appreciated 11% annually over the years. Within those averages were a series of ups and downs that made for a bumpy ride on a day-to-day basis. The stock market was a lot like a roller coaster. Appreciating that stocks going down would likely rise up again one day and that stocks rising up would likely come down again one day provided a healthy investment perspective.

Sound sleep, however, was harder to come by. If I woke up in the middle of the night, my mind went to work immediately, and I found it very difficult to drift off again. There was a tension to my life that was new to me. I worried more. There were other side effects as well.

I had always equated a day's work with a day's pay. Investing shook that notion to its core. One October morning in 1993 I woke up to find that I had made a paper profit of $30,000 overnight. That's almost twice the amount of money I earned my first year as a professor. What had I really done to earn that money? How could I explain it to anybody? How could I justify it? I felt like I had robbed a bank. I also wondered whether I would ever be able to do an honest day's work again.

Certain that I had stumbled onto the "Mother Lode," I stayed with the stock. "Fortunes are not made buying and selling stocks. Fortunes are made holding them." Whoever said that surely knew what they were talking about. I was holding on tight. I was going along for the entire ride. I had to think big if I was going to win big. I had to envision being successful.

Four months later, on a February morning in 1994, I woke up to find that I had lost that same $30,000 overnight. "Serves me right," I told myself. I had been greedy. Now I was being duly punished. When I made money in the stock market, I felt guilty about it. When I lost money, I felt I was getting exactly what I deserved. The devil had competition.

When I sold Callaway Golf early in 1994, I turned that profit into a larger one with an investment in Micron Technology, a semiconductor manufacturer whose stock appreciated dramatically later in the year. Buoyed by my luck investing in an industry I didn't know much about, I came close to investing those proceeds in an industry I knew even less about—computer data storage. My friend, Emilyn Sheffield, from Chico State University, who knew a lot about computers, was a fan of Iomega's zip drive storage disks. "Iomega," she said, "is a winner." I asked how she could be so sure, and she deferred to her friend and Macintosh specialist at Chico State, Don Penland. "If Don swears by it," Emilyn insisted, "you can count on it." Iomega's stock was selling for $3 a share. I figured I could buy 50,000 shares. I recited the mantra. "Invest in what you know. And look close to home." On both counts, Iomega failed the test. I passed on it.

A year later, in December of 1995, Iomega's stock, then selling for $51 a share, split three for one. Four months later the split shares were selling for $70 each. Following a two for one split in April of 1996, Iomega reached a high of $55 a share. In effect, had I bought those 50,000 shares for $3 apiece late in 1994, as Emilyn encouraged me to do, each one of them would have been worth $330 in the spring of 1996. You do the math.

As the months wore on, I did manage to gain an income from investing in the stock market, but I found little inherent satisfaction in it. Making money for the sake of making money was not turning out to be my cup of tea. Moreover, there was a tremendous inefficiency in what I was doing. I was investing in a way that was fundamentally contrary to all the rules. I was not diversifying, and I was investing in growth companies when I needed income. I often sold stocks way too early in their cycle because I needed money to pay my bills. My greatest strength was my stock-picking instincts. I tended to make good, and sometimes great, choices. Yet I would often buy and sell out of boredom, out of a need for something to do. Had I been holding down a regular job and investing on the side for the long run, I would have been much farther down the road to those ennobling ends I dream about.

Still, I have no regrets. I've learned a lot about the private sector through investing. While much of that learning has troubled me, it has also shown me that I can succeed outside the university. My experiential education in the stock market will yield a multitude of dividends in my lifetime, not the least of which will be an abundance of stories to tell in my old age: stories about bulls and bears, puts and calls, winners and losers, and, no doubt, more than my share of near misses.

Chapter 14

TIME FOR POOL:
THE SURPRISING WAY . . .

They say women outlive men, in part, because they have support groups to see them through life's difficulties. Men, on the other hand, isolate themselves. Outside of their immediate family, and possibly a coworker or two, men have fewer friends to call on when things go awry. Indeed, the research tells us single men and divorced men are not likely to live as long as married men and widowers are not likely to live as long as widows.

Why men tend to have fewer friends than women is not clear to me, but I wouldn't be surprised if it begins with the way men are brought up. First, they are taught that life is highly competitive. Then they are told they must make it on their own. Finally, they are admonished to stand alone against the world if need be in defense of their principles. The measure of manhood is in the ability to withstand pain, hide feelings, and project an air of confidence and autonomy.

This explains why men don't ask for directions—and why I am presently lost somewhere deep in the rural countryside of western Pennsylvania. I'm on my way to State College for an inaugural pool tournament at the home of Geof Godbey, a professor of recreation and leisure studies at Penn State. Geof invited Tom Goodale, another professor of recreation and leisure studies, from George Mason University in Virginia, and me to spend a few days shooting pool and "shooting the breeze." We will play straight pool. The first person to sink 1,000 balls wins. Whatever conversation transpires will be a bonus.

The invitation could not have come at a better time for me. Feeling adrift since my departure from San Diego State University, I'd isolated myself from my colleagues for several months. I used to stay connected through conferences, collaborative writing, and phone calls. Now I was out of the loop, especially since I didn't have e-mail. Geof, Tom, and I just happened to run into one another in late May of 1991 at a Forest Service workshop in Estes Park, Colorado. We whiled away an evening together drinking beer, exchanging barbs, and shooting pool. The competitive juices were flowing, and Geof sensed an evenly matched trio. Although it took three years to materialize, the seeds of the State College shoot-out were sown then.

I finally break down and ask for directions. I exited Interstate 79 so I could see Slippery Rock, a college town I've been curious about since my Michigan days when they announced the Slippery Rock scores at football games. Then I headed east through a maze of backcountry roads to Punxsutawney, a town I wanted to visit because of its Groundhog Day fame. Somewhere in between the two I lost my bearings, and now the gas station attendant tells me I'll be better off getting back on Interstate 80 and following the signs. Sheepishly, I heed his advice. With the time I save, I'll be able to stop at a roadside stand and pick up some sweet corn, tomatoes, zucchini, and any other produce that might endear me to my host, a devout vegetarian.

When I pull up to the Godbey residence, a pleasant split-level home overlooking "Happy Valley," Geof and Tom greet me warmly. I apologize for my late arrival and confess my navigational shortcomings. Geof smiles and then educates me about rural Pennsylvania. He says most people are surprised by the remoteness. When they think of Pennsylvania, they think of Philadelphia or Pittsburgh. They assume it's an urban state. Pennsylvania is far from urban. It's made up of hills and valleys, meandering rivers, and dense forests. When it comes to people, though, Pennsylvania is sparsely populated.

A tasty vegetarian meal awaits me inside, including freshly baked bread. Wine and easy conversation accompany the dining. It feels really good to be in the company of these two men. I am at ease. We talk about the pool-playing agenda, possible side trips to visit friends, and restaurant choices. We meet Geof's daughter, Cassandra, and her husband, Jimmy, who live in an adjoining apartment. We also meet Whiskey, the dog. Jimmy keeps a keg in the refrigerator in the garage, and he invites us to tap it. Jimmy is also a gourmet cook.

After supper, we head downstairs to get acquainted with the "field of battle." It's a good table. The balls roll true. We'll practice tonight, get a good night's sleep, and go at it in earnest in the morning. We don't know how long it will take for any one of us to sink 1,000 balls. Given the relaxed atmosphere, the good company, the proximity of the keg, and the Epicurean skills of Geof, Jimmy, and Cassandra, I really don't care. To top it off, "Whisko the Wonder Dog" likes me.

Later on, lying in bed, I reflect on this curious gathering. Both Geof and Tom are nationally renowned scholars. They are two of the best thinkers and writers in our field. They are respected for their incisiveness, for their intellectual prowess. Geof, in particular, is an imposing figure. He is 6'4" tall, with a frilly shock of white hair and a physique toned by regular games of squash. Geof, by his own admission, loves "the thrust and parry of debate, the theatrical pomposity of those who think themselves to have answers . . ."[1] He has been at Penn State long enough to have influenced the lives of scores of graduate students who have written theses and dissertations under his supervision.

Tom, on the other hand, is imposing in more subtle ways. Standing 5'3" tall, he is a master of self-deprecation. He refers to himself as "vertically challenged" in one breath and then points out that people his size are "environmentally friendlier" than larger people in the next breath. Tom was a professor for several years at the University of Ottawa in Canada before returning to the United States to teach at George Mason. Unlike Geof, the bulk of his teaching has been at the undergraduate level. Tom is regarded highly for the size of his thoughts and for his convictions. It is not uncommon for him to preside over dinner conversations on topics ranging from history to higher education, or from poetry to politics.

I am flattered to be in their company. I am also a bit intimidated. They both think clearly, express themselves clearly, and defend their points of view clearly. Wanting to hold my own, I imagine how their students must feel when "sparring" with them. Fortunately, they will not be grading me.

Morning comes too soon. Thanks to Tom, who always gets up early, the coffee is ready along with the *Centre Daily Times*. Geof has prepared yogurt, fruit, toast, and marmalade. Though the mood is laid back and the conversation light, the "boys" are itching to play pool. I am, too. We head downstairs.

Geof has prepared several score sheets on his computer. He now reviews the rules. Are we in agreement? Well, not quite.

Geof favors rules that reward strength and "slop" shots. Tom favors calling each shot and a "purer" form of play. We reach a compromise. "Slop" shots are permitted on the break. After that we must call our shots. We're ready to begin. Each of us throws a pill to see who goes first, second, and third. Geof breaks, followed by Tom and me. Whiskey curls up on the nearby sofa, oblivious to the high drama about to unfold.

We shoot pool for three hours, pausing only for an occasional snack, a draft from the refrigerator, or a visit from Cassandra or Jimmy. There are also infrequent phone calls from curious others who have heard that something "unusual" is going on at Godbey's. Apparently, what we are doing is odd, if not bizarre, for three grown men: to sequester ourselves like this, to play like this. It is the masculine equivalent of a pajama party, a sleepover. What are we up to? Who are we gossiping about?

As the tournament progresses, our personalities reveal themselves in ways that invite labeling. Influenced by Whiskey, no doubt, we have assumed our own dog-like identities. Geof is "Big Dog." Tom is "The Terrier." I am "The Retriever." Big Dog is strong and aggressive. The Terrier means business and does not let go. The Retriever is kind and wants only to please others, especially those who follow him in the rotation.

Play is punctuated by a constant banter. When The Retriever leaves Big Dog an easy shot, Big Dog reinforces him with verbal pats and promises of milk bones. When The Retriever leaves Big Dog with no shot, Big Dog admonishes him with "b-a-a-d dog!" and threatens neutering. Meanwhile, The Terrier attends to business, sinking one ball after another.

At lunch time, we pile into Geof's Hyundai and head for one of State College's eateries. Geof drives, Tom rides shotgun, and I sit in the backseat with my head out the window. Following lunch, Geof drives us by Joe Paterno's house. "JoePa" is a folk hero in Happy Valley. Geof tells us JoePa probably could be governor of the Commonwealth if he was so inclined. It's not just the winning record, Geof insists. The man has scruples that remain untarnished by his athletic and financial success. There is genuine admiration in Geof's voice.

Back at the "Godbeyrosa," we walk the fields around Geof's house. Whiskey runs ahead of us sniffing out everything in sight. All seems right with the world. We stop for a few minutes at Geof's garden to survey the vegetables. The harvest is going to be a good one. Geof delights in eating far down the food chain and in growing his own produce. He shares his bounty with Cassandra and Jimmy; Tamara, his older daughter; and friends and neighbors. There is a pastoral quality to this place that calms me. It feels civilized. With a few squash and zucchini in hand, we slowly make our way back to the house, to the basement, to the table.

Whiskey resumes her position on the sofa. We review the score sheet, trade a few quips, and throw the pills. Once again it is Big Dog, The Terrier, and The Retriever. It is still a long way to 1,000.

The afternoon features several momentum shifts. Big Dog starts strong, but he's easily distracted by his own humor. The Retriever is just happy to be playing, and his attention span is embarrassingly short. He obediently absorbs the brunt of Big Dog's "thrusts and parries" while The Terrier shoots pool. Then, all of a sudden, the afternoon session is over. The score sheet shows a clear lead dog, a dog within barking distance, and one lost dog. It's time for a break.

We head for Frank Guadagnolo's place. Frank and his wife, Deb Kerstetter, teach at Penn State with Geof. They just moved into a new home in the country, and they invited us to dinner. Their house is gorgeous. Nestled into a beautiful hillside lot by the woods, the house has a California look. Frank and Deb inquire about the tournament and humor us as we evade specifics about who's winning and losing. Then we sit down to an evening of great food and conversation. Over dessert and coffee, we listen to an "oldies" station on the stereo. Geof, an occasional dancer on Dick Clark's *American Bandstand* in the late 1950s, regales us with stories about songs and artists. He even shares a few tidbits about Justine, my favorite blond-haired girl on the show.

When we return to Geof's, we adjourn to the redwood deck, sip wine, and contemplate the fireflies. In the distance, the silhouette of Mt. Nittany is visible against the night sky. We chat about our personal lives, professional issues, and the state of our careers.

Each of us has been around long enough to have some sense of a body of work behind us, and much of what we discuss concerns what we might do differently in the future.

All three of us love to write. We have been successful writing for the field of recreation, park, and leisure studies, yet we all aspire to make a larger difference by writing for the general public about the significance of recreation, parks, and leisure in contemporary life. Breaking into the trade market, however, is difficult. Geof has made the most headway so far. It's an uphill battle, to say the least. Perhaps our time will come.

Our ages are not that far apart, but our lives are significantly different. Tom appears to be leading the most normal life. He is married with two grown sons. He is a tenured full professor and lives in Fairfax, Virginia, near the nation's capitol. Tom enjoys the history and culture that surrounds Washington, DC, but at some fundamental level he longs for his home of Cortland, New York. Geof is divorced with two grown daughters. He is also a tenured full professor, but State College, Pennsylvania, is exactly where he wants to be. I, too, am divorced and have two teenage sons. I gave up my tenured full professor position, and I remain in San Diego only to be near my boys. Tom has his personal life together. Geof has his professional life together. I have neither together.

We talk into the wee hours. The stillness is interrupted only by chirping crickets. Then, with a slight buzz from the wine, we say "good night" and retire to our respective beds. In the morning battle calls. The new day presents another opportunity to catch up, take the lead, or keep the lead, as the case may be. For now, however, sleep beckons.

We repeat this pattern for three days until, at last, we have a winner. Even though it's been a marathon and fatigue has taken its toll, it feels like it couldn't possibly be over yet. It feels like I just got here, like I was just saying "Hello," like I was just sitting down to a scrumptious dinner. Yet here we are, shaking hands and congratulating one another on a game well played. We are already referring to our first-ever pool shoot-out in past tense, and there are references to "next time" in our post-game summaries.

Who won? Before we came together for the shoot-out, we agreed that we would keep the outcome to ourselves. We would handle inquiries about who won and who lost in the same manner. When asked, "Who won?" we would answer, "Each won more than the other." When asked, "Who lost?" we would answer, "Each lost less than the other." If pressed for anything more, our answers would be unprintable.

One final evening of socializing brings the curtain down on our three-day celebration. Tom leaves at daybreak for northern Virginia. I leave later in the morning for Michigan. I will spend a few days there with my parents before beginning the long car trek back to California and my life as an independent scholar/investor. Tom and Geof will resume their lives as distinguished professors.

Little do we know what we have started. By July of 1998 we will have met for the fifth straight year in Happy Valley. The annual shoot-out has become an important ritual for each of us. Throughout the year, we discuss the possibility of changing the format, playing different games, or inviting others to join us. To date, we have come back to the same game and the same players.[2]

Every June, when the weeds are wet with summer dew, and gardens everywhere are coming into their own, The Terrier and The Retriever make their way to Big Dog's house in State College, Pennsylvania. We shoot pool, eat low on the food chain, drink modestly, and laugh heartily. We catch up on one another's lives and enjoy one another's company. I don't know if what we do qualifies as a support group or if it will lengthen any of our lives. I do know it brings considerable joy to the life I do have. For that I am grateful enough.

Chapter 15

EASY STREET

After 27 years as a public school principal, classroom teacher, and coach, my father, Derby, retired in 1970 at the age of 59. His retirement lasted as long as his career. From 1970 to 1997, he and my mother, Lucille, divided their time between Suttons Bay, Michigan, in the summers, and Port Charlotte, Florida, in the winters. My father passed away on May 17, 1997, at the age of 86, leaving a wife of 56 years, two children, and four grandchildren.

In many respects, my father's life epitomized the lives of countless men born in the United States near the beginning of the 20th century. His early life was a struggle. He was brought up in Portage, Michigan, the son of a mill worker. Life was harsh. There was little money in the family and little regard for formal education. Starting at the age of nine, my father worked long hours in the celery marshes and turned over his wages to his parents for room and board.

My grandfather, Delphonso, was stern and distant. A former lumberjack in Michigan's Upper Peninsula, he had a reputation for toughness. He would sometimes tell my dad to dig worms for fishing and then take the worms, a fishing pole, and my dad's bicycle and go fishing by himself.

After dropping out of high school, my father returned two years later to get his diploma. He asked his parents for financial help so he could attend college. His dad didn't see any point in it. If mill work was good enough for him, it was good enough for his son. He refused. Determined to build a better life for himself, my father turned to a local businessman, who loaned him enough money to attend barber college. Then he literally barbered his way through Western Michigan College at the height of the Depression.

Fortified with a college degree, a teaching credential, and a strong work ethic, dad got the first job offered to anyone in his graduating class, a teaching position in the little town of Tekonsha,

Michigan. While there, he met my mother, and they married on December 22, 1940. My sister, Carol, soon followed in the autumn of 1941, as did the Second World War. Dad enlisted in the navy and subsequently was given a direct commission as a lieutenant junior grade. He served proudly at various posts throughout the United States and ended up in the South Pacific on Saipan in preparation for the invasion of Japan when the war ended. On the voyage home, he won at poker and bought U.S. Savings Bonds with his winnings for my sister's education.

After the war, my father sought a new position in another school district rather than displace the person who had been hired in his stead in Tekonsha. The family moved to the nearby town of Mendon. While there, dad became something of a local celebrity by putting together a high school basketball team even though Mendon didn't have a gymnasium. The players practiced outside on tennis courts that had to be cleared of snow, and they shot at baskets nailed to trees. Despite the primitive conditions, his team managed to win a few games that first season. Needless to say, all the games were away.

Following my arrival in the fall of 1946, my parents made another move to the small town of Owendale in the thumb of Michigan. In those years, my father wore a variety of hats, including that of high school principal, shop teacher, agriculture teacher, coach, and bus driver. In his retirement, he talked fondly of that job and its multiple responsibilities, even though the money had not been good. He especially enjoyed the company of Roland Kretzschmer, the school custodian, and their perch fishing trips to nearby Saginaw Bay in Lake Huron. More than anything, dad really liked the people he met in Owendale.

Following a move to Fenton, Michigan, where he would serve as high school principal for six years, my father moved us once more to Farmington, Michigan. This time the move coincided with his desire to return to classroom teaching so he would not be the principal in his children's school, and so he could have summers free to spend with his family. As I think back on it, that decision seems unusual for its time: to opt for less money and prestige for the sake of other values. Dad was always making choices that befuddled his colleagues. He chose to live modestly when he could afford to live more lavishly. He drove a compact car when everyone else was driving a luxury car. He knew who he was and what he wanted from life. He was not one to wear his wealth on his sleeve.

While my father did indeed enjoy those first few years in Farmington as a classroom science and math teacher, and while our family did have some wonderful summer vacations, his administrative reputation eventually caught up with him, and he was drafted into a junior high school principal position that occupied him for the rest of his career. Farmington was growing rapidly, and schools were sprouting up everywhere. Dad was a veteran administrator, and he found great satisfaction in mentoring his assistant principals. He had good organizational skills, was a demanding but fair boss, and, in good navy tradition, was "captain of his ship."

In retrospect, my father's life was shaped profoundly by his childhood. Having worked long hours as a boy for minimal wages, and having endured a Spartan upbringing, he wanted something more out of life. His decisions to forgo the lot of a mill hand, to resist his parents' urgings to stay put, and to pursue a formal education were the consequences of an inner drive to better himself. His childhood taught him what he would always hold to be a basic truth. It was better to work with your head than with your back and hands. The way to do this was by finishing high school and going to college. This was a belief he would trumpet throughout his career to students in the public schools and to his own two children. I remember well my father saying, "The only thing of value your mother and father can give you is an education."

I always suspected my dad's relationship with his father had a big impact on his relationship with me, a relationship I would characterize as loving, but formal. Dad usually addressed me in third person. "Dan," he would say, "your mother and father . . ." I found this odd. Nevertheless, I knew my father loved me even though he never uttered the word until he was on his deathbed. He always took me fishing.

There are many ways in which dad's life seemed simple and straightforward compared to mine. His life's quest was to overcome a harsh beginning, to make something of himself, to beat the odds. The goals were a good job, a loving family, and economic security. The Depression also affected him profoundly. His challenge, he felt, was to plan in such a way that when the next Depression came, as he was sure it would, his family would be spared the hardship he had endured. Staying out of debt was paramount. Food, clothing, furniture, even cars, were bought with cash. If you couldn't pay cash, you couldn't afford it. Doing without was not a terrible state to my father. Sacrificing the present for the sake of the future made ultimate sense to him. To my knowledge, neither he nor my mother ever had a credit card.

My dad provided a comfortable and secure living for our family. In the early days, he worked summer jobs to supplement his income—shoveling coal, painting houses, and barbering. He saved money for graduate school and earned a master's degree in public school administration from the University of Michigan. Then he budgeted his money so he could pay cash for whatever the family needed. His savings paid for several summer vacations, put my sister and me through college, and ensured a pleasant retirement for his wife and himself.

My father was by no means perfect. He could be inflexible. He often saw issues as black and white, when others saw only gray. He had a discipline about him, rooted again, I suspect, in his youth, that allowed him to make life-changing decisions on the spot and then move forward undaunted. He smoked cigars and a pipe most of his adult life, but when his doctor told him to stop for health reasons, he did so instantly. When another doctor told him to eliminate sugar from his diet, he did so without hesitation. Things he had enjoyed his entire life—desserts, candies, beverages—were history then and there. He never flinched. He seemed to pride himself on his ability to go without. (Of course, my mother felt obliged to make everything he had enjoyed previously with sugar substitutes.)

My dad also had his moments toward the end of his life. While he planned well financially for retirement, he did not plan as well for filling that retirement with meaningful activity. He golfed, tended his fruit trees, did the crosswords, played computer chess, and read voraciously, but he still had too much time on his hands. His coping behavior, unintended as it was, made life more difficult for my mother. As a school principal, he had been a problem-solver. He thrived on it. After retirement, with no real problems to solve, he manufactured them. Little things became big things. Whether it was an unusual sound in the car, a neighbor's wayward pet, or the hint of forbidden sugar in his diet, he could be counted on to elevate the problem to crisis proportions. It had to be dealt with now!

My father probably could have volunteered his time in the public schools, helping kids learn how to read or do math or science. But he left all that behind in 1970 when he retired. He stopped wearing a watch, and he grew a mustache. He had earned the right to kick back, relax, and be a Monday-morning quarterback. The future was in the hands of the younger generation. He had done his duty.

I always thought dad retired too early, but mom said he was concerned about his health. He didn't expect to live as long as he did. Mom had also worked in the public schools. She was a kindergarten and music teacher for 35 years. By today's standards she was a "supermom." She did all the traditional household chores and held down another job during the day. In the morning, before school, she rousted everybody, made breakfast, and sent us on our way before leaving for work herself. After school, she prepared supper, did the dishes, and took up yet another chore that had to be done—lesson plans for the next school day. The inside of the house was her domain, and the outside was dad's. They had an understanding. On top of that, mom deferred to dad when it came to money. Even though she was earning her own salary, dad handled the finances.

Together, my parents laid a solid foundation for my sister and me. They made us feel secure and loved even as they gave us room to stretch ourselves, to take risks, to experience failure. They did not dote on us, but it was understood they were there for us if we needed them. I don't know whether this was planned or whether it was simply a reflection of who they were as people. I do know that I learned much about how to conduct myself from them, not so much from what they said, but from what they did. They modeled a caring and responsible manner of living that I admire greatly. When I am behaving at my best, I know it is my parents in me coming through. When I am behaving at my worst, I cannot help but worry about what my parents would be thinking if they knew what I was up to.

If my parents erred at all in bringing up their children, it was setting too good an example. I never heard them raise their voices against one another, let alone fight. They were always considerate and loving in the presence of others. What that meant for me, and possibly my sister, was that I felt I had a tough act to follow. Indeed, I have not been able to match my parents' matrimonial record. That has led to considerable disappointment in my life. Perhaps it would have been better if mom and dad had shown some of the blemishes that mar even the most enduring of relationships. In their absence, my expectations for my own relationships may have been unrealistic.

I have heard it said that children are not really adults until their parents are gone. By that definition, I am still not fully grown. My mother is going strong at 90. I also know that I will never be completely free of a concern for what my parents would think about my conduct. There is a part of them indelibly etched in me. I would not want to erase that even if I could. In my opinion, there has been a remarkable wisdom to their way of life. Their marriage lasted more than half a century, they were kind to others, and they did little harm to the larger world as they made their way through it.

My father lived a good, long life, and he knew it. When his time was up, he was ready. He counted his blessings. Chief among them were his pride and joy, his grandsons. In his later years, he would walk around the block two or three times a day in Florida, or to the corner store in Michigan, wearing a baseball cap or a sweatshirt advertising one of the universities his grandsons were attending— Alma College, the University of Chicago, the University of Michigan. Oftentimes, his attire and penchant for conversation would trigger a chat with one person or another about the boys and how they were faring. He never tired of bragging about them.

I think dad understood the cycle of life. As he aged, he did not begrudge the passing of time. He recognized that he had his chance, that his children were having their chance, and that his grandchildren's chance would come in time. He was excited for their future even as his own was winding down. If he brooded, it was usually over issues that threatened his grandsons' generation. Their lives mattered even more to him as he faced up to the end of his own.

My father, like so many fathers of his generation, was decent, honest, and hardworking. His life was testimony to the possibility that through hard work and perseverance one can elevate oneself in life. Dad did indeed elevate himself. He came from a difficult upbringing and molded himself into a highly principled principal who will always be remembered by those who knew, respected, and loved him as a man who, above all else, lived up to his convictions.

Chapter 16

PEGGY SUE'S DINER

Oh, yes, I'm the great pretender,
Pretending that I'm doing well,

—The Platters

J ust east of Barstow, California, near the Fort Irwin exit off Interstate 15, is Peggy Sue's Diner. Owned and operated by *the* Peggy Sue, it is a classic '50s diner, replete with red vinyl-covered booths, tabletop jukeboxes, and photos of rock 'n' roll stars on the walls.

For me, Peggy Sue's is a must stop. I don't have to be hungry necessarily, or even thirsty for that matter. It's more of a pilgrimage, a paying of tribute to a time and an age when my life was still largely in front of me, when the possibilities seemed endless. I like sitting in a booth at Peggy Sue's, sipping a chocolate malted through a straw, and listening to tunes that carry me back in time and space.

My need is such, I pretend too much,
I'm lonely but no one can tell.

It is June 18, 1997. My 1987 Dodge Caravan with 175,000 miles on it is outside in the parking lot. Everything I own is in that van. In an hour or so, I'll pull back on the freeway and head northeast across the Mojave Desert past the ghost town of Calico and then past Baker, the "Gateway to Death Valley." In another 45 minutes, I'll exit California, my home for the past 20 years, at Whiskey Pete's Casino, the final resting place of the "Bonnie and Clyde Death Car" and home of the 99-cent shrimp cocktail.

My head is spinning with thoughts of the last few months. Everything has happened so quickly. In April, I interviewed for a faculty position at Florida International University (FIU) in Miami.

The interview didn't go particularly well. FIU's priority was a senior level therapeutic recreation educator. If they could get the one they wanted, they wouldn't have the funds to hire me. I told my parents, who lived in Port Charlotte, on the Gulf Coast of Florida, that it didn't look like it was going to work out. That was okay by me, I continued, because I wanted to see my son, Adam, through his senior year of high school in San Diego. It was really a year early for me to be looking, anyway. They understood.

Three days later, my mother called from Port Charlotte to say that my father had suffered a massive heart attack. I flew to Florida to be with him. Two weeks later my sister, Carol, a registered nurse, replaced me to oversee his recovery at home. Then it was two steps forward and one step backward, a common pattern of recovery according to his doctors. We were cautiously optimistic. Then, on May 17th, my dad died suddenly.

I felt like a wishbone. My sense of responsibility to Adam pulled me toward California. My sense of responsibility to my mother pulled me toward Florida. What to do? In the end, I did what I felt I had to do. Job or no job, I was moving to Florida. But, as the gods would have it, at the last minute, FIU called to offer me an appointment as a tenured full professor. I accepted.

Oh yes, I'm the great pretender
Adrift in a world of my own,

It's funny how things work out sometimes. If my life had been more together—if I had been married, or if my children had been younger, or if my job had been more secure, or if I had a house and mortgage payments anchoring me down—I might not have been able to pick up and leave California to be with my mother in Florida. Yet it is precisely because I was not tied down in those ways that I felt able to come to her assistance. I can still remember my good friend, Bob Kuemmerling, teasing me a few years ago when I visited him at his beautiful colonial home in Gainesville, Virginia. "Dan," he laughed, "you're 44 years old, and you don't own anything!" Bob was absolutely right. But I have never really missed owning anything. Possessions have a way of possessing their possessors.

I can also remember going to my 20th high school reunion in 1984 and being blown away by other ironies in my life. There I was, out of a class of 150, among a handful of people who had

PhDs, who traveled the most, who read the most, and who, it seemed to follow, should have had their lives most intact. Yet my life was in disarray, while many of my classmates who had never left home, who had never gone to college, and who had never read much were happily married, happily employed, and happily recounting their life experiences with their classmates. The joke, it seemed, was on me. What was wrong with me, anyway?

Too real is this feeling of make-believe . . .

I have always felt happiness is overrated. There is something else I'm after, although I'm not certain what it is. To be sure, I am committed to learning, and, like my father, I value an education. But to date, my learning and my education have made my life more burdensome than blissful. It's hard for me to be carefree when I examine what is going on in the world around me. Indeed, when I teach, I begin each semester by posing the following question to my students, "If ignorance is bliss, then what is an education?" Inevitably, the students come up with something close to "education is responsibility" by term's end. And responsibility, they all agree, is a heavy notion.

Perhaps that is why I get such a kick out of Peggy Sue's Diner. It reminds me of a time when I was less burdened by the weight of the world, when I was more carefree. It reminds me of a time when I didn't know enough to be worried, when I was ignorant. Come to think of it, those were blissful times. I think my junior high school years were the best of them. I still carry images around in my head of the school itself, basketball games, sock hops, malt shops, summer jobs, pals I caddied with, and the dark-haired girl I had such a crush on, but was afraid to approach.

Tying it all together for me is the music: "At The Hop" (Danny and the Juniors), "Chances Are" (Johnny Mathis), "The Wanderer" (Dion), "The Lion Sleeps Tonight" (The Tokens). . . . Each tune evokes memories that are so vivid, so real in my mind, it is as if they happened yesterday. Rock 'n' roll music is like a glue that holds my past together, a past I struggle to hold on to, even as I can't. I find the tunes comforting.

Oh yes, I'm the great pretender,
just laughing and gay like a clown,

Even at my age, I'm afraid. This Florida job is going to be a dramatically different kind of challenge than was San Diego State. FIU is 75% minority students. Most of them work full-time. Most of them are first generation college students. Most of them expect a college degree to elevate them in life. Most of them are probably going to wonder just what it is a white, middle-aged male like me has to teach them about their world. I will, for the first time in my life, be a minority myself.

I should be excited by this. I should be energized. California is no longer where it's at. Florida is. California is no longer the bell-wether state. Florida is. California is no longer my home. Florida is. I should be looking forward to this. I should be undaunted. But, to tell you the truth, I'm apprehensive.

There is also a rush in it. South Florida, for me, is undiscovered country. There are the Everglades, the Keys, the Atlantic Ocean, and the Gulf of Mexico. There is Miami's South Beach, Art Deco, and Latin rhythms. There are mangos, mangroves, and manatees. There are shellfish. There is key lime pie. There is Jimmy Buffett. There are names like Okeechobee, Caloosahatchee, and Miccosukee that conjure up steamy, tropical images. There are ceiling fans, Panama hats, and the ghosts of Bogart and Bacall. There is going to be much for me to explore and write about in South Florida. It is, after all, Hemingway country.

But how am I going to pull this off? My mother, who I will be looking after, lives 170 miles from where I will work. And the work that will support me while I'm looking after my mother is 170 miles from her. Moving mom is not an option. Perhaps I'll live in Port Charlotte and commute. Now that would be interesting. My youngest son, Adam, would then be finishing high school in San Diego, 2,500 miles from where I would be living and 2,670 miles from where I would be working. My oldest son, Andy, would be in his junior year at the University of Chicago, 1,300 miles from where I would be living and 1,470 miles from where I would be working. My life would be disjointed to say the least.

Moreover, it would be a far cry from my Southern California lifestyle. I would have to make weekly treks back and forth across the Everglades at odd hours of the day and night. Mountains, forests, and white water would give way to flatlands, marshes, and swamps. Desert bighorn sheep would be replaced by alligators, and western songbirds would yield to eastern wading birds. But I'm ready for this. I really am. I chose it. I'm responsible for it.

There will be learning in this for me. There will be an education.

I seem to be what I'm not, you see,
I'm wearing my heart like a crown,

I never would have predicted my life would end up like this. So unsettled, I mean. I don't know what I expected really, except that growing up in a traditional midwestern family led me to believe my life would wind up similarly. My father was a member of the Kiwanis Club. He golfed regularly, bowled regularly, and attended church regularly. He tinkered around the house. He was handy. He was not afraid to look beneath the hood of a car.

I turned out different.

I slurp the last of my chocolate malted, pay my bill and my respects to Buddy Holly's muse, and do "the stroll" out to my van. I take my place in line with all the other gamblers heading northeast toward Las Vegas on Interstate 15. There is something I love about the open highway. It appeals to the dreamer in me. I think I could have been a cross-country truck driver. Maybe I will be yet. The allure is in the promise the highway holds. Who knows what's down the road, around the next bend, over the next hill? Who knows what's in store for me? My future is out there somewhere in the distance, beyond the horizon, just out of sight. But it doesn't come to me. I have to muster the courage to move toward it. I have to risk the passage.

I reach for the radio. I find the "oldies" station and tune it in to the sound of Ricky Nelson's "Traveling Man." This is great, I smile to myself. My life is still largely in front of me, and the possibilities seem endless.

Part Two—The Florida Years

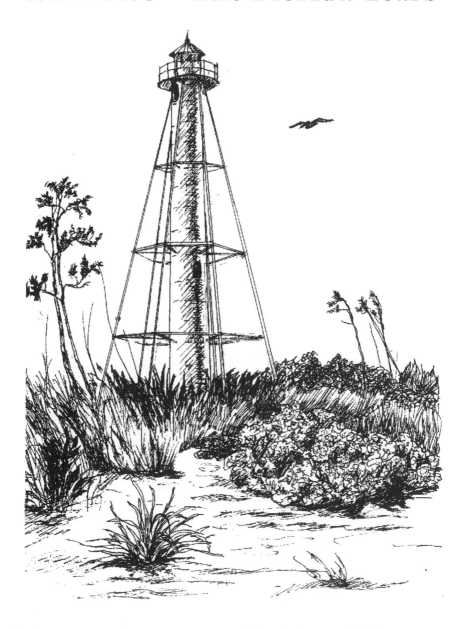

Chapter 17

FAKAHATCHEE STRAND

*You would have to want something very badly to go
looking for it in the Fakahatchee Strand.*

—Susan Orleans

My first week at Florida International University I arranged an interview with Everglades National Park's superintendent, Dick Ring. I wanted to hit the ground running, and a state-of-the-park article commemorating the 50th anniversary of Everglades National Park's creation seemed like a good way to begin.[1]

The interview with Mr. Ring went well, and upon its conclusion I asked if he could provide me with a few photographs to embellish my writing. He said he could, but he also suggested I make the acquaintance of Clyde Butcher, a landscape photographer who lives in the Big Cypress Preserve on the northeast edge of Everglades National Park. Since the Big Cypress Gallery is located along the Tamiami Trail, a road I would be traveling the next day on my way home to Port Charlotte, I decided to stop by and introduce myself.

Clyde greeted me enthusiastically. A hulk of a man, he was adorned with a wide-brimmed hat, glasses, Santa Claus-like beard, flowered shirt, cutoffs, and sandals. Clyde then introduced me to his wife, Niki, a soft-spoken complement to his Falstaffian persona. Clyde's gift, I soon found out, is creating large-format black-and-white landscape photographs, and Niki's gift is colorizing black-and-white photographs with pastel paints.

Clyde and Niki create their works of art to engage the eye in a way that conveys the beauty and fragility of the natural world. They want people to care about what they see and commit to its preservation. As I toured the gallery and listened to their story, I not only wanted to befriend the Butchers, I wanted to cultivate a working relationship with them. I also wanted to purchase their artwork, if only I could afford it.

I described my professional interests to Clyde and then asked if he would be so kind as to provide me with a few photographs of Everglades National Park to enhance my upcoming article. He graciously agreed and added that he would be happy to supply me with any more photographs I might require in the future to accompany my nature-based writing. All I had to do was ask. His attitude seemed to be that any friend of conservation was a friend of his. I sensed an immediate bond with Clyde and Niki, and as I drove away from the Big Cypress Gallery, I felt we were kindred spirits.

In the years since that first meeting, I have visited Clyde and Niki many times. They have supplied me with photographs to illustrate my articles,[2] conversed with me about south Florida environmental issues, led swamp walks for my university colleagues, and hosted me at their home behind the Big Cypress Gallery. They were also kind enough to ask me to contribute a few words to accompany a photographic retrospective of Clyde's life work.[3]

I had never faced such a daunting writing task. Clyde's photographs are often compared to those of Ansel Adams. Indeed, I think it is fair to say that Clyde is the closest living artist we have to Ansel Adams. Imagine, then, being asked to write something to embellish his exquisite black-and-white landscape photographs. I cannot tell you how inadequate I felt. But Clyde and Niki assured me they were pleased with what I wrote, and they allowed me to place my words opposite a photograph of my choosing. I selected a photograph of Utah's Escalante River Canyon,[4] a landscape near to my heart.

I also found it within myself, though barely within my budget, to purchase three of Clyde's photographs to adorn my living room walls: one of a cirrus-cloud-filled sky above the Big Cypress Preserve that measures four feet by five feet,[5] one of Cayo Costa Island on Florida's Gulf Coast that measures five feet by six feet,[6] and one of Moraine Valley in Colorado's Rocky Mountain National Park that measures four feet by seven feet.[7] There is a depth and detail to Clyde's work that takes my breath away. I get lost in his images. They stir my imagination. I will never tire of them.

There is one more thing about Clyde and Niki Butcher that I must tell you. It is not something I do lightly, but it is critical to fully understanding and appreciating the meaning of their work. As Clyde recounts it, when he first moved to Florida, he didn't see much worth photographing in the Everglades. Then, tragically, he lost his teenage son, Ted, in an automobile accident. Clyde retreated into the wilderness with his grief, a wooden box camera, and black-and-white film. Weeks later he emerged with masterful images of the Everglades to form the foundation of what now is an internationally acclaimed body of work. I don't know what Clyde experienced on that photographic soul search, but two recent books about and by him give some indication: *Seeing the Light/Wilderness and Salvation: A Photographer's Tale*[8] and *Clyde Butcher: Nature's Places of Spiritual Sanctuary.*[9]

What I find so moving and inspirational about Clyde and Niki Butcher is their ability to turn a devastating loss into something good and beautiful. I admire them for that. I'm not sure I could have done it. The strength of character it must take to not only go on with their lives, but to retain their optimism, sense of purpose, and commitment to a larger calling, is nothing short of ennobling.

In August of 1999 Clyde invited me on a photo shoot to the Fakahatchee Strand, a long narrow swamp forest on the western edge of the Big Cypress Preserve. Our goal would be to photograph the elusive ghost orchid, a seldom seen endangered plant that grows nowhere else in the country. Clyde's close friend and fellow photographer Oscar Thompson had been looking for the ghost orchid for 50 years. As luck would have it, a state field biologist had just discovered what Oscar had been searching for so long and hard. Clyde had already made one journey to the Fakahatchee Strand to photograph the flower, so he knew its exact location. It would require a two-mile walk in waist-deep water, crawling with snakes, alligators, and mosquitoes.

Serving as Clyde's "grip" on a photo shoot in a miserable swamp was not high on my "to do" list, but I didn't want to miss out on the chance to observe him at his craft. When we arrived at the trailhead near the remote village of Copeland, Clyde reassured me that since he didn't hear any frogs croaking, we probably wouldn't have to worry too much about snakes, since frogs were the snakes' primary food. I found little comfort in his logic, and I couldn't quite believe what I was doing as I took my first step into the water and felt the cold surging up my legs to my waist. It didn't help my confidence when Clyde provided me with a long stick and strict orders to check my footing before every step and to be on the lookout for "critters."

To say I was scared to death is an understatement. For one thing, another new acquaintance of mine, Everglades airboat guide Ernie Redwing, had warned me that snakes don't have to surface to bite you. It also didn't help when Clyde regaled me with stories the night before our photo shoot about how he had to be hauled out of the muck from time to time with a rope and a truck when he got stuck up to his torso in one quagmire or another. What if Clyde had a heart attack? What if I had to haul him out? The thought horrified me.

Like Clyde, I didn't see much to admire in the Fakahatchee Strand at first, let alone photograph. I was edgy. With each step I fully expected to feel the chomp of a gator's jaws or the sting of a water moccasin or cottonmouth. My imagination ran wild. Gradually, however, a different sensation began to wash over me. The water was cool and clear, not warm and murky. Clyde insisted we could drink the water, and then he did.

Moreover, the footing was solid, not soft. This, Clyde went on to say, is why developers so love to drain south Florida and then build on it. The limestone base just a few feet below the water's surface provides a solid foundation for constructing most anything. As we sloshed on, Clyde described the introduction of the melaleuca, an Australian tree that was brought to Florida in 1906 as an ornamental plant. Melaleucas soak up so much water they can dry out an acre of wetlands a day. Real estate developers had melaleuca seed scattered over the Everglades in the 1930s to hasten the drying out of what was thought to be a useless swamp. Today, the State of Florida and the federal government are undertaking the monumental task of trying to eradicate the melaleuca as part of the Everglades restoration process.

As we penetrated deeper and deeper into the Fakahatchee Strand, the cool air temperature surprised me. The summer sun was directly above us, but the forest canopy sheltered us from the heat. Royal palms towered overhead, and cypress trees dotted the landscape. Clyde continued discussing the history of the Fakahatchee, including its appeal to loggers and hunters of water birds for their decorative plumage in the late 19th century, and I eventually stopped worrying about snakes, alligators, and nonexistent mosquitoes. The Fakahatchee Strand was turning out to be something other than what I thought it would be. It was not forbidding. It was inviting. It had an otherworldly feeling, and it teemed with live things.

After an hour of slogging through waist-deep water, we came upon the spot where *Polyrrhiza lindenii*, also classified botanically as *Polyradicion lindenii*, known more commonly as the ghost orchid, had wrapped its delicate roots around the host tree. But the lovely white flower with the pouting lip and long fluttering tails was no more. There was nothing left but the roots.

"Not to worry," Clyde said cheerfully, and his attention turned immediately to a newly discovered elephant orchid blossoming in a nearby tree. I stood in silence watching him work. He carefully positioned his "Clyde-O-Wide," as he affectionately calls his home-made box camera, on a tripod for multiple shots of yet another beautiful and delicate creation of nature. After each shot, Clyde handed me the used photographic plate for safekeeping, and I handed him a new one. Oblivious to time, I felt the healing power of what Clyde was doing, and the sensation overwhelmed me.

In those moments, I was reminded of two passages I'd read recently, one from Susan Orleans's *The Orchid Thief* and another from *Seeing the Light*. "Being an orchid hunter," Orleans said, "has always meant pursuing beautiful things in terrible places."[10] Yet that was not really what I was observing. I was observing a large man who had suffered a large loss gently positioning a large-for-mat camera to capture for eternity the image of something so tiny, so fragile, and so wondrous as a flower—not in a terrible place, but in a wonderful place, a place Clyde had taken the time to know and understand.

The passage from *Seeing the Light* recounted a storm Clyde had weathered off the coast of Baja California many years ago aboard the *Sea Shanty*, his newly acquired 35-foot sailboat. The storm was so harrowing and came so close to capsizing the boat and dispatching those on board that, when land was finally reached, one of the crewmen leapt from the *Sea Shanty* to kiss the earth. Clyde, on the other hand, was ecstatic, for "he'd ridden out a storm, only to discover it had blown him directly to where he'd wanted to go."[11] As I reflect on Clyde and Niki Butcher, it seems to me that their lives have been a continuous weathering of storms, and the biggest storm of all, the loss of their son, Ted, has brought them back to nature, a place they, too, had always wanted to go.

Chapter 18

WASTING AWAY IN BOCA GRANDE

I am kicking back on the patio of the South Beach Bar and Grill on southwest Florida's Gasparilla Island sipping a piña colada. Sitting across the table from me is Ingrid Schneider, a visiting professor from Arizona State University.[1] Ingrid is delightful. She is upbeat and full of life. We have a few hours to while away on the island before heading back to Miami and our respective lives.

Named in honor of the 16th-century pirate Juan Gaspar, Gasparilla Island's sole community is Boca Grande, site of the nation's premier tarpon tournament each summer and vacation spot for President Bush's extended family each winter. A sleepy, unincorporated village, Boca Grande is beginning to wake up, and I fear its charm will soon give way to commercialism and crowding. For now, however, I can nurse my piña colada, enjoy Ingrid's company, and think my thoughts.

Looking out on the aquamarine water of the Gulf of Mexico, it is easy to forget who I am and how I got here. The waves lapping onto the shore mesmerize me with their repeated questions. "Why would you want to live anywhere else? Why would you want to do anything else but what you are doing right now?" I am caught off guard by the interrogation. Indeed, at the moment, aspiring to do anything else with my life seems silly.

Inside the bar, ceiling fans turn lazily, and bronze, middle-aged waitresses bedecked in flower-printed blouses and khaki shorts trade wisecracks with the customers. A dance floor and band equipment stand idly by. At night, we are told, the place jumps, but now, at midday, it is sluggish. It is as if someone has turned off the clock. Being on Gasparilla Island means not being rushed. It is a place for vegging out.

The scene before me invites contemplation. I have experienced this feeling before when trekking across the Sierra Nevada, hiking in the Grand Canyon, or sitting quietly by Grand Traverse Bay in Michigan. There is something about being in the company of

nature that unlocks me from everyday life and opens me up for
introspection. Immersed in nature, I reflect on what I am doing
with my life, and on what, if anything, I have accomplished. Perhaps the feeling can be explained by the simple fact that I am under
the spell of a power much greater than I. In nature's presence, I am
forced to admit that no matter what I achieve in life, it is destined,
relatively speaking, to be small potatoes.

This realization, while humbling, is not entirely unwelcome.
Oftentimes, when I feel I have the weight of the world on my
shoulders, when I am convinced that everything that needs to be
done depends on me alone, I find relief in a walk in the woods or in
a stroll along the beach. My load lightens perceptibly. Nature is an
elixir, a tonic that frees me from the burdensome illusion that the
world cannot get along without me. It reminds me that whatever I
make of myself, life will go on, like the water in front of me, wave
after wave, without end.

I wonder if Ingrid has similar feelings? Maybe I will ask her
someday, but not today. It would be—how should I put it—im-
prudent. Ingrid is at a different stage in her life. She is near the
beginning of her voyage. I, on the other hand, am farther out to
sea. Where it will end is anybody's guess, but my journey is far
enough along that it feels like time to check my bearings, to see if
I am on any sort of course, let alone the one I started out on.

Cynicism, you see, is what I fear most. Cynics are frustrated
idealists, and I was raised an idealist. I was brought up in an intact
family where fairness and justice held sway. But having been on my
own for some time now, and having experienced something of the
larger world, I have learned that life is rarely fair and just. Reconcil-
ing that fact with the ideals my parents instilled in me has always
been difficult. Sometimes I think my solid upbringing only primed
me for a bigger fall.

I suppose everyone reaches a point in life when they begin to
question the tack they are on, when they begin to second-guess
their career choices. I have been embroiled in that questioning
period for a long time now. When I began my career I wanted to
change the world. Now I would be happy if I could just change
myself. My life, it seems, has been a continual readjustment of goals
downward, a pattern befitting a budding cynic.

If we live long enough, we are bound to get roughed up some.
How to maintain enthusiasm for life in the wake of such beatings?
How to remain optimistic? For me, part of an answer resides in the

hope that comes with keeping company with people who are less beat up than I. They are like fresh recruits as yet unscarred by battle. They give new life to things. They offer their own kind of relief. They are also an elixir, another kind of tonic that relieves me from that same burdensome illusion that the world cannot do without me. Their presence reassures me that no matter what influence I might have on things, life will go on in my absence, perhaps even for the better.

It will be interesting to follow Ingrid's career. I wonder if she will stew over the same things I do, or if she will stew over different things? I think men and women may have more in common than we care to admit, but since men are not encouraged to open up very much, we may never know. For my part, the older I get, the more taken I am with things near and dear to me. I am less interested in worldly affairs and abstract ideals and more interested in the people around me. The real miracles of life, I am now convinced, reside in everyday actions of everyday people who go largely unnoticed. Why is it, I wonder, that so many people do what is needed and what is right when nobody else is looking? How do they develop character and then abide by it? What is the source of their conviction?

I am not very religious, but I do feel a strong attraction to values often characterized as religious. Aspiring to follow the Ten Commandments makes sense to me even if you do not believe in a god, because they are good rules of thumb for anyone living in a community of others. And though I have gone through a divorce, I value the institution of marriage, especially when it comes to giving children a good start in life. I really believe parents who instill worthwhile values in their children and then raise them successfully on modest means have more to teach me about what is important in life than any high-paid CEO, or even the president, who seemingly holds the fate of the nation in his hands. My guess is that it is parents who really hold the fate of the nation in their hands—parents and teachers.

I have had the particularly good fortune to be surrounded by great teachers all my life. The difference they have made to the quality of my existence is immeasurable. The little things they have said or done that have made me feel worthy, that have made me feel needed, that have made me feel wanted, are beyond words. For the life of me, I do not understand why we do not value teachers more, especially elementary and secondary school teachers,

teachers who work with children when they are young, when they are most receptive to learning, when they are most open to life's possibilities. Those teachers are worth their weight in gold.

Maybe Ingrid will grow into one of them. I have watched her in the classroom. If she brings the same care to her own children someday that she brings to her college students, she is bound to be a good mother, too. Her challenge, of course, will be in juggling her parental responsibilities, spousal responsibilities, and professional responsibilities. Knowing her as I do, I know that Ingrid will want to do it all. But can she? Should she? For many people, the question soon becomes which responsibilities to lateral to a willing spouse, or perhaps even drop altogether. How does one prioritize? In Ingrid's case, she will have to work it out with her husband, Dan. He, too, is young, vibrant, and full of promise. How to divvy up what needs to be done so that Ingrid and Dan can both experience fulfillment? As my good friend, Tom Goodale, avows, marriage is turning two into three, not two into one. The trick will be in doing justice to her, him, and them, and not necessarily in that order.

The greatest disappointment of my life is my failed marriage. The moral guilt is something I manage well enough, but it is a wound that will not heal. The fact that there were children involved accounts for much of the pain. To her credit, my former wife, Carla, has worked diligently with me to minimize the effects of the divorce on our children, but the rippling effects continue to be felt after almost 20 years. There is no end to them in sight. The "coulda, shoulda, wouldas" rule. I know it is not fashionable to carry around a lot of guilt these days. It does no good, the self-help books say. It gets you nowhere. Better to do away with it, get beyond it, start anew. I appreciate what they are trying to say. On the other hand, I think it was Ernest Hemingway who said that feeling guilty is the only evidence we have that human beings have a conscience.

Meanwhile, the waves continue to roll in, depositing layer upon layer of shells onto the beach in front of us. Coquinas, glistening in the sun, burrow into the sand as each wave pulls back into the Gulf. In time the shells will lose their luster and fade into a sun-bleached sameness. A few of them will be noticed and picked up by beachcombers taking time out from their busy, productive lives for a well-deserved rest. Then they will go back up north again to

Michigan, Ohio, or Indiana and return to work so they can earn the wherewithal to visit the beaches of Boca Grande one more time.

Were I to do it over again, I would drop some things I held on to and pick up some things I dropped. I would enjoy the moment more. I spend so much of my time trying to make sense out of yesterday in the hope of building a better tomorrow that I often leave little time for today. The problem, of course, is that while my mind preoccupies itself with the past in preparation for the future, my body is confined to the present. The result is a fundamental disconnect between my mind and body, an occurrence that oftentimes leaves me fragmented, if not dysfunctional. Reducing the gap between my mind and body so that I might enjoy more thoroughly the here and now is—I confide to my piña colada—a stellar idea.

I would also savor parenting more. No matter what I accomplish professionally in my life, it will never surpass the satisfaction I feel in having witnessed the growth and development of my two children into socially responsible adults. I can still remember my oldest son, Andy, scampering across the lobby of the Eugene, Oregon, airport in 1978 when he was barely one year old, climbing into my arms, and hugging and kissing me. The smile on his face is forever etched in my brain. It was one of the greatest moments in my life. A simple greeting between father and son. Isn't it curious that the achievements I feel best about, my two children, are common ones shared by millions of people? The most important work is within reach of us all. The greatest satisfactions are right there also. Being a loving person matters more than anything else.

This has been a glorious day. I do not want it to end. I do not want to leave the island. I do not want to go back to Miami. I do not want to leave Ingrid's company. I do not want to go back to work. I do not want to grade papers. I do not want to attend committee meetings. Most of all, I do not want to grow cynical. Neither do I especially want my children to grow up, nor do I want them ever to grow cynical, either. I want the distance between their ideals and their reality to dissolve before them. I want them to rejoice in the present moment. I want them to marvel at life's unfolding and not consume themselves with what they should or should not have done in the past or what they should or should not do in the future. I want them to find someone to spend time with and delight in, and I want them to find the solace in nature that can heal and nourish them so they, too, might someday work their way back to the car—as I am doing now—and start the engine and return to what they know they must do, though no one else may be looking.

Chapter 19

CONFESSIONS OF A TECHNOLOGICAL RESISTANCE FIGHTER

Sometimes when I listen to myself talk, I hardly recognize the source. This is especially so when it comes to technology. For reasons I cannot quite comprehend, I remind myself more and more of my father when he used to tell me how much more difficult things were when he was young, how much tougher conditions were, how much harder it was to get anything done. While the point of his lectures always seemed to be that the younger generation seldom appreciates how good they really have it, I heard something else in his words, something I do not think he intended to communicate, but something that was there nonetheless. It was the unspoken message that those difficult times, those tougher conditions, those harder tasks, like them or not, were responsible for molding my father's character. He was who he was not because things came easily to him in life, but because he had to work hard for them. The qualities he drew on to succeed—discipline, perseverance, self-sacrifice, and a tolerance for delayed gratification—were forged not through ease and convenience, but through struggle.

Would my father have traded indoor plumbing, electricity, refrigeration, the automobile, television, the polio vaccine—indeed, a longer, more comfortable life—for those harsher character-building days of his youth? No, I don't suppose he would have. But technology is not an either/or proposition. The principal lesson of my father's musings was that advancing technology brings with it both benefits and costs. And while others are better suited to discuss the benefits, I, as my father's son, am going to direct your attention to what this same advancing technology may have cost us along the way.

I am what social critic and communications theorist Neil Postman calls in *Technopoly* a technological "resistance fighter."[1] This
does not mean I shun technology. I am not a Luddite. I take advantage of many modern conveniences. But I am also someone
who tries to keep a certain psychological distance from technological innovation, preferring to cast a critical eye on what others often
embrace uncritically as the wave of the future. Moreover, I question many of the assumptions underlying our culture's unabashed
enthusiasm for advancing technology: namely, that efficiency is always good, that getting somewhere sooner rather than later is always desirable, that the answers to life's big questions are always to
be found in more data.

I am old-fashioned enough that when I "reach out and touch
someone" I prefer that someone be within arm's reach. And though
I use e-mail, I prefer the feel of stationery and the personality reflected in cursive writing. I frequently bemoan the loss of a sense of
community that has accompanied our increasingly mobile society.
And I fear our love affair with computers, rather than bringing
people closer together, is leading toward greater social isolation. I
am, in sum, from the tradition of Henry David Thoreau, who concluded that most modern inventions were but improved means to
an unimproved end. But enough about me. You get the idea.

When I am invited to give a talk, I almost always request a slide
projector. Why? I don't know. I guess it is a knee-jerk reaction. My
students at the university, raised on television, prefer visual images
to words. Words are too slow for them. They grow impatient when
we work in that medium. And when I require them to read a book,
they roll their eyes. Afterward, they always insist the author could
have made the case in fewer pages, in fewer words. I would kill for
students who would say to me they were sorry a book wasn't longer,
that it was too bad the book had to end. In their world, words,
especially the printed kind, are out of favor. College students used
to rely on *Cliff's Notes* when they didn't want to read a book. Now
they pray the book I've assigned them has been made into a movie.

Historians tell us the Lincoln/Douglas debates lasted up to seven
hours, and that citizens in attendance paid attention throughout.
The arguments would often be long and convoluted, and the language complex. Yet the audience stayed tuned. Now I hear that
Good Morning America is losing significant market share because
ABC made the mistake of hiring two hosts who were more brainy
than beautiful, who pushed substance over sizzle, and who wanted

to make a show that mattered. Clearly, they were out of step with the times. They didn't understand the world of "infotainment." As Postman avows, thinking does not play well on television. There is not much to see in it.[2]

Those same historians tell us any one of the first 15 presidents of the United States could have walked the streets of any city, town, or village in the nation and not be recognized. They were known, if they were known at all, by their written words. When I say "Patrick Henry," if anything comes to mind, it is likely the words "Give me liberty or give me death!" But when I say "Oliver North," what likely comes to mind is the image of a Marine Corps lieutenant colonel sitting stiffly in front of a microphone before a Senate sub-committee. That's because Oliver North belongs to the Age of Television while Patrick Henry belonged to the Age of Typography.

Just as typography was a technological innovation that transformed us from an oral tradition by "freezing" speech in written form, television is a technological innovation that transforms us from an expository tradition by "freezing" images on a screen. This is significant, Postman avows, because the forms of our human conversation influence the ideas we can conveniently express. And what ideas are convenient to express inevitably become the important content of our culture.[3]

Think about a watershed event in American politics, the Nixon/Kennedy debates. In a national poll conducted immediately after those debates, people who listened to them on the radio thought Nixon prevailed. People who watched the debates on television thought Kennedy prevailed. Nixon won with his words, while Kennedy won with his appearance. Kennedy, of course, went on to win the election, and the debates were considered a turning point. Politics have never been the same.

In the Age of Typography, there was little relationship between the shape of a human being and the shape of her or his ideas. One's physical appearance was largely irrelevant. In The Age of Television, one's physical appearance is everything. William Howard Taft, the 27th president of the United States, would have little chance of being elected were he standing for office in the Age of Television. His multi-chinned, 300-pound frame would get in the way of most any idea he would try to communicate, just as Richard Nixon's five o'clock shadow, beads of perspiration, and nervous manner did in the 1960 presidential debates.

What we are left with, according to Postman, is a great struggle between these two technologies—typography and television—to control our minds. First, there is the printed word, with its emphasis on logic, sequence, history, exposition, objectivity, detachment, and discipline. Second, there is television, with its emphasis on imagery, narrative, presentness, simultaneity, intimacy, immediate gratification, and quick emotional response. I shall leave it up to you to decide for yourself just which technology is prevailing in this struggle, but I would now like to focus on some of the implications I see in all this for leisure in our lives.

According to John Robinson and Geof Godbey in *Time for Life: The Surprising Ways Americans Use Their Time*, watching television is, by far, the number one leisure pastime in the United States.[4] On average, Americans spend between 15 and 20 hours per week in front of the tube. Nothing else we do in the name of leisure comes close. Nothing. The impact of this amount of television watching on our culture is not entirely clear, but there are several ominous signs.

I have already touched on some of the implications for our children. They come to school expecting to be entertained, and they are not inclined to work at anything that doesn't come easily. They want their learning to come in tightly woven colorful packages like presents under a Christmas tree. And they expect their teachers to be nothing short of Santa Claus. We can hardly blame them, I suppose, because we raise them on *Sesame Street* and *Mr. Rogers' Neighborhood*. So now they sit passively in the classroom—whether it be in an elementary school, middle school, high school, or college—and wait for the "show" to begin.

This lifestyle, and I think it's fair to call it a lifestyle, comes at the expense of our children's physical fitness as well. According to the President's Council on Physical Fitness, our nation's youth are more unfit and overweight than ever before. If a sound mind and sound body do in fact go together, then we must be concerned on both fronts about the deleterious effects of the Age of Television.

Finally, if spending so much time in front of the TV weren't bad enough, research studies indicate that we don't really enjoy it that much, that television viewing fosters passivity and grumpy moods, that it is far down the list of what we report as satisfying leisure pastimes. Why, then, do we watch so much television? We seem to be creatures of habit with an infinite appetite for distraction. We do what comes easily. One can only wonder what will become of us when the computer is wedded to the television? For my part, I find it disturbing that the Internet is increasingly being referred to as the "playground of the 21st century."

What does this portend for leisure in our lives? Some people argue that the leisure services profession should reposition itself as a player in the midst of this sea of technological change, that it should get in front of the curve and make it work to its advantage. I have a different perspective.

In my opinion, the future of leisure is as an antidote to this mindless infatuation with labor-saving, time-saving, energy-saving devices. Its mission should be to provide a healthy alternative to the increasingly sedentary and isolated lives of a citizenry made passive and complacent by advancing technology. Its charge should be to reintroduce struggle into people's lives, to get people up and out of their easy chairs, away from their televisions, away from their computers, out their doors, back to nature, and, most important of all, back into one another's company.

Its charge should be refined further to provide people with new and engaging contexts within which to create meaning in their lives, lives made increasingly less meaningful by those same labor-saving, time-saving, energy-saving advances in technology. Whether volunteerism will be one of those contexts, or environmental stewardship, lifelong learning, a renewed commitment to our children, or all of them in some combination, therein lie the future benefits of leisure.

Technology, it seems to me, is neither friend nor foe. It is both. Technology is not either/or. It is this and that. Technology is not value-neutral. Each technology brings with it a program for social change, however subtle. Technology has made our lives easier, cleaner, and longer, to be sure. But it has also cost us. In our exuberance over what technology does, we are frequently oblivious to what technology undoes. To be ignorant of this, to be uninformed, is to be the tool of technology, not the toolmaker.

With the possible exception of health care, I cannot, for the life of me, see any real advantages to a technological mindset hell-bent on helping us live our lives at a faster clip, making less work for us to do, saving us time and energy that, in the final analysis, is our life itself. I think Will Rogers had it right when he said, "Half our life is spent trying to find something to do with the time we have rushed through life trying to save." The questions we never seem to get to, the really important questions, are these: To what use do we put the advantages of our technological innovations? What do we do with the time and energy we save? What do we do with the lives we save?

Until we address these questions and come up with worthwhile answers, I reserve the right to remain skeptical of technology's contributions to the quality of our lives. I, like Aldous Huxley in *Brave New World*, reserve the right to brood over our adoration of technologies that undo our capacity to think.[5] I reserve the right to worry about a citizenry that seems less and less interested in reading a book. I reserve the right to question the wisdom of giving people so much information that they are reduced to passivity and egoism. More than anything else, I reserve the right to fear, as Huxley did, that we will become "a trivial culture, preoccupied with some equivalent of the feelies, the orgy porgy, and the centrifugal bumble puppy."[6] In the end, I, too, worry that what we love will ruin us.

Chapter 20

THE PROFESSOR WHO MISTOOK HIS LIFE FOR A STAT

I would like to begin by citing Patricia Stokowski's commentary in the *Journal of Leisure Research* entitled "Trophy Hunting in the Shadow of the Castle Keep."[1] I cite Professor Stokowski for three reasons. First, I want to demonstrate that I actually read *JLR*. Second, I want to demolish the good professor's hypothesis that no one is likely to ever cite her article. Third, I want to share my amusement regarding Dr. Stokowski's exchange-theory-based proposition that we academics do not publish in order to be read. We publish, she posits, merely to be published.

I must confess I'd never seen publishing in this light before, as an end in itself, and not as a means to an end. By this measure, the 1998–1999 academic year was a very good one for me. I had three papers accepted for two conferences, both of which were canceled. Picture my glee in monitoring the subsequent SPRENET conversations when I learned that I could, in good conscience, list those papers on my curriculum vitae even though I had not delivered them. The important point was they had been accepted for delivery. I, in turn, was spared both the dollar expense of attending the conferences and any psychic expense that might have come my way from critiques of my presentations. That I could avoid such angst and still have my papers "count" was almost too good to be true.

Imagine my dismay, then, when a few months later, Professor Geof Godbey from the Pennsylvania State University insisted I actually show up at a conference in Nashville to discuss the question of whether recreation, park, and leisure studies scholars have anything to say to the larger world. I trust you will agree with me that at some fundamental level Professor Godbey just doesn't get it. After all these years, he still doesn't comprehend the nature of the game. Nevertheless, out of loyalty to him, I showed up anyway—

out of loyalty, that is, and the fact that getting on the program was the only way I could, in good conscience, ask Florida International University to pay my way to the Grand Ole Opry.

I titled my talk "The Professor Who Mistook His Life for a Stat." I chose this title for three reasons. First, it suggests in a clever way that I read beyond our field. It is important to do so, I think, if we aspire to make a difference with our thinking and learning in a bigger arena. Outside reading alerts us both to what is going on elsewhere and what matters elsewhere, and it also attunes us to different kinds of language that are spoken elsewhere. In the absence of such reading, the dangers of disciplinary insularity, isolation, and irrelevance that are discussed at great length by professors Jordan, Roland, Samdahl, Kelly, Pedlar, Stewart, Stokowski, Dunn, Madrigal, and Dahl in that same issue of *JLR* heightens considerably.

Second, "The Professor Who Mistook His Life for a Stat" hints at a special kind of neurosis plaguing students of recreation, park, and leisure studies. Rooted in a basic sense of insecurity about who we are and if, and how, we matter, this neurosis saps our energy and retards our growth and development as a community of scholars. Like some attention-starved child, we hunger for affirmation from the outside world, an outside world, I hasten to add, that is plagued by its own kind of sickness. Lacking a healthy self-concept, we rely on other ill people to tell us how we are doing.

Third, and most important, "The Professor Who Mistook His Life for a Stat" conveys a sense of the main point I wished to make that day—our work amounts to more than being social scientists. If recent discussions in the literature are any indication, understanding that there is more to life than science, that there is more to us than science, however obvious it sounds when I say it, is good medicine for us all.

I have been influenced tremendously over the years by a social scientist named B. L. Driver. When I was a graduate student at the University of Michigan in the mid 1970s, Driver had just edited *Elements of Outdoor Recreation Planning*,[2] a seminal text rethinking recreation and leisure and their associated implications for practice. In that book, Driver claimed the role of social science, as part of the planning process, was to provide decision makers with technical information upon which to base planning and policy decisions. He drew a clear line between providing information (the purview of social scientists) and acting or not acting upon that information (the purview of planners and policy makers). As an aspiring social scientist, I took that distinction to heart. But I confess I have always found it wanting. As a job description, it didn't do much for me in the 1970s, and it does even less for me now.

There are three reasons why I feel this way. First, to separate ourselves from the implications of our work, to say the use to which our learning is put is not really our concern, is to deny the existence of a significant part of who we are, the part of us that is not social scientist, the part of us that is citizen of a larger community. To my way of thinking, our work derives its principal meaning from its utility to that larger community. Why distance ourselves from its application? Why allow our work, and ourselves, to be dismissed as academic?

Part of a response, I suppose, would be that when we act as social scientists, there is a purity to our work that is guaranteed by the canons of scientific inquiry, a purity that inevitably is soiled by the down-and-dirty politics of professional practice. Better to steer clear of such contamination by confining ourselves to the laboratory—to the university—where we can live a more sanitary existence. The problem I have with this response is the second reason I am troubled by the assertion that our professional obligation is limited to supplying information upon which others may or may not base decisions. As far as I know, we can never prove anything. We can only fail to disprove things. This creates an intellectual tentativeness that makes it difficult for us to say much of anything with certainty. We are, by education, prone to qualification. While I understand the scientific need for this, I also understand that others who are not so constrained are busily acting. To be bystanders, then, when our incomplete information is more complete than the information being acted upon is, to me at least, goofy. If, as social scientists, we wait to be absolutely sure about something before we speak up, we are destined to be a silent lot.

Third, I find it unfulfilling to be solely a data dispenser. Judging by the intensity of the Benefits Based Management campaign, I gather Bev Driver has found it less fulfilling as well, as must have Mike Csikszentmihalyi, Geof Godbey, and John Robinson when, based on their experience sampling and time budget diary research, they criticized the impact of television on contemporary life, as must have Tom Goodale when he agreed to serve on the advisory board of TV Free America, as must have John Hemingway when he applied those same criticisms of television to an analysis of the weakening foundations of a strong form of citizenship so vital to the healthy functioning of a participatory democracy. We are all obliged to speak up when we believe we have something important to say.

I am less certain about the form such communication should take. Writing for publication is only one way of speaking up. Professing our insights in the classroom and at meetings, workshops, and conferences is another, as is taking an active role in our communities beyond the university. We are not lacking for opportunities here. Figuring out the most effective ways to proceed is another matter. The Academy of Leisure Sciences, for example, has posted a series of white papers on its web page discussing the importance of various aspects of recreation, parks, and leisure in contemporary life. While this is a commendable outreach effort, getting recreation, park, and leisure studies scholars to agree on a strategy for communication, let alone agree on the content of what should be said, strikes me as the equivalent of trying to herd cats.

I have always equated writing with tossing a pebble into the ocean. Whether it sinks to the bottom, never to be heard from again, or whether its rippling effects reverberate on some distant shore, is really out of our hands. We must proceed largely on faith when offering up our thinking for public consumption. We never know if or when our written or spoken words will strike a responsive chord.

In *Science and Human Values*, Jacob Bronowski posed the question, "Is You Is or Is You Ain't Ma Baby?"[3] He was inquiring about the relationship between scientists and their work. It's a good question to ponder. The nuclear physicist Robert Oppenheimer responded to Bronowski thusly (and I paraphrase): We know that our work is both an instrument and an end. A scientific discovery is a thing of beauty, and our faith—our binding, quiet faith—is that knowledge is good in and of itself. But our work is also an instrument for our successors who will use it to probe elsewhere and more deeply, and it is an instrument for the affairs of humankind.

So it is with us as social scientists, so it is with us as people. We are at once instrument and end, teachers and discoverers, actors and observers. We understand there is or ought to be harmony between the knowledge we uncover and its service to the larger world.

If you have been reading carefully, perhaps you have detected an undercurrent to my thoughts. I have spoken of social science both as an end and a means to an end. I have spoken of the joy of inquiry and the beauty of discovery. And I have spoken of an obligation to elevate the implications of our findings to a higher plane, of taking our learning to "The Show," as it were, of applying it to help solve the personal, social, and environmental problems of our time. All the while we are engaged in this enterprise, society patronizes us, society encourages us, society frees us to go wherever our thoughts take us. For some of us, at least, this borders on a life of leisure, a life of privilege that is still, at the beginning of the second millennium, just a distant dream for most people.

To be sure, we may not be well read by others, but that can be said of most any academic discipline. And we have our moments. I see references to our work from time to time in my general reading. I saw Garry Chick's work cited recently in *Psychology Today*[4] as well as Godbey's and Robinson's in James Gleick's book, *Faster*.[5] I also see our work indirectly every time I read about one of our students' accomplishments in the field, or in Leo McAvoy's case, when I read one of his former student's Anna Pigeon murder mysteries set in a national park.[6] So let's not be too hard on ourselves. It's a big ocean out there.

There is also, I suspect, a temporal problem. Does it ever occur to you that we may be living before our time? Does it ever occur to you that we may be farther along in our thinking, that we may be more knowledgeable than most of our contemporaries? Does it ever occur to you that the society in which we live needs our help and our guidance even if it does not yet know it? Granted, few of us may be around long enough to savor the fruits of our individual labor, but our children will be. That is reason enough to sustain our efforts—that and knowing *A Sand County Almanac* was published after Aldo Leopold's death.

Chapter 21

I'M BACK IN THE SADDLE AGAIN

In the shadow of California's Mt. Whitney, nestled between the eastern escarpment of the Sierra Nevada and the little town of Lone Pine, are the Alabama Hills. Named in honor of a Civil War battleship by 19th century prospectors sympathetic to the Confederacy, the Alabama Hills are a curious geological oddity. As old as the Sierra Nevada itself, the hills appear ghostly and forlorn, surfacing in clusters of brown, rounded rock, providing a sharp contrast to the snowcapped peaks rising above them.

It is this contrast that accounts for the Alabama Hills' claim to fame. Even if you have never visited them, you most certainly have seen the Alabama Hills. For more than 70 years, they have provided the setting for Hollywood motion pictures and TV Westerns. Hopalong Cassidy rode Topper here, Roy Rogers rode Trigger, and the Lone Ranger rode Silver. You've seen Audie Murphy shoot it out from behind these rocks too, and John Wayne, and Gary Cooper. The Alabama Hills provide the ideal backdrop for filming a chase scene, an ambush, and a stickup. They are quintessentially Western.

I have come to the Alabama Hills to star in a Western of my own making. I'm on a pilgrimage to find one rock—*the* rock— Gene Autry Rock, a tall, cucumber-shaped chunk of stone featured in the 1937 film *Boots and Saddles*.

"Why, exactly, do you feel compelled to act this way?" my Dale Evans wants to know.

"I don't know," I reply. "I only know I have traveled the width of the continent to seek out this rock. It is something I must do. Perhaps only cowboys can understand."

From my saddlebag (briefcase) I pull out *On Location in Lone Pine* by Dave Holland. It's a treasure map of sorts, pointing the way to various gulches and gullies in the Alabama Hills where Hollywood's greatest stars have thrilled us with tales of yesteryear. Holland promises to unlock the many secrets of location shoots and bring me closer to my matinee idols.

First, the book instructs me to head straight west out of Lone Pine toward Mt. Whitney on Whitney Portal Road. Just like Humphrey Bogart in *High Sierra* (1941), I can hear the gas station attendant boasting, "You're lookin' at the pride of the Sierras, brother. Mt. Whitney. Highest peak in the United States—14,501 feet above sea level. Say! I see you have an Illinois [Florida] license plate! You're a long way from home, aint'cha?"

(Bogart [Dustin] frowns at him.)

"You must excuse me. I . . . I get lonesome here. And when a customer shows up, well, I—maybe I talk too much."

(Bogart [Dustin]) "Lonesome, eh? Yeah, I can see how you would get lonesome out here."

At Movie Road, I take a hard right and pick up Roy Rogers's trail from his first starring feature in 1938, *Under Western Stars*. Soon, however, the trail fades into dust, and I am left to ponder the barren landscape in front of me. There are no mileage markers here. No street signs. Only line drawings of the general vicinity and scattered dirt roads leading off in every direction.

On my immediate left are the "movie flats" where chase scenes played out in Tom Mix's *Riders of the Purple Sage* (1925) and wagon trains crawled westward in *Brigham Young, Frontiersman* (1940). In the distance, somewhere on my right, is *The Lone Ranger* (1938) ambush site, the place where outlaws killed every Texas Ranger but one, leaving a lone survivor, a lone Ranger, to carry on.

"This is great!" I chuckle, as we wind our way back into the hills. I can almost hear the pounding of horses' hooves, gunfire, and shouts of "Take cover!" At any moment I expect to see The Cisco Kid riding toward me at a gallop. With each mile, I am carried farther and farther back into time to a childhood full of Wild West fantasies and play.

According to the guidebook, segments of *Bonanza* were filmed near here in the 1950s and '60s, though what I remember most about *Bonanza* is the opening theme song that accompanied me to bed every Sunday night at 9 p.m. I can still hear my dad saying, "Good night, Dan. Remember, tomorrow is a school day," as he settled into his easy chair to watch the Cartwrights fend off another threat to the Ponderosa.

I grew up on a steady diet of TV Westerns, and many of them were filmed right here: *Annie Oakley*; *Have Gun, Will Travel*; *The Lone Ranger*; *Wagon Train*; and *Wild Bill Hickock*. Segments of *Death Valley Days* were shot here, too. Do you remember who narrated them? That's right. Ronald Reagan, the 40th president of the United States. And during commercials he would sell Twenty-Mule Team Borax Soap. Who'd a thought . . .?

Those programs sparked my fascination with the American West and fired my imagination. I played at being a cowboy all the time, and I dreamed of actually going "out west" someday. My dad made me a hobbyhorse when I was three, and I trotted all over the house.

The West, in my mind, was a place where everything turned out right, where good always triumphed over evil. Little did I know that Hollywood screenwriters carefully packaged the "West" for me. As Wallace Stegner was fond of pointing out, the mythic figure of the lone Western hero, the rugged individualist, was far from the truth of the matter. Survival in the Old West had a lot more to do with cooperation between and among individuals than it did with any one individual being quicker on the draw. Nonetheless, it feels good now to pass among the spirits of my childhood heroes, however fictitious they may have been.

I take a long, slow swig from my canteen (bottled spring water). The liquid coolness brings back memories of one of my favorite songs, "Cool Water," by the Sons of the Pioneers. Below me is the parched Owens Valley, a valley that used to be green. That was before the Los Angeles Water and Power District bought up much of the land in the 1920s to lock up water rights for the burgeoning Los Angeles Basin. Southern California, I confide to my sidekick, is parasitic by nature. Left to its own resources, it would shrivel up and die. Its cool water is carried in from elsewhere, too; hence the great struggle over Northern California's Mono Lake. Although environmentalists appear to have won that showdown, it will be years before Mono Lake's water level returns to normal. In the meantime, as I take one more swig from my canteen, Southern California hankers to quench its thirst as well.

There is also the problem of geography. Knowing something about it, as I do, can lead to difficulties when attempting to suspend one's disbelief in front of a motion picture screen or TV set. Not long ago, I saw *Maverick* (1994), starring Mel Gibson, Jodie Foster, and James Garner. In one scene, the characters were pictured in the Alabama Hills just below Mt. Whitney, while in the very next scene they were pictured 100 miles to the north in Yosemite Valley. The illogic offended my sensibilities.

Even more far-fetched, on top of all the Westerns set in the Alabama Hills, are scores of other movies filmed here that were supposed to be about other parts of the world. *Gunga Din* (1939), for example, features elements of the Alabama Hills as the Khyber Pass. While such trickery works well enough on the uneducated eye, seeing Mt. Whitney in the background of what is supposed to be the border between Pakistan and Afghanistan can ruin one's appetite for a film.

I dismount (get out of the car) to check my bearings, but nothing makes sense to me. The so-called landmarks all look alike. Evidently, I am lost. This is tough for a cowboy, even a 21st century cowboy, to admit. As the afternoon wears on, I am becoming increasingly flustered. Every rock looks the same. Every direction looks the same. Other than the constant presence of Mt. Whitney in the background, I am disoriented. How will I ever find Gene Autry Rock?

On a hunch, I dismount once more, consult Holland's book, and huff and puff my way up to some grotesquely shaped boulders. There is a vague familiarity about them. I can't be sure whether I've seen them in movies about the American West, Old Mexico, Argentina, or India. They just feel right somehow. Surely, these must be the ones. In a few minutes, though, I am ready to give up the chase once and for all, as nothing familiar reveals itself to me.

Then, as I scan the horizon one last time, I see an odd-shaped rock far and away across the canyon. It is not Gene Autry Rock, but I know I have seen it before. I get out Holland's book and—lo and behold—it is Gary Cooper Rock, an overhanging slab that Cooper hid under in *Lives of a Bengal Lancer* (1935). Running for it, I soon stand where Cooper stood, hiding from the same enemy. And just like Cooper, I pause for dramatic effect. . . . It's a smaller space than I expected. Cooper must have been a smaller man than I imagined him to be. Now, isn't that the truth? Hollywood makes movie stars out to be bigger than life, but if you ever see one of them in person, or if you ever see their footprints in the sidewalk in front of Graumann's Chinese Theater in Los Angeles, or if you ever actually stand in a space they once stood in, they almost always shrink a size or two.

Leafing madly through the pages of Holland's guidebook, I see where Gene Autry Rock is in relation to Gary Cooper Rock. It can't be more than a few hundred yards away. What luck! After two hours of putting up with the sun, wind, and dust, I'm about to hit pay dirt. I am about to get my man.

Unfortunately, after another half-hour of futile searching, and with darkness fast approaching, I'm ready to pack it in. Then—suddenly—I spot the cucumber-shaped silhouette I've been looking for. Gene Autry Rock! And now that I've found it, it seems so obvious. I run for it. Gleefully.

I am now standing on the exact same spot where Gene Autry sat on the back of his horse in *Boots and Saddles* in 1937. It doesn't matter that the Bengal Lancers rode by this same rock in 1935, that Hopalong Cassidy found Shorty's body here in 1946, or that the Indian chase scene in *How the West Was Won* (1962) was filmed right here, too. What matters is that I have finally found what I've been looking for. I've finally reconnected with my boyhood hero. And for this one moment, this one delicious moment, I, too, am back in the saddle again.

Chapter 22

REMEMBERING MANZANAR

"I want to ride to the ridge where the west commences,
Gaze at the moon until I lose my senses.
I can't look at hobbles and I can't stand fences,
Don't fence me in . . ."

—Cole Porter

What I remember most about Roy and Mickey Okimoto is that my parents thought they were wonderful neighbors. We lived in a middle-class subdivision in Farmington, Michigan, and the Okimotos occupied the corner house next door. Roy ran a garage, was an excellent mechanic, and owned a race car. Mickey was a dutiful mother and homemaker. Until recently, I never knew why they left California in the early 1940s to move to Michigan, or, for that matter, why they returned to California during my high school years in the mid 1960s. I only knew they were hardworking, friendly people, and that my parents held them in high regard.

To appreciate the Okimotos' story, it is necessary to place it in the context of a larger story that unfolded immediately after the Japanese bombed Pearl Harbor on December 7, 1941. In the hysteria that followed, all Japanese Americans living on the West Coast of the United States were viewed as a threat to national security. They included *Issei*, first-generation Japanese who migrated to the United States between 1890 and 1924 and who were prevented by law from becoming naturalized citizens; *Nisei*, second-generation children of the *Issei* who were American citizens by birth; and *Sansei*, third-generation children of the *Nisei*, most of whom were infants during the Second World War.

Led by Lt. General John DeWitt, the zealous commanding officer charged with ensuring the security of the West Coast, pressure mounted to force the three generations of Japanese

Americans to the interior of the country, where they would be less
"dangerous," or to place them in internment camps for the dura-
tion of the war. While the Okimotos moved to the Midwest, others
did not. More than 100,000 people of Japanese ancestry soon were
incarcerated by the authority vested in Executive Order 9066, signed
into law by President Franklin Delano Roosevelt on February 19,
1942.

Manzanar, the first of 10 such prison camps, was opened on
March 25, 1942. Located in California's Owens Valley in the shadow
of Mount Williamson, it was bounded by barbed wire and guard
towers. Manzanar, meaning "apple orchard" in Spanish, would
eventually confine 10,000 people, the majority of them American
citizens, until its official closing on November 21, 1945. Unlike
the infamous concentration camps of Nazi Germany, Manzanar
would not come to be known for killing. It would come to be
known, however, as a place where the 14th Amendment to the
United States Constitution, guaranteeing citizens equal treatment
and protection under the law, was sacrificed hastily for the sake of
"military necessity."

Life at Manzanar unfolded in an outwardly normal fashion. There
was a community newspaper, a cooperative, a manufacturing plant,
a hospital, churches, and a school with a gymnasium and playing
fields.[1] Inmates were referred to euphemistically as "evacuees," and
the prison itself was called a "War Relocation Center." But the
"residents" were in fact prisoners of war, locked up solely because
their faces were an exact likeness of the enemy. If they tried to leave
the compound, the military police had orders to shoot them.

To add insult to injury, the imprisoned families were forced to
liquidate their belongings before being sent to Manzanar. This included businesses, land, and houses. The internees were thus deprived of their livelihood, property, and freedom. This was especially hard on the *Nisei*, who prided themselves in making an hon-
orable living in the United States of America, their native land.
Taking away their possessions and their jobs—not to mention their
civil rights—was terribly degrading, and many families disintegrated
in the aftermath.

Work at Manzanar was limited to manufacturing camouflage
nets to support the war effort and growing crops to make the prison
camp self-sustaining. The *Nisei* were accomplished farmers, and
they were able to transform a portion of the dusty, windswept Owens
Valley into fertile fields. Still, the vast majority of prisoners were

professionals without professions. The psychological damage was devastating.

For the children of Manzanar, there were school, friends, and extracurricular activities. But here as well the effects of confinement were deeply felt. In *Farewell to Manzanar*, an autobiographical account of prison life told through the eyes of a child, Jeanne Wakatsuki Houston recalls her older brother Bill leading a dance band called The Jive Bombers and singing Glenn Miller arrangements of *In the Mood, String of Pearls*, and *Don't Fence Me In*. Bill refused to sing the lyrics of the last song in protest to the authorities who were denying him his freedom.

The injustice at Manzanar did not go unnoticed. The camp's second director, Ralph Merritt, called on a friend, Ansel Adams, to photograph for posterity what life was like behind the barbed wire and guard towers. The result, *Born Free and Equal*, published in 1944, was vilified by many Americans, and in some places the book was burned. Nonetheless, the tide of public opinion was beginning to turn, and by December 1944, the U.S. Supreme Court had ruled that loyal citizens could not be held in detention camps against their will.

The question of loyalty was always in the air. From the beginning, skeptics felt that Americans of Japanese ancestry would side with their ancient, Oriental homeland rather than with their newly adopted Western country. Such doubts were less often raised about German or Italian Americans. The grounds upon which to base suspicions of Japanese Americans' loyalty to the United States were tenuous. Indeed, many of the internees signed loyalty oaths and then served admirably in the Armed Forces. Moreover, the most decorated unit in the history of the U.S. military, the 100th Battalion of the 442nd Regimental Combat Team, made up entirely of Japanese Americans, fought the Second World War with great courage and sacrifice throughout Italy and France.

Manzanar today is but a wisp of its former self. The pagoda-like sentry houses are still standing, as is the community auditorium, as is the "soul consoling tower" erected in the center of the cemetery at the rear of the camp. But the 504 barracks have long since been torn down, as have the guard towers, the compound's hospital, and all other administrative buildings. Designated a National Historic Site in 1992 by President Bush, the Manzanar "War Relocation Center" now awaits the interpretive touch of the National Park Service. What story, I wonder, will it tell?

Manzanar represents a dark chapter in American history. That it existed at all is testimony to civilization's thin veneer, a reminder of how vulnerable our democratic way of life can be when strained and stressed. But the opportunity Manzanar presents us now to set the record straight, to own up to our past mistakes, and to discuss what we have learned from it illustrates the strength of our democracy as well. That the park and recreation profession, through the National Park Service, has been assigned this important educational role says a lot about the centrality of our field in helping make this a better nation.

Remembering Manzanar is but one way to remind ourselves of the pivotal educational role our profession can, and ought to, play in getting our nation's story right. Similar opportunities present themselves at Independence Hall in Philadelphia, the Statue of Liberty on Ellis Island, The Little Bighorn Battlefield in Montana, the birthplace of the women's rights movement in Seneca Falls, New York, and Martin Luther King Jr.'s home in Atlanta, among many others. Being entrusted with these stories reflects the faith placed in our profession by the American people to render a truthful accounting of our cultural heritage. In this regard, safeguarding freedom of choice, a sense of fair play, and equal treatment and protection under the law is what the park and recreation profession ultimately is about. We must never forget that.

When the Second World War came to its horrific end with the bombing of Hiroshima and Nagasaki in August 1945, my father was stationed on Saipan in the South Pacific, awaiting what he was sure would be an even more horrific invasion of Japan itself. He came home from that war with good reason to hate the Japanese. Yet if he harbored such feelings, he never expressed them to his family. Based on his friendship with Roy and Mickey Okimoto, I am left to conclude that he found it within himself to distinguish between nationalism and racism, between governments and people, between enemies and neighbors. I would like to think that my dad, were he alive today, would nod his head in quiet approval of the message now greeting visitors at the gates of Manzanar: "May the injustice and humiliation suffered here as a result of hysteria, racism and economic exploitation never emerge again."

Chapter 23

IS THIS HEAVEN?

In Meredith Willson's 1957 Broadway hit, *The Music Man*, Professor Harold Hill, a fast-walking, smooth-talking outsider from Gary, Indiana, tries his hardest to convince the good citizens of River City, Iowa, to forsake the evils of pool for the saving grace of a marching band. "You've got trouble," he says, "right here in River City, with a capital 'T' and that rhymes with 'P' and that stands for Pool!" Chided by his fellow traveling salesmen as a "bare-faced, double-shuffle, two-bit thimble rigger" who "doesn't know the territory," Professor Hill nonetheless casts a spell over the citizens of River City and is about to capitalize on his flimflam when salt-of-the-earth Marian, the librarian, steals his heart and saves him from himself.

I am going to weave elements from *The Music Man* throughout this essay. Indeed, almost every point I will make emanates from it. That's because *The Music Man*, more than anything else, is a morality play. It is about bad values attempting to subvert good values, and it is about good values prevailing in the end.

I am well aware that I, too, am a professor, and an outsider to boot. Unlike Professor Hill, however, I will not try to sell you a bill of goods. Even if I wanted to, I would refrain, because the citizens of River City taught me that Iowans are "so stubborn they can stand nose to nose for a week at a time and never see eye to eye." But they also taught me that Iowans will "give the shirt off their back and the back to go with it" to help a neighbor in distress. So allow me to begin with an earnest payment. I promise that not only will I not try to bamboozle you by convincing you that Iowans are something they are not, I will entrust you with the responsibility of finishing my essay for me. The last words on this matter, I guarantee you, will be yours.

On May 17, 1997, my father passed away unexpectedly in Port Charlotte, Florida, leaving his wife of 56 years in my care. While we did our share of grieving, our family was also very grateful for

Dad's long life, a life marked by conviction of purpose and moral integrity. So, rather than dwell on the past, our family discussions quickly turned to the future. During the last years of my father's life, he had discouraged my mother from driving, monitored most every morsel that went into her mouth because of his concern for her late-onset diabetes, and chosen to stay put, eschewing travel because it would take him and his wife away from their trusted medical caregivers.

However terrible the passing of her lifelong partner, I tried to make the case to my 90-year-old mother that she was now liberated in a way she hadn't been before. I would not be standing over her like Dad did. She was going to have to use her own judgment when it came to driving and eating. And, oh, by the way, I would gladly take her anywhere in the world she wanted to go. If she wanted to see the Eiffel Tower, I would take her to Paris. If she wanted to see the Great Wall of China, I would take her to the Orient. If she wanted to see Alaska's Inland Passage, I would accompany her on that voyage as well. I encouraged mom to take her time and think it over, but she said there was no need. "Dan," she said softly, "if it wouldn't be too much trouble, I'd like to go back home to Ida Grove, Iowa."

Two months later I was sitting on the front porch of my cousin Al Schreiber's farmhouse, gazing into a star-filled sky. It was so still, so peaceful, save for an occasional chirp of a cricket, and I was filled with the sweet fragrances of a summer's night. Though I have never lived in Iowa, I thought at that moment that I never wanted to leave. It felt like home to me, or the way I thought home ought to feel. And as I watched the fireflies punctuate the darkness, I was reminded of the author Jim Harrison and a story he wrote set in Iowa called "The Woman Lit by Fireflies." That association, in turn, reminded me of something else Harrison had written, something to the effect that Iowa is one of only two places he knows in the United States that actually remind us of what America thinks she is like.

I agree with Mr. Harrison. I believe Iowa is what America would like to be when she grows up. But because of our adolescent culture, our juvenile state of mind, our almost childlike preoccupation with the superficial and transitory, we are not cognizant of it. We are as awestruck teenagers mesmerized by all the wrong things. We are a society hung up on appearances. If Iowa were a girl or a boy it would be the kind we parents would counsel our sons and daughters to marry. "Oh sure," we'd say, "You want to show off your independence, let your hair down, be irresponsible, sow some wild oats. That's okay. We understand. That's what New York, Florida, and, especially, California are for. But when you come to your senses, when you mature, when you finally grow up, you'll come to understand the values that give life its most enriching and enduring meaning. Then you'll want to come back home and marry Iowa."

If Iowa has a problem, and I seriously question the premise, it would have to be that it is before its time. The nostalgic, bucolic images of Grant Wood's "American Gothic," Robert Waller's *The Bridges of Madison County*, and Phil Alden Robinson's *Field of Dreams* notwithstanding, Iowa is without question one of the most forward-thinking states in the union. Its high school students score the highest in the country on the SAT. Its citizens have the highest literacy rate in the nation. Iowa City has the highest percentage of residents with a college degree of any town in America. (Surely there must be a joke in there somewhere. "Did you hear about the Iowa grad who moved from Iowa City to Ames, thereby lowering the intelligence quotient of both communities?") Iowa's cost of living is low, and Iowa has a low crime rate. Iowa is wired electronically. Now, I am not an expert on jobs, but I think the *Des Moines Register's* editorial on Wednesday, October 27th, 1999, titled "Focus on the Good Life" may be onto something. When it comes to Iowa's quality of life, build it and they will come.

But that's far from the whole of it. The name "Iowa" is derived from an American Indian word for "beautiful land." The name is significant, I think, because more than any other state in the union, almost everything worth cherishing about Iowa is rooted in the soil. This is of no small consequence in a country that is now 85% urbanized. We Americans are quickly becoming detached from our biological moorings. We don't know any more where our food comes from, where our sustenance comes from, where our life comes from. Most of us have lost touch with our fundamental ground of being, the wellspring from which all blessings flow. Iowans are still close enough to the land to can keep this sense of connection alive in their children and in visitors to their state. If you are not aware of it, you should know that the greatest environmental ethicist of our time, Aldo Leopold, was born and raised in Burlington, Iowa, and that one of our country's greatest environmental writers and teachers of writing, Wallace Stegner, was born in Lake Mills, Iowa.

These are men whose thinking was before their time also. They both saw land as a community, and they saw human beings as plain members and citizens of it.

But that's still not the whole of it. Psychologists tell us human beings are proximal by nature. We like being close to one another and enjoying one another's company. In Iowa, especially small-town Iowa, there is still a fighting chance to preserve, celebrate, and nurture this aspect of our humanity in a way that much of the rest of America cannot. Borrowing from Iowa's own Chuck Offenburger, "You know you're in small-town Iowa when . . . you don't need to use your car's turn signal because everybody knows where you're going . . . when Third Street is on the edge of town . . . and when you dial a wrong number but wind up talking 15 minutes anyway." The gripe against small towns has always been that everybody knows everybody else's business. Well, I've got news for you. The United States of America is rapidly becoming a transparent society where everybody is going to know everybody else's business anyway, no matter where we live. Under the circumstances, give me friends and neighbors.

But we're still not quite where I want to take you in your thinking. If I had any use for advertising, which I don't, I would urge Iowa's governor to put up billboards at both beginnings of Interstates 80 and 35 proclaiming, "We grow more than corn in Iowa! We grow . . ." And then, on a rotating basis, I would fill in the blank with "environmental awareness," "highly educated children," and, most importantly, "democratic values."

When reading Ames newspaper editor Michael Gartner's 1997 speech to the Story City Chamber of Commerce, I was struck by just how pivotal a role Iowa has played in cultivating the ideal of freedom in the United States. Iowa was the first place where the Supreme Court chose not to recognize slavery—well before the Civil War. Iowa was the first place where, in 1869, 12-year-old Susan Clark, "of the colored race," successfully sued the Muscatine school board, striking down their segregation policy. Indeed, "Iowa opened its schools to children of all races nearly 100 years before the Supreme Court of the United States ordered an end to segregation." Iowa was the first state to admit a woman to the bar to practice law. And Iowa was instrumental in the establishment of groundbreaking precedents for both the doctrines of equal protection under the law and the separation of church and state. As Mr. Gartner concludes, "freedom is what Iowa is about." And as Iowa reminds the rest of the nation every four years, it is where the democratic process of choosing our next president begins.

This brings me to the role of leisure services in Iowa's future. For leisure, too, is about freedom, volition, and choice. But more than anything else, as the ancient Greeks taught us, leisure is about choosing to live one's personal life in a way that enhances the quality of public life. Leisure services, at their best, are a form of social glue that helps bind us together as a nation. Properly planned, they help cultivate a strong form of citizenship so vital to the healthy functioning of a participatory democracy. I know these things to be true, but they did not originate with me. You could have asked Karla Henderson, a native of Coggon, Iowa, who is, in my judgment, the individual most responsible for giving a voice to women's leisure in the United States. Or you could have asked John Hemingway, educated at both Grinnell College and the University of Iowa, who is one of our country's leading scholars when it comes to thinking and writing about leisure's potential as a contributing force in shaping our democratic way of life. Please allow me to say it once more. They grow more than corn in Iowa.

We live in increasingly frenetic times. Everything is speeding up. Everything is becoming a blur. We are being swept away by the attendant values accordingly. Economic efficiency rules. We see the Gross Domestic Product as a measure of progress when it really only measures the rate at which we go through limited natural resources. We assume getting somewhere sooner rather than later is always desirable. We assume newer is always better than older, and, therefore, that younger must be better than older also. Yes, my friends, I'm afraid we've got trouble, right here in the U.S. of A, with a capital "T," and that rhymes with "V," and that stands for "Values."

How easy it is to forget what matters most in life. How easy it is to lose our way. Do you remember, by chance, the lyrics from the song "Till There Was You" in *The Music Man*? "There were bells on the hill, but I never heard them ringing. . . . There were birds in the sky, but I never saw them winging. . . . And there was music and wonderful roses, they tell me, in sweet fragrant meadows of dawn, and dew. . . ." "Till There Was You," in this case, refers to Iowa. America is in desperate need of an antidote to cure what ails her. America needs salt-of-the-earth Iowa to steal her heart and save her from herself.

At the end of *The Music Man*, a little boy named Winthrop challenges Professor Harold Hill's faith. "Is there a band?" the boy asks. "I always think there's a band, kid," Hill replies. Whatever his faults, the professor is a dreamer, a visionary. I trust Iowans are, too. They have an extraordinary opportunity to model right livelihood, to lead the United States of America by example. Never forget that *The Music Man*, ultimately, is about Iowans working together, despite the odds, to build a better community. That the vehicle for this miracle is made out of clarinets, trumpets, and trombones does not surprise me, nor would it surprise Karla Henderson or John Hemingway. Neither are we surprised that the context for the *Field of Dreams* is a baseball diamond. Leisure, at its core, is about individuals in community. It is about civic engagement and civic responsibility. It is about building a better quality of life for all.

As I prepare to put down my pen, I know, in my heart, that I envy Iowans. I envy them their beautiful land, their beautiful communities, and their beautiful planning opportunity. Though I am an infrequent visitor, let me say once more that Iowa feels like home to me, or like home ought to feel. I know what Professor Harold Hill meant when he said he was about to skedaddle, only to get his foot "caught in the door." I also know how Shoeless Joe Jackson felt when his field of dreams bewildered him. For I, too, am bewildered by the State of Iowa, and like Shoeless Joe, when he trotted back out into the cornfield at the end of his day of play, later on this evening, when—in my mind's eye—I wind my way slowly through the cornfields of central Iowa to Des Moines and board a plane bound for Miami, I, too, will feel the need to stop and look back one last time, just like Shoeless Joe did, and ask, "Is this heaven?"

Chapter 24

SATURDAY NIGHT AT THE
LAZY "B" BAR AND CAFE

I fell in love with Montana in 1957. I was 10 years old. My parents took my sister, Carol, and me to the edge of the Bob Marshall Wilderness for a summer vacation and turned us loose. I waded the streams in blue jeans and tennis shoes, fishing for brook and rainbow trout with freshly caught grasshoppers. I played the line out gradually, allowing the hopper to float naturally downstream through the riffles and deeper holes. Then I worked the bait upstream in fits and starts, trying to entice a trout into striking. I can still feel the anticipation of a splash and the numbing cold of surging water as it pressed in on my legs, ankles, feet, and toes. Even now, almost 50 years later, I count those days as the happiest of my life.

We stayed at the Bruckert Ranch, a dude ranch located 30 miles west of the little town of Augusta. The gravel road from Augusta circled Haystack Butte and then climbed into the Lewis and Clark National Forest and higher still into the Benchmark area of the northern Rocky Mountains. The farther up we went, the rougher the road got. Eventually, it proved too much for the left front tire of our '55 Buick. My dad surely must have had second thoughts about his choice for a family vacation as he changed the flat tire. Our spirits were soon lifted, however, when we came upon homemade welcome signs affixed to pine trees on each side of the road: "Hi Dan!" "Hi Carol!" "Hi Derby!" "Hi Lucille!"

The D. A. O'Dell family from Moses Lake, Washington, greeted us. The O'Dells were former neighbors from Fenton, Michigan. D. A. was a pharmacist who served on Fenton's school board, where he got to know my father, the town's high school principal. I can still picture D. A.'s drugstore. As a boy of seven or eight, I sipped cherry colas at the soda fountain and dreamed of being a pharmacist myself one day. I especially liked the drugstore's coolness in the summer. After the O'Dells moved to Washington state, they stayed in touch with our family and encouraged us to share a summer vacation in Montana. The O'Dells had crafted the welcome signs.

The Bruckert Ranch was primarily an outfitting camp for big-game hunters. The main quarry were elk, bighorn sheep, mountain goats, bear, and deer. In the off-season, the owners, Dan and Donna Neal, rented cabins for $25 a week. Guests could ride horses for three dollars a day; take pack trips into the "Bob" for heftier fees; fish for brook, rainbow, and golden trout in nearby Wood Lake, Fairview Creek, Straight Creek, and the South Fork of the Sun River; and otherwise enjoy the tranquility and fresh air of the Rocky Mountains.

Our cabin was rustic; it had neither plumbing nor electricity. We fetched water from a nearby mountain stream, stored perishables in a clean new garbage can set in the same stream, cooked on a wood-burning stove, and made use of an outhouse behind the cabin. We soon found out that a badger had laid claim to the path between the cabin and the outhouse, and it would often chase us as we made our way to and fro.

The Bruckert Ranch was heaven on earth to a 10-year-old boy. Early in the morning, I'd leap out of bed, jump into my clothes, run outside, and swat a dozen or so grasshoppers with my baseball cap while they were still sluggish in the dewy grass. I put the hoppers in a jar with air holes in the lid and then ran to my favorite fishing hole on Fairview Creek. Most mornings, I'd bring my limit of trout back to the cabin in time for Mom to cook them up for breakfast. I'd spend the rest of the day scouting out new fishing holes, hanging around the corral, feeding the horses sugar cubes, harassing chipmunks and fool's hens, shooting my BB gun, and just being a boy.

On special days, we rented horses and rode to Pretty Prairie, five or six miles into the "Bob." Once there, we picnicked and fished for larger rainbows at the confluence of the South and West Forks of the Sun River. This is where I learned to fly-fish, and my favorite dry fly was the Crazy Goof, a grasshopper imitation I purchased at Dan Bailey's Fly Shop in Great Falls. On the way back from one of our rides to Pretty Prairie, I found a sun-bleached deer antler rack next to the trail. I took it home and mounted it as a project for my school shop class. The antlers still adorn a bedroom wall in my folks' cottage, with a little boy's cowboy hat hanging from the prongs.

Other days, we rode horses to the fire lookout atop Patrol Mountain. The last few hundred feet along the mountain's crest were breathtaking. The wind whistled all around us as a 360-degree panorama of the Continental Divide opened up. I gripped the saddle horn with all my might as Skeeter, my trail horse, plodded along, indifferent to the steep slopes on either side. We brought mail and other supplies to the fire lookout and then listened raptly to stories of grizzly sightings, lightning strikes, and other accounts that stirred my imagination.

Upon returning to the ranch, Dan Neal turned the livestock loose for the night. The trail horses and pack mules grazed in clusters of three or four, and Dan hung bells on the lead animals in each group. Then, in the predawn hours, we'd be stirred from our sleep by the distant sounds of bells clanging as Dan or one of his wranglers herded the stock back into the corral. Dan certainly knew his animals. When we rented horses, we'd gather in the corral and wait for him to announce which ones were ours for the day. Mom, who was not accustomed to horseback riding, always got Baldy, a gentle horse entrusted with carrying eggs on pack trips into the Bob Marshall Wilderness.

Occasionally, we'd wake up to learn that Dan had been out all night fighting a forest fire. In the 1950s, the Forest Service tried to put out fires, even naturally caused ones inside wilderness areas. Dan knew the "Bob" like the back of his hand. He once found alongside the trail in pitch blackness a pair of tennis shoes that my sister had lost on a ride back from Pretty Prairie.

In the evening, we'd gather around the kitchen table and play Crazy Rummy with the O'Dells by the light of kerosene lamps. I still recall D. A.'s booming voice, ribald character, and storytelling. As the evening progressed, Mom always saw to it that everyone was well supplied with food and drink. Then, all too soon, it would be bedtime. I'd drag myself off to the adjoining room, change into my flannel pajamas, climb into one of the big four-posters, and burrow down under the covers. As I tried to eavesdrop on the adults in the next room, the exhaustion from a full day's play would quickly carry me off into a deep sleep.

Those summer days could have lasted forever as far as I was concerned. I loved the routine of waking up early to the muted sounds of bells and hooves, catching grasshoppers, trout fishing, exploring the ranch, horseback riding, day-hiking, playing cards, and then collapsing into bed. I had never been so happy. It was as

if the Bruckert Ranch were a world unto itself, and the thought of
leaving it behind to go back to Michigan and another school year
was almost too much for a young boy to bear.

On the day of our departure, Donna Neal invited us to the
main lodge, where she served up a breakfast of sourdough pancakes. The elk antlers on the wall, Donna said proudly, were within
one inch in width of being a world record. There were also photos
of huge bull trout caught on the White River in a remote part of
the "Bob." As we ate, Dan stopped by to say good bye and remind
us to keep our eyes open for the goat licks on our way back to
Augusta. Then, after breakfast, Donna gave my mom some sourdough starter to take home so we could eat sourdough pancakes
throughout the year in remembrance of the Bruckert Ranch. I didn't
want to leave, and I teared up as we drove away.

On our way back to Augusta, Dad stopped the car briefly, near
the spot where we had the flat tire coming in, to view the goat licks
Dan had told us about. Sure enough, we saw through binoculars
several tiny white "specks" inching their way across what appeared
to be a vertical rock face high above us. Then we continued working our way down, out of the mountains, ever so slowly, so as not
to puncture another tire. All too soon, the Bob Marshall Wilderness, the Bruckert Ranch, and the Lewis and Clark National Forest
were left behind us.

Our family enjoyed Montana so much that we returned every
other summer during my growing-up years—1959, 1961, and
1963. I looked forward to going out west with such excitement
that I would pack and then live out of my suitcase for months in
advance of our vacation. My parents, especially my mom, must
have gotten a kick out of it, because living out of a suitcase forced
me to be neat and tidy when most boys my age delighted in being
just the opposite.

The magic of that first summer flavored all of our subsequent
trips to Montana, even though the Bruckert Ranch changed over
time. On August 17, 1959, while at the ranch, we felt the after-
shocks from a powerful earthquake that obliterated a campground
near West Yellowstone, Montana, killing several people. The next
morning we found cracks in the earth, and Fairview Creek, nor-
mally clear, ran brown with silt and mud. In 1961, we returned to
find electric lights and a refrigerator had replaced kerosene lamps
in our cabin and the need for a garbage can set in the stream to
keep our food cold.

I loved the rustic character of the ranch, and I whined and whined about spoiling it with such "improvements." My mother lent a sympathetic ear, and it never occurred to me that she might have welcomed the changes herself. Indeed, as I think back on the significance of those summers to my own growth and development— not to mention my eventual career choice—I am now ashamed to admit that I hardly ever thought about my mom as someone having preferences of her own. To me, she was the Rock of Gibraltar. Mom was always there, attending to our family's every need, cooking and cleaning and otherwise going about the business of being the primary caregiver. She possessed strength of character and a work ethic that revealed themselves simply in the way she behaved. I could always count on Mom. I can still picture her, ever resourceful, on our family camping trips, heating stones, stuffing them in athletic socks, and then placing the socks at the base of our sleeping bags to keep our feet warm.

Our family vacations were almost always outdoor-oriented and on the primitive side. We camped a lot, rented a cabin once or twice on Lake Huron's shore, and traveled cross-country by car to see America's scenic wonders. Always frugal, Mom packed picnic lunches to get us off on the right foot and then cooked whenever we stayed at a motel with a kitchenette. In hindsight, it is clear to me that our family vacations were designed primarily to please my dad or me or Carol. For Mom, family vacations meant cooking and cleaning under inferior conditions.

Please don't jump to the wrong conclusion. I think Mom derived considerable pleasure from seeing her family members enjoy themselves. I think she defined how she was doing by how we were doing. Mom was from a large Iowa farm family, and she grew up catering to others. She helped feed and clothe hired hands. She taught school in a rural one-room schoolhouse. Then she spent 35 years teaching kindergarten in three Michigan communities while raising a family. Her whole life, it seemed, consisted of service to others. Yet I can't help but wonder from time to time if she might have wanted things to be different somehow. In an age when so many women take pride in being liberated from deferential and subservient roles, I sometimes wonder just who was my mother, really, and what was she thinking?

I regret I did not talk more to Mom about these matters before she died in the summer of 2002. I regret she may have felt she had to yield in family matters. I regret I may not have known what

Mom was really thinking because she always seemed to go along quietly with my father. Mom was such a good team player, such a good supporter of the family unit. I sometimes fear that not to have known her innermost feelings and thoughts may mean I did not really know my mother at all. On the surface, she seemed to understand and accept her helpmate role. But looking back on her life now, it's the rare glimpses of another side of her that give me pause to wonder about her true nature.

My favorite story about Mom occurred on one of those beloved Montana vacations. It was customary on the last Saturday evening of our stay at the Bruckert Ranch for the adults to drive to Augusta for a night on the town. The destination was the Lazy "B" Bar and Cafe, Augusta's principal "watering hole." On one such occasion, a grizzled saxophone player named Gabby was in need of an accompanist on the piano. D. A. blurted out for all to hear that not only could Lucille Dustin play the piano, she had played "in every goddamn bar east of the Missouri River!" My dad, who ordinarily would have put a stop to such things, was otherwise occupied in a conversation with Gabby's wife, Opal, a strikingly beautiful Blackfoot Indian. Mom spent the entire evening at the keyboard accompanying Gabby, harmonizing on songs, and downing all the free Tom Collins she could handle.

I learned of this from Mom herself, and it was she who told the story best. When recounting it, her eyes sparkled with a certain mischievousness, as if that Saturday night at the Lazy "B" Bar and Cafe had given her a chance to really let loose and shine. She revealed a social side of her being that evening that was often subdued in the presence of my father. I was not to see that sparkle in her eyes on a regular basis until after his passing. Then, and only then, did certain dimensions of Mom's personality begin to flourish that I had seldom, if ever, seen before—a quick wit, a strong sense of humor, and an adventuresome spirit. In her last few years, there was a blossoming.

My mom lived a beautiful life. I say this because her time was spent largely in service to others. She demonstrated an uncommon wisdom in her social orientation, in her strong sense of connectedness to the larger world. I would like to think that whatever compromises she might have made for the sake of her husband, son, and daughter were knowingly and willingly made and that she felt the benefits to family harmony and unity far outweighed any costs she might have incurred along the way.

My mother, along with my father, certainly gave Carol and me a solid foundation upon which to build our lives. I know whatever compassion is in me has come largely from Mom. While Dad was formal and distant, Mom was warm and giving. While Dad modeled Kohlbergian-like autonomy, Mom modeled Gilligan-like caring and connectedness. I think Mom was a better person for it. Yet even as I write this, even as I take comfort in the thought that my mom lived an extraordinary 94 years, I will always be haunted by those same two questions: "Who was my mother, really, and what was she thinking?"

Chapter 25

FREE SPIRIT

" On your left!" I glance over my shoulder to make sure I haven't drifted into the fast lane. I have spent the better part of the week hugging the extreme right side of the highway. I'm drafting behind a cyclist with paraplegia, and it's taking all my energy to keep my Crestwood Free Spirit upright on this steep hill. My $85 bicycle is clunky and slow, and these Iowa hills are like gigantic roller coasters. I am wedded to the "granny" gear, and my mantra is taken directly from "the little engine that could." Whoever told me Iowa is flat didn't know what the hell he was talking about.

I am one of 10,000 people participating in the *Des Moines Register's* 32nd Annual Great Bicycle Ride Across Iowa. Affectionately known as RAGBRAI, it is seven days and 500 miles of ups and downs. I have never spent this much time on a bicycle in my life. My behind has form-fitted to the bicycle seat, my legs ache, and my hands are gnarled from gripping the handlebars day after day. We began the ride in Onawa near the Missouri River, and we will finish in Clinton on the Mississippi River. For now, however, I am trying my best to remember how I got myself into this fix.

It's partly Karla Henderson's fault. A native Iowan, she had wanted to do this ride for a long time. I learned of it only recently. Like Karla, I, too, have a fondness for Iowa, and a recent visit to my mom's homestead near Ida Grove cemented the deal. Together, Karla and I formed the "Crazy Goofs," including her friend Delaine Deal and my wife, Kathleen. We took a training oath, goaded each other into sticking to it, and then made plans to join up at RAGBRAI the last week of July. Two weeks before the ride, Karla got her feet stuck in her clip-in pedals, fell off her bike, and broke her wrist. Relegated to the support team, she is now doing RAGBRAI in an air-conditioned truck, all the while, I might add, being an incredibly good sport about it.

"Car back!" The call goes up the line as a vehicle approaches from the rear. RAGBRAI's organizers don't close the roads to motorized traffic. Instead, they choose sparsely traveled two-lane highways and then broadcast the route widely. By and large, automobiles and trucks stay away. It's what cyclists do to themselves that sometimes is cause for alarm. On this trip, for example, a rider was killed the first day on the road between Mapleton and Schleswig when he was going down one of those roller coaster hills at breakneck speed. There was a small crack in the center of the pavement, and the man was thrown head over heels when his front tire wedged in the crack. The incident has cast a pall over this year's ride.

Though RAGBRAI is not billed as a race, the diversity of participants guarantees a spectrum of attitudes and approaches to the 60-to-80-mile days. The bicycles range from high-end racers to road bikes to hybrids to mountain bikes to clunkers like my Crestwood Free Spirit. There are also tandem bikes, recumbent bikes, custom bikes of all shapes and sizes, and even an occasional unicycle. Riders are encouraged to get their 60 to 80 miles in between sunup and sundown. Some finish well before noon. Others, like me, are lucky to finish by dusk.

RAGBRAI is a celebration of humanity, togetherness, and small-town Iowa. The stream of cyclists passes through as many as 10 communities a day, and every one puts out the welcome mat for the thirsty, hungry, and, in my case, tired riders. When we entered Eagle Grove two days ago, a couple dressed as eagles greeted us from their perch high in an old oak tree. From pancake breakfasts at the local fire department to lunch at the American Legion Hall to dinner at the Methodist church, each day brings its own freshness. It didn't take long for me to get into the swing of things, despite the loss of feeling in my derriere.

One of the things I enjoy most about RAGBRAI is the sense of humor that permeates the ride. People enter as individuals or in groups. The beauty of groups, in addition to the camaraderie, is the opportunity to come up with clever names. My favorite group name so far is the "Donner Party" from Truckee, California. People tell me the T-shirts they wore last year proclaimed, "We eat the slow ones!" This year's shirt announces, "We're back for seconds!" Then, of course, there are the "Wisconsin Dairy-Aires" and "Team Mega-sore-ass." Even my wife, Kathleen, has joined in the fun. The third day out, on our ride from Ft. Dodge to Iowa Falls, she surprised me with a custom-made T-shirt that has "This space for rent!" emblazoned across the back. The humor rests in the fact that my Crestwood Free Spirit is so slow that I can't seem to keep pace with anybody. "If you're going to be passed by 10,000 riders each day," Kathleen chuckles, "you might as well capitalize on it."

It's hard to explain why I didn't buy a new bicycle for this ride. Most everybody else has a Trek, Cannondale, or Specialized to get her or him through to Clinton in the most comfortable manner possible. It's not that I'm cheap. It has more to do with my general worldview. If this is a ride for people of all ages, shapes, and sizes, then shouldn't it also be a ride for bicycles of all ages, shapes, and sizes? Shouldn't my Free Spirit have just as much right to be ridden in RAGBRAI as any of those other fancy makes and models? I'm democratizing the event, that's all. At week's end, when we're all dipping our front tires into the Mississippi River to celebrate the completion of the ride, my Free Spirit will be right there alongside Kathleen's Cannondale. Is there not a certain beauty in that?

Earlier in the week, I wasn't sure my Free Spirit was going to make it to the finish. I wore out the front derailleur the second day by spending so much time in the "granny" gear. Fortunately, it lasted until day's end when the problem was identified. The bike repairmen who accompany RAGBRAI took one look at it and said they couldn't do anything for me. I had to find someone who "specialized" in Huffy-type bikes. So I took my Free Spirit to an old-fashioned bicycle shop in downtown Ft. Dodge. I would have purchased a new bicycle on the spot if they had told me mine was beyond help, but they didn't. On the contrary, a very nice man with tattoos and a beard said he thought he could make my Free Spirit like new. He then spent more than an hour putting on a new front derailleur and generally cleaning up the bike. When I asked him what the damages were, he said "Twenty-two dollars for parts and four dollars for labor." I gave him $40 and told him to have dinner on me. Suffice it to say, I will always have fond memories of Ft. Dodge, Iowa.

In addition to the colorful names that make RAGBRAI so much fun, there are colorful characters as well. I have especially enjoyed meeting "Tiny Tim," who rides an itsy-bitsy bicycle like the ones clowns ride in the circus. He tells me that it takes two to three times the energy to pedal his bike across Iowa as it does a regular bike. He's an extraordinarily fit man in his 60s who loves to laugh and joke around with everyone he meets. He also makes me feel better about riding my Free Spirit. "Gears are for wimps," he says. Then there is "Holiday Lady," who changes her costume every day of the week to celebrate a different holiday. Since RAGBRAI always takes place the last week in July, one of those holidays is guaranteed to be her birthday. Yes, "Holiday Lady" expects gifts.

"Pork chooooooops!" It is midday, and the unmistakable call coming from the pink school bus up ahead gets my attention. I glance over my left shoulder and begin the risky passage across several lanes of bicycle traffic to get safely off the road. There, in the front yard of a big Iowa farmstead, is a portly man with a wad of cash sitting under an umbrella. A long line of people slowly passes by, each forking over six dollars for a humongous two-inch-thick pork chop. Under any other circumstances, it would be pure gluttony to devour an entire one of those things. But in the middle of a RAGBRAI day, it somehow seems justified. There is nothing better to keep those wheels turning than one of Mr. Pork Chop's pork chops.

Unless, of course, you are fond of Chris's Cakes, Tender Tom's Turkey, Pastafari, Beckman's Ice Cream, or a host of other goodies served up by traveling concessionaires that accompany the tidal wave of humanity across the state. When you begin the ride, you think you are bound to lose weight by week's end. When you end the ride, you know you've gained at least five pounds. It doesn't seem theoretically possible to ride a bicycle 500 miles in a one-week period and gain weight. But believe me, I can tell you from experience that it's not only possible, it's a sure thing, a guaranteed proposition, a done deal. You can bet the farm on it.

As the days wear on, our routine is firmly established. We get up at 5:00 a.m., break camp, and ride a few miles. We stop for a roadside breakfast burrito, orange juice, and coffee. We ride again, stopping next for a freshly baked slice of homemade pie and ice cream. We ride again, stopping next for a midday gyro, "walking" taco, or pork chop. After lunch, we ride again, stopping next for watermelon or a freshly roasted ear of corn. We ride again, stopping next for ice cream at Beckman's. Then, just as we're about to burst, we make one final push to the overnight town and the Brancel Charter campsite, where, with any luck, Karla will have already pitched our tent and stowed our gear. You've gotta love it. A beer or two while swapping stories from the day's ride, a hot shower, and then it's time to search out the most appealing dinner at the local church or high school gymnasium. By then it's 7:30 p.m., and bedtime.

"Rumble!" Once again I am jolted back to reality. It's too late for me this time, and I ride my Free Spirit over the speed bumps at a fast clip. The washboard effect rattles my teeth and reminds me that it's a good idea to pay attention to what I'm doing. Being on a bicycle for so many hours a day lends itself to daydreaming—especially during the morning hours. As I ride by Iowa's corn-fields, their bucolic nature arouses a strong sense of nostalgia in me, a longing for something I can't quite put my finger on. Whether I'm trying to picture what it must have been like for my mother to grow up in Iowa during the early part of the 20th century or whether I'm just wishing I could live in simpler times, there is something about Iowa that smacks of the good life.

After seven days pedaling across the state and with Clinton just over the next hill, I feel compelled to put this ride into some sort of perspective. What is the source of RAGBRAI's appeal to me, any-way? It's the grown-up equivalent of recess. For one week of the year, it's okay for me to be carefree and childlike. I can strap on my helmet, tug on my fitted gloves, and pedal. It's as innocent as it gets in this sophisticated and complex world of ours. I can be a kid again, riding down the highway with a sparkle in my eye, a smile on my face, and a sense of wonder about what's in store on the road ahead. The world is my oyster. It's basic exercise, good food, and lots of fun, plain and simple.[1]

Chapter 26

MAPPING THE GEOGRAPHY
OF HOPE

After my sophomore year at the University of Michigan, I returned to the Bob Marshall Wilderness with a friend to backpack into the Chinese Wall. To my surprise, spring floods and a Forest Service airstrip had changed forever the Benchmark area where I fished as a boy, and for the first time I entertained thoughts of dedicating my life to the protection of wilderness. Obviously, those childhood vacations in Montana had a profound effect on me. Viewed retrospectively, they provided not only a wonderful context for my growing-up years, they provided fertile ground for stimulating my imagination, for exploration and make-believe, and for dreaming my future. They also provided, as it turns out, the inspiration for my life's work. The fact that I am writing these words almost 50 years later is clear trace evidence of the depth and durability of the meaning of wilderness in my life.

But, of course, the case for wilderness cannot stand on one story alone. As Bev Driver once wrote, "Who cares what wilderness means to any one individual? The important question is what does it mean or not mean to representative samples of users and nonusers."[1] Bev was right, I suppose, at least from a scientific perspective. So you might ask Perry Brown about his boyhood excursions into the Sierra Nevada or Roderick Nash about hiking as a 10-year-old in the Grand Canyon or Gary Snyder about his youthful forays into the wilds of the Pacific Northwest. Or take a more formal survey of other individuals across the United States, or in most any other place on the planet, about the origins of their love of nature.

Like Snyder, many people, I think, would speak of an immediate, intuitive, deep sympathy with the natural world that was not taught them by anyone.[2] It is this deep sympathy, this deep sense of affiliation with nature, that I most encourage wilderness social scientists to explore. Where does this sympathy come from, if it comes at all? How does it express itself? What other forces influence it? Can it be taught? And how does this deep sympathy affect our behavior, our sense of place in the world and, ultimately, our growth and development as human beings?

Theologian Sally McFague reasons "all things living and all things not living are the products of the same primal explosion and evolutionary history and hence are interrelated in an internal way from the very beginning. We are distant cousins to the stars," McFague says, "and near relations to the oceans, plants, and all other living creatures on our planet."[3] If she is correct, a deep sense of attachment to the land should come as no surprise. We are, after all, made up of the same ingredients.

Environmental psychologists Rachel and Stephen Kaplan explain these same deep stirrings in terms of our species' age-old penchant for information about the natural world to enhance our prospects for survival in it.[4] If the Kaplans are right, a deep sense of connectedness to nature should still come as no surprise. We are, after all, intimately dependent on the natural world for our sustenance.

Then there are the poets and philosophers among us, many of whom see wild nature as the divine manifestation of God.[5] If they are right, a feeling of sacredness toward the land should not surprise us either. We are, after all, the self-conscious part of His creation, the part that, by design, reflects on the meaning and purpose of things.[6]

I don't know to what extent any of these speculations about our relationship with nature reflect a ray of truth, but I do know that I am intrigued by the possibilities. Indeed, throughout the first half of the 1990s, I worked on a book called *Nature and the Human Spirit: Toward an Expanded Land Management Ethic* with 50 other contributors from many walks of life, all of whom felt that a spiritual bond with nature is a palpable, researchable topic.[7] While I remain optimistic about our ability to shed light on these hard-to-define and hard-to-measure spiritual values through the practice of social science, I am going to confess a doubt or two about the prospects of ever reaching the full depth of their meaning. And while I'm at it, I might as well also confess that even though I have spent much of my adult life pondering the meaning of wilderness to humankind, I often wish I were that little boy again in Montana who simply loved to fish and drink the water at his feet without having to think.

I speak to you not so much as a social scientist but as a wilderness enthusiast, as one who feels the call of the wild even as I have trouble articulating it. But that, of course, is the challenge—to tease out the meaning of wilderness to people like me, however inadequate our self-reports, however ineffable our feelings. The challenge is magnified by the fact that what we are seeking to understand is invisible.[8] Mapping what Wallace Stegner once called "the geography of hope" is really mapping the geography of the human mind, a geography that more often than not seems unfathomable.[9]

We are not unlike Fra Mauro, the 16th-century cartographer to the Court of Venice, whose lifelong dream was to make a perfect map, one that represented the full breadth of Creation. "I speculate," he confessed.

> Mapmakers are entitled to do so, since they readily acknowledge that they are rarely in possession of all the facts. They are always dealing with secondary accounts, the tag ends of impressions. Theirs is an uncertain science. What they do is imagine coastlines, bluffs, and estuaries in order to make up for what they do not know. How many times do they sketch in a cape or bay without knowing the continent to which it might be attached? They do not know these things because they are constantly dealing with other men's observations, no more than a glance shoreward from the rigging of a passing ship.[10]

I'll let you draw your own analogies. Suffice it for me to say that since we cannot really see what is going on inside other people's heads, since we must rely on secondary accounts and the tag ends of impressions, ours, too, is an uncertain science. I say this not to discourage us from our quest for understanding, but to emphasize that when it comes to mapping the invisible worlds of others, there is always a danger of seeing something that is not there and not seeing something that is there. Any notation of landmarks, and their subsequent assignment to continents, should thus be understood as the most tentative of undertakings.

What I am hinting at here and what I am celebrating in my own way is the incredibly rich, diverse, and often unique makeup of that part of each and every one of us that is not body.[11] While we social scientists may make sketch maps of the human mind that are useful in very general ways for wilderness planning and management, as we probe deeper and deeper into the invisible worlds of others, the landmarks we uncover inevitably become more specific, more personal and unique. The resulting maps, while richly textured and finely detailed, are not likely to be very useful for predictive purposes. This was Driver's point about personal accounts of wilderness meaning. They may be fascinating to read, but they are seldom generalizable.

There is an indeterminism in all this that I find wonderfully maddening. It feels wonderful to the poet in me. It feels maddening to the social scientist in me. What to do? How to handle it? If, as Roderick Nash reasons, wilderness is not so much a place as it is our response to a place, we humans have considerable latitude in terms of what we make of wilderness.[12] It is this openness of meaning, I think, that is our hope for the future. Wilderness symbolizes unbridled potential. It is a source to be interpreted creatively. The question, it seems to me, is not so much what does wilderness mean to us, but what do we want it to mean?

Wilderness experience, as Mike Patterson, Alan Watson, Dan Williams, and Joe Roggenbuck recently conceived it in a paper in the *Journal of Leisure Research*, may be thought of as human experience characterized by situated freedom, in which the wilderness sets boundaries that constrain the nature of the experience, but within those boundaries people are free to experience wilderness in unique and variable ways.[13] The authors go on to characterize wilderness experience as an emergent phenomenon motivated by the not very well-defined goal of acquiring stories that enrich our lives.

I began with a personal story that has taken 50 years to unfold, a story, I might add, that remains unfinished. Multiply my story by countless others waiting to be told by wilderness enthusiasts across the earth, each of whom, through encounters with wild nature, comes to better understand her or his place in the world. Pay attention to each and every detail of their stories, and rejoice in the thickness of your data. Pencil in your landmarks, and assign them to continents as best you can. Then, like the 16th-century cartographer Fra Mauro, prepare yourself for the world's infinite capacity to surprise.

Chapter 27

WERE YOU EVER OUT IN THE GREAT ALONE?

On a point of land extending into a cold northern Minnesota lake, a solitary figure sits in quiet contemplation. There is a hush in the air. Distanced from civilization by the remoteness of his surroundings, Sigurd Olson ponders his relationship with the larger living world.

Gradually, "a soft undercurrent of sound like the coming of a wind from far away or something long remembered"[1] fills the air. Olson soon recognizes the sound for what it is, the whistle of a train winding its way through his beloved North Country. He is filled with mixed emotions. On the one hand, he fondly recalls his youth when a train whistle signaled the end of a long wilderness trek and his return to civilization and the comforts of home. On the other hand, he now finds the sound vaguely disturbing, and he asks himself whether the whistle has come to symbolize something else—the relentless advance of civilization and an end to the wilderness he knows and loves.

"The Whistle" was published in 1958 in a book called *Listening Point*.[2] At the conclusion of the essay, Olson reconciles his ambivalent feelings.

> Without that long lonesome wail and the culture that produced it, many things would not be mine—recordings of the world's finest music, books holding the philosophy, the dreams and hopes of all mankind, a car that took me swiftly to the point whenever I felt the need. All these things and countless others civilization had given me, and I must never again forget that because of the wonders it had wrought this richness now was mine.[3]

Like Sigurd Olson, I, too, appreciate what civilization has given me. I understand that the contrast between wilderness and civilization accentuates the good things both have to offer, and I understand how the existence of one helps give definition and meaning to the existence of the other. The principal difference between Sigurd Olson's reaction to the sound of that train whistle and mine can be explained, I think, by the simple fact that "that long lonesome wail and the culture that produced it" is now almost 50 years farther down the track.

The question I want to explore with you is the nature of this relationship between wilderness and civilization. Specifically, I want to focus on what I perceive to be the relentless advance of civilization with insufficient regard for its detrimental effects on the physical and psychological aspects of wilderness, or what I will call the wilderness "without" and the wilderness "within." I want to alert you to what I fear will be lost along the way if this advance is left unchecked. I then want to build a case for a different kind of future: a future characterized by a civilization that exercises restraint and that consciously makes room for both kinds of wilderness.

In 1975, when I was a doctoral student at the University of Minnesota, one of the first questions posed to me during my oral comprehensive examination was the following: "What are the implications of recombinant DNA research for wilderness?" To say that I was stunned by the question is an understatement. I didn't really know what the examiner, a futurist named Arthur Harkins, had in mind. I was at a loss for words, and I sat there for what seemed like an interminably long and awkward time. Finally, my department chairman, John Schultz, took pity on me and bailed me out by rephrasing Harkins's question for the entire committee. "If we are on the verge of understanding the basic building blocks of life, what's to stop us from putting that knowledge to good use by creating new wilderness areas whenever we want them?"

Fortunately, I didn't have to respond to the question, because another committee member, a salty old forestry professor named Larry Merriam, jumped in and tangled with Harkins for quite some time about his far-fetched and unduly optimistic view of the human potential. That was just fine with me. All I really wanted was to have those two hours pass as quickly as possible. Having survived that, I soon forgot Arthur Harkins's preposterous question—until, that is, quite recently.

My reading of late has reminded me how apropos it was, and is, to call Arthur Harkins a "futurist." I am referring most directly to two books by Bill McKibben, *The End of Nature*,[4] published in

1989, and *Enough: Staying Human in an Engineered Age*,[5] published in 2003. In the first book, McKibben reasons that those places that are home to wild beasts, those unfettered places, those untrammeled places, those places largely free of the imprint of the human hand, are no more. The advance of civilization has reached a point where there is really no place left on planet Earth that is without human influence in one form or another. There is, in the words of Aldo Leopold, no "blank spot" left on the map.

As disheartening as this is, I am even more disheartened by the line of thought presented in McKibben's more recent work, *Enough*. In it he examines the possibility of living in a world shaped by germline genetic engineering and the damage it would do to our humanity. Germline genetic engineering, if you are not familiar with it, refers to our fast-approaching capability to manipulate the genetic makeup of human beings through the alteration of sperm and egg cells. With regard to this capability, McKibben acknowledges our curiosity, ingenuity, and inventiveness as a species, while simultaneously brooding over the ramifications of acting upon them. As Wendell Berry asks in response to McKibben's book, "Are we willing to submit our freedom and our dearest meanings to a technological determinism imposed by the alignment of science, technology, industry and half-conscious politics?"[6] "Is it possible," he inquires further, "for us to refuse to do something that we can do?"[7]

The relentless advance of civilization, it seems, has reached a point where it not only threatens the wilderness "without," but it threatens the wilderness "within" as well. In the same way we have cut back and tamed the physical wilderness through the application of science and technology, we are now on the brink of cutting back and taming the psychological wilderness inside each and every one of us. In the same way advancing civilization has reduced the number of question marks attendant to self-willed land, it now threatens to reduce the number of question marks attendant to self-willed people.

Imagine a future when basic germ cells can be altered before birth to guarantee certain traits. We might welcome such alterations if they reduce or eliminate major congenital birth defects or other catastrophic human maladies. But if they are employed to eliminate simple differences between and among people like height and weight, eye and hair color, the size of one's nose, and the shape of one's teeth; or if they are employed to enhance athletic or

artistic abilities or a host of other human characteristics now com-
posing our diversity, then there is cause for alarm, and there is
reason to step back and think through the implications.

McKibben's fear is that if we will be able to guarantee specific
attributes in our children that will give them a competitive advantage in life, the prospect will be irresistible. And once we start down
that path, who would dare not come along? Who would run the
risk of depriving her or his children of that competitive advantage
when all others about them were guaranteeing it for their children
before birth through the manipulation of life's basic building blocks?

McKibben goes on to point out that if such procedures were
prohibitively expensive, only the wealthy would be able to engage
in them, resulting in a bigger and bigger genetic gap between the
haves and have-nots. Furthermore, should germline genetic engineering be within reach of us all, the relative advantage of employ-
ing it would be reduced, as everybody's prospects would be similarly elevated. Nonetheless, he foresees a genetic "arms race" as
everyone would try to outdo everyone else.

McKibben then examines a whole host of additional rippling
effects that would undoubtedly flow out of such an engineered
world—most of them bad. For example, how could we be confident that success in life would be the result of individual effort? If
an individual performed well, it could simply be that she or he was
engineered to perform well. It might not have much to do with
the individual at all. It is not unlike our current uneasiness over the
possibility that it might not really have been Mark McGwire who
broke Roger Maris's home run record, but the steroids in Mark
McGwire. If germline genetic engineering is perfected, it will be
increasingly difficult to distinguish between the individual and the
engineering. McKibben fears we may even engineer ourselves out
of existence.

If this kind of future comes to pass, something essential inside
us will have been lost. Much of the magic and mystery will have
gone out of life, the uncertainty that comes with being born into
the world not knowing one's gifts, of having to discover them for
oneself, and the challenge of having to make the most of them.
Engineering ourselves out of every imperfection, out of every hardship, would mean engineering ourselves out of many of life's great
lessons, lessons that can only be learned through failing and then
trying again. It would not only be the blank spots on the map
"without" that would fade into oblivion. The blank spots "within"

would fade away as well. If most everything of import were pre-programmed, what would become of meaning making? What stories would be worth telling if their endings were a foregone conclusion?

In 1930, historian T. J. Whipple proclaimed,

> All America lies at the end of the wilderness road, and our past is not a dead past but still lives in us. . . . Our forebears had civilization inside themselves, the wild outside. We live in the civilization they created, but within us the wilderness still lingers. What they dreamed we live; and what they lived we dream.[8]

The world we inhabit has indeed become more and more civilized as we have repeatedly cut back and tamed wild nature. What our forbears dreamed, we do now live. But it is the latter half of that sentence, the half that says "what they lived we dream," that haunts me. For if the state of being wild has been diminished over time, the opportunity to experience wilderness and the dreams associated with it have also been diminished. And in a society that is now 85% urbanized, one can only wonder what losing touch with wilderness might mean in the long run? What would life be like if there were nothing but the sound of a train whistle? And should that day come, how could the wilderness within us remain alive?

It is, then, not so much the lessening of the physical space we call "wilderness" by the relentless advance of civilization that I want you to ponder, important as that is; it is the concomitant lessening of our opportunity to think wilderness-inspired thoughts, to consider the meaning of any remaining blank spots on the map, to find refuge in what Wallace Stegner once called "the geography of hope,"[9] because that same advancing civilization will have cut back the wilderness inside each and every one of us. It is the prospect of losing the wilderness "within" through germline genetic engineering that unnerves me.

This brings me back to Wendell Berry's question, "Is it possible for us to refuse to do something that we can do?" Is it possible for us not to go down the road of germline genetic engineering? Or, if we do go down that road, is it possible for us to limit ourselves in terms of the applications that present themselves? McKibben is skeptical. I just don't know.

What I do know is that our species has made incredible scientific and technological strides forward over a relatively short period of time. I know further that the speed with which these advances bear fruit is exponentially fast. "When the Human Genome Project was first proposed," for example, "critics said it would take 10,000 years; its backers said they'd be done by 2010. The project was finished early in 2000."[10] The problem is that there is a significant lag time between our understanding of what we are capable of doing technologically and our understanding of what we ought to be doing ethically.

Don't get me wrong. I am neither a "bioluddite" nor an alarmist. I just think we need to slow down and think through the wisdom of doing what we can do before we do it. Having just read Jared Diamond's book *Collapse*[11] with a special interest in what he has to say about the fate of Montana's Bitterroot Valley, I appreciate how we get ourselves into environmental fixes when blinded by economic and technological shortsightedness. Under the circumstances, attempting to envision the long run, erring on the side of conservation when we aren't sure about the short- or long-term consequences of our actions, and trying our best to safeguard future options, just seems prudent to me.

We live in times characterized by an unbridled enthusiasm for technology. We see the future as full of limitless possibilities, and we believe it is our destiny to continually overcome our limitations, to break barriers, to reach for things that exceed our grasp. This way of thinking is euphoric, and it is full of unrestrained optimism typical of futurists like Arthur Harkins. It is also marked by impatience. Woe to the stick-in-the-muds who would hold us back from striving to become more than we presently are, from reaching our human potential, from experiencing transhumanism. To technological enthusiasts, humankind's progress can best be measured by our ongoing stream of inventions and by our increasing ability to change the face of the earth. These are the champions of germline genetic engineering. Their motto is "Forward, ever forward."[12]

As McKibben reminds us, however, the rejection of limits, including the limits imposed on us by our own mortality, is not the only path we humans can take. There is another path, a less-traveled path, which not only recognizes our human limitations, but also embraces them. This path has led us to different kinds of inventions, inventions that act not as catalysts to the advancement of civilization, but as brakes on that advancement. This is the path that has led us to protest nuclear weapons after their creation, to employ nonviolent civil disobedience as a method of political change, and to invent the concept of wilderness.[13]

Wilderness areas "are crucial ecologically," McKibben says,

> but in some ways their greatest value is philosophic: here are places where people have actually decided to take a step back. Where they've decided that other species, other needs, are more important than ours.[14]

That we have the capacity to exercise this kind of restraint is what makes our species unique. Our particular gift is that we possess self-awareness. We can step outside ourselves and reflect on what we are doing, right and wrong. Then we can do something about it. This is what sets us apart from other living things.

There is ample scientific and technological progress going on in the Western world. There is quite enough engineering of the human condition. There are plenty of catalysts for change. What is really needed in our society is something akin to the sound of Sigurd Olson's train whistle to symbolize its opposite—not the relentless advance of civilization, but a civilization tempered by restraint. Perhaps it should be the call of a loon, the howl of a timber wolf, the bugle of an elk, or the woofing of a grizzly bear. I don't know.

What I do know is that there is no better place for absenting oneself from the sound of Olson's fast-approaching train than wilderness. There is no better place in this increasingly transparent society for finding privacy, for finding solitude. There is no better place for gathering one's thoughts. There is no better place for considering one's relationship to the larger living world. There is no better place for reflecting on the opportunities and obligations attendant to being human. There is no better place for weighing our ethical responsibility to the rest of the community of life. There is, in sum, no better place for thinking through the costs and benefits of an advancing civilization than through the experience of its antipode—wilderness.

Roderick Nash describes wilderness as a moral resource.[15] He reasons that its continuing existence is testimony to humankind's capacity to show restraint. I could not agree more. I do not for one moment doubt our ability to do away with wilderness. But in so doing, I fear we would be doing away with ourselves as well. Aldo Leopold understood this when he shot a wolf and then saw the fierce green fire die in its eyes. In that moment he knew that in killing the wolf he had killed part of himself.[16] Keeping the wilderness "without" alive is a way of keeping the wilderness "within" alive as well. Safeguarding wilderness is a way of safeguarding our role as plain members and citizens of the larger community of life. It is a way of acknowledging that we do not know all the answers to life's big questions, that we will never know all the answers. As Nash concludes, in the end, wilderness preservation is a gesture of planetary humility.[17]

Twenty-five years ago, Leo McAvoy and I proposed the idea of no-rescue wilderness in the *Journal of Forestry*.[18] The proposal was not grounded in machismo. On the contrary, our proposal was a reaction to an article published in the *Sierra Club Bulletin* by William Leitch called "Backpacking in 2078."[19] Leitch envisioned a future when

> heavy recreational use of the public lands coupled with an 'insurance mentality' would force resource managers to employ every technological weapon in their arsenal to protect the environment from people and people from the environment.[20]

In the story, wilderness managers, not wilderness recreationists, were in control of the wilderness experience. The prospect was abhorrent to us. We decided to make a case for its antithesis, a wilderness where recreationists themselves would be unbridled and unfettered. "Big Brother" would be barred from interfering, and wilderness sojourners would be free to interact with nature on its own terms. Though our no-rescue wilderness proposal has not been widely embraced in the intervening years, the need for it seems greater to me than ever. For what William Leitch offered up as science fiction, just like the question Arthur Harkins offered up on the implications of recombinant DNA research for wilderness, is now not so far-fetched after all.

My fondest hope is that we will always be able to count on wilderness as a sanctuary within which we

> can take refuge from the relentless advance of our own tools, from everything modern and mechanical that we have created in the name of progress. . . . Wilderness must also remain that special place we visit when we feel the need to remind ourselves of our human frailty, a place to which we return again and again to gain a healthier perspective on our lives."[21]

I don't want us to lament the loss of the Bob Marshall Wilderness in the same way John Muir lamented the loss of Hetch-Hetchy. I don't want the "Bob," like Glen Canyon, to be something fondly remembered by fewer and fewer people over time. I want our children and our children's children and children throughout time to be able to call on the words of Robert Service—not in past tense, but in present tense, in their here and now, whenever that might be—as they gather around the campfire with their friends and reflect on past, present, and future wilderness adventures. I want them forever and always to be able to ask eagerly of one another:

> Were you ever out in the Great Alone, when the moon was awful clear, and the icy mountains hemmed you in with a silence you most could hear; with only the howl of a timber wolf, and you camped there in the cold . . . while high overhead, green, yellow, and red, the North Lights swept in bars? Then you've a hunch what [my words have] meant . . . hunger and night and the stars.[22]

Part Three—Synthesis

Synthesis

What have I learned about myself in relation to the larger world as a result of my journeys outward and inward? How am I trying to incorporate that learning into the conduct of my everyday life? The final two essays coalesce my thinking about these questions. They synthesize my book and experiential learning regarding my place in, and obligations toward, the larger community of life.

Chapter 28

LIKE LIGHT PASSING THROUGH A PRISM[1]

Born on September 13, 1946, Daniel L. Dustin is the culmination of a loving reunion at the end of the Second World War between navy lieutenant Derby D Dustin and his wife, Lucille. Now an aging baby boomer and "slightly" graying at the temples, Dustin, like so many of his contemporaries, is engaged in a tragicomic struggle to repeal the Second Law of Thermodynamics (at least as it applies to him). Recently, however, he has begun to own up to his inevitable winding down, and his attention has turned accordingly to the question of whether his life has in any significant way mattered.

My intent here is to examine various aspects of this poor soul's existence, and in so doing illuminate his outlook on life. More specifically, I demonstrate at the outset that the person writing these words is not who he appears to be—indeed—that there is much less to him than meets the eye. In this regard, I show that he hardly exists as an individual at all anymore, and that what is left of him is composed of little that is unique or original to him.

If I stopped at this point in the writing, you might conclude, as did Shakespeare's MacBeth, that life—well, at least Dustin's life—is but a "brief candle . . . a tale told by an idiot, full of sound and fury, signifying nothing." But I do not stop here. For I then demonstrate that there is another way in which the person recording these thoughts is not who he appears to be—indeed—that there is much more to him than meets the eye. In this regard, however brief the candle of his physical existence, I argue that he has more than his mere "hour upon the stage," that he is part of a larger everlasting presence that gives his temporary being meaning and purpose.

Finally, I explain how this individual's understanding of himself has prompted him to think, write, and act in certain ways—ways, that, however effective, have been intended to promote social change. Whether what I have to say resonates with you or not will depend, I suspect, on the degree to which you empathize with this writer. And while that is, to be sure, your affair, I can assure you for what it's worth that this essay most certainly resonates with him.

I can say best what I have to say by talking first about immortality. I shall open the matter with a question. Here I am, serving up my thoughts; and there you are, consuming them. Our mental lives are in contact. The question I would put is this: how far can we consider this mental life we are sharing to be immortal? And more particularly, I would ask you a question I have often asked myself. What is this Dan Dustin who is writing to you?

Now what do you suppose our little conference amounts to? What is happening now? You are Mr. So-and-so or Mrs. So-and-so or Ms. So-and-so or, if you must, Dr. So-and-so, and someone called Dan Dustin is communicating with you. That is what most people will call self-evident fact. That is what will pass muster as the truth of the matter. But is it altogether true? Let us go into things a little more precisely. I will talk about my side of the discussion, but what I have to say will apply quite well to your side also.

This Dan Dustin, who was born a little more than five decades ago, has in the years since gone here and there and done this and that. His words are here, some thought that may be considered to be his is here, but are you sure that all of him is present? May I point out that, far from all of him being present in this discussion, very much of him is not present anywhere. The greater part of him is no longer in existence. It is dead. It is past and forgotten. He is already, for the most part, as dead as his grandfather.

Let me explain a little more fully what I mean by this. Consider the childhood of this person. I will tell you of one incident in it. In 1952, he was a rambunctious kindergartner, full of life and without caution. One day he had a terrible accident. Running from school to his parents' waiting car in a downpour, he was broadsided by a tackle on the high school football team and knocked unconscious into a mud puddle. It must have seemed like the end of the world to this little boy. This body I have with me still bears a scar. What a storm of feeling, what a fuss it must have been!

Yes, but what do I know of it now? Nothing, nothing except what my mother told me of it; nothing else at all. All the fear, all the feelings, all the details of the event have gone out of my conscious existence. All that is really quite dead. Now, can I really say that child of five years of age is here? You will say, perhaps, "Of course he is." There is the scar. And if that five-year-old child had not existed, how could this present man exist?

But wait a moment. That grandfather of mine. He was a lumberjack in Michigan's Upper Peninsula. I know that for a fact, just as completely as I know for a fact that little boy was knocked unconscious in 1952. And also, be it noted, if my grandfather had not existed, the present writer could not exist. My nose and my eyes would not be the shape and the color they are. If the scar is Danny Dustin of 1952, the eye is Delphonso Dustin of 1889. So, by the same test, if that child is alive here, his grandfather is alive here; and so far as one is dead and forgotten, so is the other. There is the same physical continuity. There is the same forgetfulness.

Now this idea that the Dan Dustin who is writing these words is not all of Dan Dustin is a very important part of what I am trying to say. It is not only that I who am writing am not in any real sense that child of 1952, but it is also that I am not a certain angry young man of 25 who in 1971 was struggling to reconcile his enlistment in the army with a growing disillusionment with the army's mission. I have photographs of him as he was then. I have stuff that he wrote. And for the life of me I cannot identify my present self with him. I have left him behind almost as completely as I have left my grandfather behind. On the other hand, I have recently been spending a lot of time with my youngest son, Adam. We share many ideas, and we have very similar mental dispositions. I feel at present much more closely identified with him than with that young Dan Dustin of 1971 or even with the Dan Dustin of 1985, who, I find from an old photograph, wore a scruffy beard and wandered alone much of the time in and out of the Grand Canyon.

And now let us turn to another aspect of this curious inquiry. I have tried to demonstrate that this person talking to you is very much less than who he appears to be, that he is, from my point of view, already very largely dead. But it is also the case that he is very much more than who he appears to be. Remember, we are thinking about what is immortal in ourselves. Now Dan Dustin never started that topic. It came to him. He heard people talking about it and preaching about it. He read about it. People who died in Egypt 5,000 years ago and whose names and faces and habits and sins are utterly forgotten were talking about it. Plato, Buddha, Confucius, and St. Paul have all had something important to say on the matter. That discussion came into our lives as we grew up. We may participate in it, change it a little, before we pass it on. It is like a light passing through a prism, which may test it, refract it perhaps, polarize it perhaps, and send it on again changed. We are the prism. The thoughts existed before we were born and will go on after we are finished with altogether.

Now here, then, is the heart of what I am trying to say to you. Either this will seem the most lucid of realities or the most fantastic of speculations. Here, I say, is this Dan Dustin who is writing, and he is—I have tried to show—so far from being immortal that the greater part of him is already dead and gone forever. But also over and above this Dan Dustin is something else, a living growth and a continual refining of ideas, a thought process that is bringing our minds together. And this thought process has lived already thousands of years ago and may, so far as we know, passing from mind to mind and from age to age, continue its life forever. We are mortal persons responding to the advance of perhaps immortal ideas. We are not ourselves only; we are also part of human experience and thought.

Well, I hope I have made my meaning clear thus far. You may not agree with me exactly, but I hope you have understood me so that I can go on to the next point I wish to discuss with you—the question of what is an individual. It is a question that joins very closely to these ideas about immortality. How is the individual related to the species? How is the part related to the whole? How is the one related to the many?

I suppose the ordinary and obvious answer to this question of what is an individual would be to say it is a living being detached from the rest of the world. It is born or hatched as a definite, distinctive self; it maintains itself for a certain time against the rest of the universe; and at last it dies and comes to at least a physical end. But is that an impregnable statement?

Go first to the biologist. She will tell you that most plants seem much more individualized than they are. You can take a plant and break it up into a number of plants. Are they new individuals, or are they fractions of the old one? You can even take two plants of different species and graft them together. What is the grafted plant, a new individual or one or both of the old ones? Trees seem to be much more individual than they really are, just as mountains do. It is a disposition of our minds to think of them as individuals.

And it is not only the plant kingdom that is wanting in individuality. Think of Dolly, the sheep, or, once again, Dan Dustin, the designated organ donor. Were Dustin's eyes to find one new home, his lungs another, and his heart a third, where would his individuality be then? Or, for that matter, where would be the individuality of the donees? Our particular individuality, it seems, does not penetrate our interiors.

And when we turn from the biologist to the psychologist, we get still more remarkable revelations about this individuality of ours, which at first seems so simple. We learn of minds split and divided against themselves. Think of Dr. Jekyll and Mr. Hyde. Quite a number of us go some little way toward such a change. Which of us, indeed, has not a better self and a worse self?

Well, I trust this abbreviated appeal to biology and psychology demonstrates my skepticism toward the idea that this Dan Dustin of mine is really the completely independent, separate, distinct being that it is our habit of mind to consider him. Perhaps my individuality, my personality, seems to be more distinct than it is. Perhaps it is—how shall I put this—a convenient biological illusion.

How, then, do I finally feel about this person writing to you? I have already tried to show that as a matter of fact a lot of him is already dead stuff and irrelevant stuff, and I have tried to show that this thought that is reaching out to you is something very much more than him. Indeed, the words on these pages would not have been expressed at all were it not for Roger Mannell's thoughts on "self as entertainment,"[2] Karla Henderson's thoughts on "complete participant observation,"[3] H. G. Wells' thoughts on H. G. Wells,[4] and so on. It is as if all of these people are making themselves heard through this one individual's voice. Dustin himself, however, is little more than a conduit, whatever else he may seem.

When it comes to introspection, then, I feel strongly that I am something very distinct from this Dan Dustin who eats and sleeps and drives back and forth across the Florida Everglades. I have to use his voice, see with his eyes, experience the pain of any physical misfortune that comes to him. He is my window on the world and my mouthpiece. I have to think in his brain, and his store of memories is my only reference library. I doubt if I can think or feel or act as an individual without him. But I do not feel that I am he.

Make no mistake about it. I take a great interest in him. I keep him as clean as I can and am always on the watch to prevent him getting sulky, dull, or lazy—not always, I must confess, with success. He has to be petted and persuaded. I like to be told he is good and remarkable, just as I like to be told my car is a good one. But sometimes I wish I could get away from him—heavens, how I wish it at times! He is clumsy in all sorts of ways and unbeautiful. His instincts and appetites are dreadful. He begins to show signs of considerable wear. The reference library in him might be better arranged and the brain cells quicker at the uptake. But he is all I have to keep me in touch with the world. When he goes, I go. I am silenced forever.

Now there is nothing original in this sense of detachment from myself. Most people get to something of the sort. When we are young, we identify ourselves with ourselves very completely and fiercely. But as we ripen, or as we age, or as we marry, or as we have children, the separation widens. Our individuality is, so to speak, an inborn obsession from which we all escape eventually. A consciousness of something greater than ourselves—the immortal soul of our species or whatever—then takes control of the direction of our lives.

This brings us to the vantage point from which I write. I have come to it, dare I say, naturally through a half century of living. I share it not because I want to convert you to my way of thinking or convince you of the clarity of the view, but because it explains why I think what I think, why I write what I write, and why I act the way I act. When it comes to understanding me, it has predictive power.

When I first started to write, I wrote for myself. Now I write for my children. When I first started to write, I saw leisure as an opportunity to do whatever one found pleasure in. Now I see leisure as an opportunity to find pleasure in doing the right thing. When I first started to write, I was preoccupied with individual growth and development, with self-fulfillment in autonomous Kohlbergian terms. Now I am taken with questions of individuals in community, with relationships, in connected and caring Gilligan-like terms. These shifts in focus, I submit, have paralleled closely changes in my own sense of self over the years.

Occasionally, this point of view has led me to make decisions that have pained the part of me, and the parts of others close to me, that I have characterized as tiny and transitory—our mortal selves. Witness my resignation from San Diego State University a few years ago over a matter of principle. That decision cost me a whole lot of money, precipitated a feud between my better and worse selves that lingers to this day, and came at a time when, unbeknownst to me, my oldest son, Andy, was about to decide the University of Chicago was the only place for him.

I bring this up because I think it is important that anyone who claims to write with social change in mind attempt to practice what she or he preaches. The truest test of our worldviews is the degree to which we employ them in our own lives, is it not? Advocating for social change in our writing while modeling something else entirely in our living will not go undetected. It will cheapen our words.

At the same time, imperfect beings that we are, our expectations of self and others should be tempered by humility and compassion. If we insist that the preaching of what ought to be is the domain only of those who never themselves transgress, we are in for either a world of silence or a world of hypocrisy. All I think we have a right to insist on is sincerity. And when, from time to time, someone preaches water and drinks wine, it is not necessarily an act of insincerity. It may simply be that the preacher is human. (I feel compelled to say this, of course, to cover for all my past, present, and future transgressions.)

If I am something of a social leveler, it is because I don't want one individual to be deprived the opportunity leisure affords to live a virtuous life. I don't want people to be left out. Almost everything I have written is predicated on that fear—that someone, somehow, is going to be left out because of something we do. I don't want to be responsible for that. And so, like the Man of La Mancha, I set out, through my writing, to right wrongs, correct injustices, and make injured things whole.

This brings us back to where I began, to the question of whether my life has in any significant way mattered. I am reminded of a conversation I had while walking with Bev Driver outside his cabin near Centennial, Wyoming, soon after I decided to resign from San Diego State. Bev has always been good for me in the same way that cod-liver oil is good for a sickly child.

"Dan," he said, "I understand why you feel the way you do, but are you really sure you want to do this? You're a nice fellow, and that means when you die someday, a few people—maybe 10 or 20 if you're lucky—are going to take a few minutes out of their day and reflect on you and your life. Then they're going to get on with theirs."

What Bev was driving at, of course, was that I was overreacting, that I was being melodramatic, that I was being quixotic. Toward what end, he wanted to know, were my actions directed? What was I trying to accomplish? What, if anything, would be done differently by that university as a consequence of my departure? Who, in essence, cared?

Bev was right, I suppose, but I resigned anyway. It's hard to explain why, but in a fundamental sense I couldn't help it. It's who I am. I cared. And when I say "I," I'll stop here and let you figure out for yourself just who it is that's talking now.

Chapter 29

GARDENING AS A SUBVERSIVE ACTIVITY

We live in a crazy world. Or so it seems. Weather reports in Los Angeles admonish millions of us not to go outside because of the poor air quality, and we do not even flinch. At the same time, the plight of two—count them—two gray whales trapped in an Alaskan ice floe captures national attention, tugs at our hearts, and prompts calls for immediate action. Meanwhile, halfway around the globe, we are gripped by the news of one American's abduction by Middle Eastern terrorists while in our own backyard the deaths of thousands of Americans every day from preventable automobile accidents, heart disease, smoking, and the consumption of drugs and alcohol go unnoticed.

What's going on here? Why is it that we are oblivious to the real environmental hazards threatening our existence on this planet while preoccupying ourselves with transient matters that are, in the course of things, likely to be of little consequence? Why do we behave the way we do? And what can we do about it?

I have come to believe that we human beings are biologically ill-equipped to deal effectively with the environmental problems confronting the world today; that there is a fundamental mismatch between the nature of those problems and our ability to perceive them and do something about them; and that if we are to have any hope of turning things around, we must better understand the causes of the mismatch so that we might begin to act in the light of our limitations as a species as well as our potentials.

To foster that understanding, it is first necessary to appreciate the context out of which we present-day humans evolved. Such appreciation is difficult to effect because of the immensity of the time involved, but it can be made easier by condensing that time into the equivalent of one calendar year. If midnight, January 1st represents the "Big Bang," the origin of the universe, then every day thereafter represents approximately 41 million years. At this rate, the formation of the Earth does not even take place until September 14th. Dinosaurs emerge on Christmas Eve only to disappear by December 28th, the same day flowers bloom for the first time. We human beings do not make our entrance until 10:30 p.m. on New Year's Eve. Finally, all of recorded human history takes place in the last 10 seconds of the year.[1]

This cosmic calendar illustrates vividly two essential points about human evolution. First, the climb up from our watery origins was a long and laborious one, consuming over three months of the year. Second, our ability to change the face of the Earth in cataclysmic ways has happened only in the last one second.

Embedded in these numbers is the source of our human predicament. They reveal that our mental machinery, the way we take in the world and make sense out of it, was forged eons ago. Indeed, scientists tell us there has been no appreciable change for thousands of years in either the size of our brain or the way the brain functions. What this means is that almost all of our biological evolution took place long before the times in which we live, and long before we fashioned tools powerful enough to destroy the Earth.

Biologically, we are wired for a world that no longer exists. Our nervous system was formed in a relatively stable environment where only recognition of dramatic changes in our immediate surroundings—a sudden movement, a breaking branch, and unfamiliar noise—spelled the difference between life and death. In that world it paid to filter out the familiar, the commonplace, the slow to change. We learned over a long period of time to take note of certain things and to ignore the rest. It is a way of processing the world that characterizes us still.

What we have inherited is a mental mismatch of gigantic proportions. On the one hand, we are biologically predisposed to concentrate on the transitory, the fleeting, the passing moment; hence our concern for the precarious position of two gray whales trapped in the ice and our interest in the sudden kidnapping of an American overseas. On the other hand, that same biological predisposition discourages us from noticing changes marked by a slower cadence, changes that take years or even decades to be felt; hence our obliviousness to the gradually eroding quality of the air we breathe and our disinterest in commonplace deaths resulting from familiar hazards of contemporary life.

The problem is that most environmental crises jeopardizing the Earth have not announced themselves. They have proceeded at a snail's pace, too slow to signal our alarm, and too fast to adapt to biologically. This is true of deteriorating air and water quality, the greenhouse effect, ozone depletion in the atmosphere, acid rain, vanishing species, the destruction of tropical rain forests, the leeching of nutrients from farmland, urban sprawl, overpopulation, toxification of nuclear wastes, and the decline and fall of quality recreation opportunities and environments. One has to wonder, given the large gap between the pace of biological and cultural evolution, just what will become of us? We are not unlike television's *The Simpsons*, Neanderthal-like creatures struggling to survive in a world of our own making that, nonetheless, seems out of control.

Exacerbating the situation is our age-old habit of simplifying the world in which we live to facilitate its understanding. Since we can't possibly process all incoming stimuli, we have evolved mental sorting mechanisms to filter them. These default positions of the human mind automatically channel our thinking in certain ways.[2] They encourage us to "look for discrepancies in the world, to ignore what is going on constantly, and to respond quickly to sudden shifts, to emergencies, to scarcity, to the immediate and personal, to 'news.'"[3] What they result in are mere caricatures of reality, caricatures that may have worked well enough in bygone times, but that obscure rather than clarify the reality of our present world.

The *Exxon Valdez* incident is a case in point. When the tanker ran aground in March of 1989, discharging millions of gallons of oil into Prince William Sound, the suddenness of it all, the sense of urgency, the emergency, triggered our primeval "fight or flight" response. It was tailor-made for the default systems of the human mind. It was news. It was an environmental crisis that announced itself. If only Captain Hazelwood had not been drinking, we reassured ourselves, everything would have been just fine. Or would it?

What was obscured by the commotion over the *Exxon Valdez* disaster was the reality of a disaster of larger proportions, a disaster that would have been fueled by the *Exxon Valdez* if only it had delivered its cargo to port intact. If the 10,000,000 gallons of oil that despoiled the Gulf of Alaska would have reached the gasoline tanks of America's automobiles, they would have fed into the much larger environmental crisis caused by the increased spewing of carbon dioxide into the atmosphere. That crisis, however, is not one our default systems are designed to register. Indeed, the global warming crisis is all too reminiscent of the "boiled frog" syndrome. Put a frog in a pan of slowly heating water, and the frog will not detect the gradual rise in temperature. It will sit there until it boils to death. Is it possible that we human beings are not much different?

Our caricatures of the world not only misrepresent its complexity, they also lead us to adopt solutions to problems that are themselves caricatures or simplifications of what needs to be done. We are attracted to the promise of a quick fix or magic bullet to cure what ails us when what is really needed is the discipline of a long-term commitment, a long-term program of care, a long-term change in behavior. Health fads come quickly to mind, as do pie-in-the-sky promises of aspiring politicians, as does the naive notion that if Exxon is forced to shell out enough money, everything will be just fine. The prescriptions for our maladies are touted as fast and painless and, to make them palatable, are advertised as being of no significant cost to anyone. Is it any wonder they are seldom of significant value to anyone?

We are, in sum, living in a world of accelerated change where our cultural evolution, our creativity, our inventiveness, our technological know-how, far outpaces our biological evolution, our ability to perceive the consequences of our actions and do something about them. We are increasingly out of step with our own nature.

For most of human history this has not been a significant problem. That's because, "humanity, until very recently, lived almost entirely on its 'income'—solar energy captured by green plants in fields, on farms and in forests by the process of photosynthesis. Now, thanks to cultural evolution, humanity is living largely on its 'capital'—nonrenewable resources."[4] We are living on our savings. One of the principal questions of our time, both for the individual family and for the human family as a whole, is how long can this go on?

As Robert Ornstein and Paul Ehrlich argue persuasively in their book *New World New Mind*, our triumph has not been in adapting to or understanding the natural world, but in transforming that world to make it a more hospitable place for our species. The irony results from the Pogo-like realization that in this triumph we have become our own worst enemy and that, barring a fundamental change in the way we live our lives, we may do ourselves in from within.

If we are to extricate ourselves from this predicament, we must recognize our shortcomings and mend the error of our ways. We human beings are fortunate in this sense because we have the capacity to step outside ourselves, to observe and reflect upon our own circumstances. Self-awareness distinguishes us from other life forms and offers us the possibility of recovery from ill-conceived acts. So it is that the same process of cultural evolution, the same process that is responsible for our major environmental crises, offers us the hope of turning things around. If this same creativity, this same inventiveness, this same technological know-how, can be recast in ways that consciously allow us to change our thinking, then there is still hope for a healthier and happier future for us all. The burning question, of course, is how do we go about doing it?

I have little hope that political leaders will solve our environmental problems. I say this for two reasons. First, politicians are ill-suited to offer leadership in dealing with environmental crises. Crises that evolve over long periods of time, or that demand long periods of commitment to resolve, or that demand long and costly programs of care to mitigate, or that demand significant changes in individual behavior to be done away with, simply do not play well to the voting public. What politician in his or her right mind is going to take a stand on an issue that will principally benefit generations of voters yet unborn? Politicians understand this. They know they must promise immediate results if they are to get elected. They also know that to have any chance of getting reelected they must give the appearance, however false, that everything is progressing on schedule. Successful politicians are masters of the caricature, of presenting the illusion that everything is hunky-dory. It is a skill akin to acting. If recent history teaches us anything about politics, it is how well such acting works on the American public. If it teaches us anything else, it is that, however entertaining, masters of this craft are not likely to get the job done.

Second, and more important, I do not see the major environmental crises confronting the world primarily as public problems. Indeed, the ease with which most of us are inclined to elevate such problems to a global level puzzles me. What we seem to be saying, in effect, is that if only this business or that business would behave responsibly, if only this public agency or that public agency would behave responsibly, if only this country or that country would behave responsibly, if only they . . . they . . . they. . . . Why is it that we always blame someone else?

We are the ones who demand increasing amounts of gasoline for our cars. We are the ones who eat beef raised in Central and South America. We are the ones who spray chlorofluorocarbons into the atmosphere. We are the ones who insist on a bigger house in the suburbs. We are the ones who dream of visiting exotic and faraway places. We are the ones who are never satisfied with what we have. We are the ones who don't know the meaning of enough. We . . . we . . . we are the guilty ones. We need look no farther than into the nearest mirror to see who is really responsible for the state of the world.

We also need look no farther than into the nearest mirror to see who really is in a position to do something about the state of the world, to see who really is in a position to make a difference. Garrett Hardin, in *Filters Against Folly*, admonishes us to "never globalize a problem if it can possibly be dealt with locally."[5] By globalizing problems, we shove them away to some distant authority so we can evade culpability. It's a way of turning our problems into "their" problems. It's a way of getting out from under the burden of responsibility. In the long run, it is failure's way.

What can one individual do to make a difference in this world? There are several things. First, let me be clear about expectations. If my reasoning has been persuasive, if the environmental crises facing us are as monumental as they appear to be, if as much of our evolutionary biology works against the effective resolution of these crises as I think it does, then obviously I can prescribe no simple remedies. On the contrary, all I can prescribe are ways in which an individual can proceed in the context of his or her own life. In doing so, I recognize the cumulative possibilities, the potential synergistic effects of individual actions considered collectively, but I do not dwell on them. To do so would be to obscure the significance of that one individual who, against all odds, seizes the initiative. That individual, whoever she or he may be, is destined to be the real savior of this planet.

As a first step, I recommend the conscious slowing down of our lives. This recommendation may seem illogical in an age when everything else is speeding up, when we feel heightened pressure to keep up with the Joneses, but that is precisely why downshifting is called for. Recall that our "old" minds are programmed to respond quickly to visceral issues, to the rapid unfolding of events. We are designed to be quick on the draw. Yet sudden reactions to surface appearances result in short-lived, poorly chosen courses of action.

"New-mindedness" demands removing ourselves from the immediacy of things, pondering the long-term implications, thinking before we leap. New-mindedness means developing the habit of stepping back from the fray.

The Yellowstone fires of 1988 are illustrative. Remember the hullabaloo over the crackling events? Remember the clamor, the uproar over what ought to be done? Remember the concern for the immediate economic consequences for tourism? Remember the politicians demanding William Penn Mott's resignation as National Park Service Director because his fire policy did not bring a quick solution to that "horrible ecological disaster"?

Fortunately, calmer heads prevailed. Director Mott was not removed from office. The fires gradually were subdued with the assistance of God-given snow, and within a year of the fires' extinction the scientific community had concluded that the fires were not the disaster they were made out to be, that they were likely part of an age-old pattern of periodic burnoff. But what if we had allowed the heat of our emotional or political response to dictate our course of action? Where would those policies have led us in the long run?

Do you remember as well that all the while our national attention was fixed on Yellowstone, all the while our senses were glued to the smoldering imagery, all the while our caricature of the nation's first national park going up in smoke was calling us to action, thousands of miles away to the southeast a national park was really dying, and continues to die, a slow and insidious death? While the Yellowstone fires may have captured our flair for the dramatic, for the theatrical, for "news," the death of Florida's Everglades National Park for the lack of a drink of water goes virtually unnoticed. Old minds can be excused for that oversight. New minds cannot.

Perhaps by slowing down we will be better able to see such unannounced crises and do something about them. Perhaps by slowing down we will begin to appreciate more deeply the backdrop against which our human drama unfolds. Perhaps by slowing down we will be more inclined to give that backdrop its proper care. I know such a slowing down will not come easy. I know it will demand a conscious effort, a disciplining of the mind. I know as well that we have it within ourselves to effect such a slowdown if we so desire.

Second, I recommend scaling down our list of "necessities," of consciously living below our means. This, too, is a tall order. There is an old saying among backpackers that what one doesn't carry in one's head one must carry on one's back. I think the saying can be applied to the general conduct of our lives also. If, indeed, we are living increasingly on our savings, on the Earth's limited nonrenewable natural resources, then it behooves each and every one of us to draw as little as possible on that savings, to carry proportionately more of what is necessary to live full and satisfying lives in our heads. We need to measure the fullness of our lives not by the number of our possessions, but by the quality of our relationships with others and by the degree to which we continue to learn and grow intellectually, spiritually, and emotionally. We need to get the weight off our backs, to lighten our physical loads.

I wonder why this is such a difficult thing to do? Philip Slater, in *The Pursuit of Loneliness*, questions the custom of sacrificing our lives for the accumulation of dead things.[6] Where is the wisdom in expending our life's energy for the sake of things that in and of themselves are lifeless, for things that do not have the capacity to receive or tender affection and care? Where is the meaning in that kind of existence? Wouldn't it be better to recognize such things for what they are, mere fillers for an otherwise hollow life, and turn our attention to issues that really matter?

Third, I recommend stepping down from our anthropocentric pedestals to assume a more humble position among the creations of the Earth. I encourage us to cultivate a lifestyle characterized by reverence and restraint. Just as we are awed by our own accomplishments, by our own ingenuity, we must exercise the humility that allows us to be awed by all that is beyond our making and our ken.

We must never forget that history is written by the "winners." There are histories untold and future histories waiting to be written. Who will write our history? Do we ever consider the possibility that it will be written by somebody or something other than ourselves? Will our history be written by the wind swirling over America's Great Plains, made parched and lifeless by shortsighted agricultural practices? Will our history be written by the silence of a planet made barren by the greenhouse effect? Will our history be written by the cold and emptiness of an Earth no longer fit for life because of a nuclear holocaust? Or will our history be written by our children in celebration of their parents' good sense in mending the error of their ways and in developing new patterns of behaving and relating to the world around them?

If I were asked to propose a tangible first step, an individual initiative that would lead us in the right direction, a revolutionary change in human conduct that would shake the very foundation of contemporary life, something our children could take great pride in writing about someday, I would propose that each and every one of us plant and tend a garden. Gardening, it seems to me, is the quintessential metaphor for all that I have been trying to say.

It is difficult to rush a garden. Planning is called for. Preparation of the soil is necessary. Decisions about what to plant, where to plant, and when to plant must be made. This all takes time. The weather matters. Precipitation is important. Temperature is a concern. One needs to think about the long term, about the relationship between this year's planting and future plantings, about the ability of the soil to rejuvenate itself, about the recycling of wastes.

At the outset, "a person who undertakes to grow a garden at home, by practices that will preserve rather than exploit the economy of the soil, has set his [or her] mind decisively against what is wrong with us."[7] Gardening demands slowing down and stepping back from the fray. It is an antidote to the accelerated pace of contemporary life. It is calm and calculating. It is marked by a slower cadence, a beat in step with the seasons. But gardening is more than that.

Gardening is also taking responsibility for the condition of one's own plot of ground. Gardening, if done organically, is a way of improving a piece of the Earth.[8] Unlike public officials or bureaucrats who talk in generalities from afar about the proper stewardship of the land, gardeners are down on all fours, with rolled up sleeves, actually doing something about it. They are "serving the world's future more directly and surely than any political leader, though they never utter a public word."[9] They are illustrating that responsible husbandry of the Earth's natural resources is carried out by individual citizens in everyday life.

Gardeners are also scaling down their dependency on middlemen for life's sustenance. As Wendell Berry points out, "most of the vegetables necessary for a family of four can be grown on a plot of forty by sixty feet."[10] By reducing the need for the grocer, and the need for a car to get to the grocer, and the need to seek pleasure beyond the bounds of one's own backyard, the gardener is involved directly in reducing the drain on the Earth's bank of limited natural resources, on the Earth's savings. The gardener is relearning the ability to live on the Earth's income, on the solar energy captured by green plants by the process of photosynthesis. The gardener is acquiring knowledge that leads toward greater self-sufficiency, toward a way of living that is based on the wisdom of carrying more in one's head than on one's back. Gardeners are choosing to live below their means.

Finally, gardening is a way of living the connectedness that defines our relationship with the Earth. Gardeners are in step with their own nature, a nature forged in close proximity to things natural, a nature inextricably intertwined with the larger community of life. While delighting in the day-to-day progress of their work and the gradual appearance of the fruits of their labor, gardeners recognize their vulnerability to larger forces—to unexpected droughts, to sudden storms, to drastic changes in temperature. Gardeners are both proud of, and humbled by, what they have accomplished. They are happy with their lot and are aware that things could have turned out otherwise. Gardeners know there are thanks to be given.

Perhaps you are bewildered by this essay? Here we are, after all, confronted by environmental problems of devastating proportions and all I have to offer is the planting of a garden. Where are my slogans, my petitions, my protest songs? Where are my references to civil disobedience? The world is falling apart before our very eyes and I can't even muster a drum roll, a clanging of cymbals, a rally to arms. I should be stirring everyone up, but instead I try to calm us down. I should be inciting us to immediate action, but instead I suggest tending a garden over time. Gardening. Some subversive activity that is. I should be shouting at the top of my lungs for all the world to hear, but instead I lower my voice and speak to you personally about what it is you can do to make a difference in the context of your own life. What's going on here? Why do I behave the way I do?

The future is open-ended. It is history waiting to be written. Whether we human beings will be treated kindly by future historians depends, I think, on the degree to which we begin to act with increasing recognition of our obligations to others, with an increasing sense of humility about our place in the order of things. On an evolutionary scale, we are not so far removed from the animal kingdom. We have strong genetic ties to the past. But we also have the ability to rise above our bonds and dream of worlds unknown. That ability, and our capacity to make such dreams come true, give us cause for hope and fear. The challenge facing our human family is unparalleled. How we will respond to it is a question that is up in the air.

Notes

Chapter 1: In Search of Rescue

1. Watts, A. (1951). *The Wisdom of Insecurity*. New York, NY. Vintage Books.

2. Leitch, W. (1978). Backpacking in 2078. *The Sierra Club Bulletin*, Vol. 3, No. 1, pp. 25-27.

3. For further reading about the no-rescue wilderness idea, see:
McAvoy, L., Dustin, D. (1981). The Right to Risk in Wilderness. *Journal of Forestry*, Vol. 79, No. 3, March, pp. 150-152;
Wagar, J. (1981). Comment on "the Right to Risk in Wilderness." *Journal of Forestry*, Vol. 79, No. 3, March, pp. 152-153;
Allen, S. (1981). Comment: No-Rescue Wilderness—a Risky Proposition. *Journal of Forestry*, Vol. 79, No. 3, March, pp. 153-154;
McAvoy, L., Dustin, D. (1981). The Right to Risk in Wilderness a Rejoinder. *Journal of Forestry*, Vol. 79, No. 5, May, p. 284;
McAvoy, L., Dustin, D. (1983). In Search of Balance: a No-Rescue Wilderness Proposal. *Western Wildlands*, Vol. 9, No. 2, Summer, pp. 2-5;
McAvoy, L., Dustin, D. (1984). No One Will Come. *Backpacker*, Vol. 12, No. 5, September, pp. 60-62, 64-65, 88;
McAvoy, L., Dustin, D., Rankin, J., Frakt, A. (1985).Wilderness and Legal Liability: Guidelines for Resource Managers and Program Leaders. *Journal of Park and Recreation Administration*, Vol. 3, No. 1, Winter, pp. 41-49;
Peterson, D. (1987). Look, Ma, No Hands! Here's What's Wrong with No-Rescue Wilderness. *Parks & Recreation*, Vol. 22, No. 6, June, pp. 39-43, 54.

4. Masters, E. (1962). *Spoon River Anthology*. New York, NY: Collier Books.

Chapter 2: The World According to Gorp

1. Thoreau, H. (1854). *Walden*. Boston, MA: Ticknor & Fields.

2. Twain, M. (1948). *Life on the Mississippi*. New York, NY: Penguin Books.

Chapter 3: The Myth of Comfort

1. Sax, J. (1980). *Mountains Without Handrails.* Ann Arbor, MI: University of Michigan Press.

2. Orwell, G. (1950). *Coming Up for Air.* New York, NY: Harcourt Brace.

3. *Newsweek.* (1983). Battle Over the Wilderness. July 25, p. 28.

4. Orwell, G. (1949). *Nineteen Eighty-Four.* New York, NY: Harcourt Brace Jovanovich.

5. Murchie, G. (1978). *The Seven Mysteries of Life: An Exploration in Science & Philosophy.* Boston, MA: Houghton Mifflin Co.

6. Ibid., p. 484.

7. Steinhoff, W. (1975). *George Orwell and the Origins of 1984.* Ann Arbor, MI: The University of Michigan Press.

8. Learner, L. (1982). *Ascent: The Spiritual and Physical Quest of Willi Unsoeld.* New York, NY: Simon and Schuster.

9. Naisbitt, J. (1982). *Megatrends.* New York, NY: Warner Books.

Chapter 4: The Wilderness Within: Reflections on a 100-Mile Run

1. On July 23, 1988, I set out to run 100 miles across California's Sierra Nevada. I had trained for the Western States 100, an organized run that takes place annually in the Lake Tahoe region of northern California. Because of its increasing popularity, participants in the Western States 100 are determined by lottery. Unfortunately, my name was not drawn. So I decided to run 100 miles on my own. This essay re-creates the psychology of that run. It describes what was going on "in here" while the rest of my body was dealing with "out there." I first presented this essay as a 45-minute talk while running on a treadmill at the Congress for Recreation and Parks in Indianapolis, Indiana, on October 9, 1988.

2. Teale, E. (1954). *The Wilderness World of John Muir.* Boston, MA: Houghton Mifflin.

3. Thoreau, H. (1937). *Walden.* New York, NY: The Modern Library.

4. Heller, J. (1962). *Catch-22.* New York, NY: Dell.

5. Thoreau, H. (1854). *Walden.* Boston, MA: Tichnor & Fields, pp. 81-82.

6. Leonard, G. (1974). *The Ultimate Athlete.* New York, NY: Avon Books.

7. Service, R. (1907). The Quitter. In *The Best of Robert Service.* New York, NY: Dodd, Mead & Company.

8. Navajo chant.

9. Momaday, N. (1968). *House Made of Dawn.* New York, NY: Harper & Row.

10. See McAvoy, L., Dustin, D. (1989). Resurrecting the Frontier. *Trends,* Vol. 26, No. 3, pp. 40-42.

11. Olson, S. (1965). From a speech at the Ninth Biennial Wilderness Conference, San Francisco, CA.

12. Whipple, T. (1930). *Study Out the Land.* Berkeley, CA: University of California Press.

13. Marshall, R. (1937). The Universe of the Wilderness is Vanishing. *Nature Magazine,* April, p. 236.

14. Wolfe, L. (1938). *John of the Mountains: The Unpublished Journals of John Muir.* Madison, WI: The University of Wisconsin Press.

Chapter 5: Inside, Outside, Upside Down: The Grand Canyon as a Learning Laboratory

1. For additional reading about my perspective on "nature's university," see:

Dustin, D. (1980). "Watered Down" Course Work. *Journal of Physical Education and Recreation*, Vol. 51, No. 3, March, pp. 55, 58, 61;

Dustin, D. (1981). A Bear of an Examination. *California Parks & Recreation*, Vol. 37, No. 2, April/May, pp. 25-26;

Dustin, D. (1981).Classroom and Experiential Education. *Improving College and University Teaching*, Vol. 29, No. 4, pp. 166-168;

Dustin, D. (1985). Outdoor Recreation Leadership: The Limits of Responsibility. In *Proceedings of the 6th Annual Intermountain Leisure Symposium*, Logan, Utah: Utah State University, November, pp. 16-17.

Chapter 6: The Incident at "New" Army Pass

1. Upon returning to San Diego, I gathered everyone together for a final debriefing. I said I would always remember this group as the luckiest I ever led, because they had survived my blunders. I also knew that my apologies, however sincere, were not enough to make up for my poor leadership. I had violated a trust. I wrote Kevin a check for $300 to compensate him for the loss of his camera and a coat.

Chapter 7: The Barrenlands

1. For more information about their programs, contact Wilderness Inquiry at 808 14th Ave. SE, Minneapolis, MN 55414-1516: 800-728-0719: or info@wildernessinquiry.org.

2. Back, G., Sir. (1836). *Narrative of the Arctic Land Expedition to the Mouth of the Great Fish River*. London: J. Murray.

3. Venice, as it turned out, had three broken ribs. All things considered, it was a modest price to pay.

4. We never did determine what had hold of me. Several years later, however, after two additional episodes with similar symptoms, I was diagnosed with diverticulosis, a painful, but common malady that comes with age.

5. Olesen, D. (1989). *Cold Nights, Fast Trails*. Minocqua, WI: North-Word Press.

Chapter 8: Fly-Fishing With B. L. Driver

1. Driver, B., Tocher, R. (1970). Toward a Behavioral Interpretation of Recreational Engagements: With Implications for Planning. In *Elements of Outdoor Recreation Planning*. Ann Arbor, MI: University Microfilms, pp. 9-31.

2. Little did we know that this initial get-together in 1992 would culminate in the publication of *Nature and the Human Spirit: Toward an Expanded Land Management Ethic* in 1996 by Venture Publishing, State College, Pennsylvania.

Chapter 9: Coyote Gulch

1. Rich Schreyer died in March of 1991. Those of us who knew Rich cherished him not only for his intellect, which was remarkable, but for his being, which was warm and nurturing. My memory of Rich will always be intertwined with Utah's canyon country, a landscape he dearly loved.

2. Schreyer, R. (1988). The Freedom to Be Human. In D. Dustin (Ed.) *Wilderness in America: Personal Perspectives*. San Diego, CA: San Diego State University's Institute for Leisure Behavior, pp. 15-22.

Chapter 10: Back in the USSR

1. This is a recounting of my sabbatical visit to the Soviet Union in the spring of 1989. I include it here because, for me, it was as much a wilderness journey as any of the others I've written about. Indeed, it was a solitary excursion into the unknown. Much has happened in what was the Soviet Union since I wrote these words. Leningrad is now St. Petersburg, the Baltic States are free again, and Boris Yeltsin is an international household name. There is still the question of how history will ultimately judge Mikhail Gorbachev, and more important, what will become of the new Commonwealth of Independent States. For my part, I am pulling both for him and the future of his motherland.

2. See Dustin, D. (1991). Soviet City Parks. In *Proceedings of the 12th Annual Intermountain Leisure Symposium*. Provo, UT: Brigham Young University, pp. 30-32.

3. See Dustin, D. (1989). Backpacking Sitting Down: Reminiscences from the Great Siberian Railroad. In *Proceedings of the 10th Annual Intermountain Leisure Symposium*. Provo, UT: Brigham Young University, pp. 16-19.

4. See Dustin, D. (1990). Monopolizing the Great Siberian Railroad. In *Proceedings of the 11th Annual Intermountain Leisure Symposium*. Provo, UT: Brigham Young University, pp. 176-179.

5. Hardin, G. (1977). What Marx Missed. In *Managing the Commons*. San Francisco, CA: W. H. Freeman and Company, pp. 3-7.

6. See Dustin, D. (1989). The Legacy of Lake Baikal: Interpretation in the Soviet Union. *Journal of Interpretation*, Vol. 13, No. 4, pp. 4-6.

7. See Dustin, D. (1991). Peace, Leisure, and Recreation. *Parks & Recreation*, Vol. 26, No. 9, September, pp. 102-104.

Chapter 13: Betting On Big Bertha

1. Witt, P. (1993).The Changing Proportions of My Life. In D. Dustin (Ed.) *For the Good of the Order—Administering Academic Programs in Higher Education*. San Diego, CA: San Diego State University's Institute for Leisure Behavior, pp. 115-123.

2. Goodale, T. (1990).On Professing, Publishing, and Sometimes Writing. In D. Dustin (Ed.) *Beyond Promotion and Tenure: On Being a Professor*. San Diego, CA: San Diego State University's Institute for Leisure Behavior, pp. 79-91.

Chapter 14: Time for Pool: The Surprising Way . . .

1. Godbey, G. (1990). On Reading and Professing: Recounting a World of Privilege. In D. Dustin (Ed.) *Beyond Promotion and Tenure: On Being a Professor*. San Diego, CA: San Diego State University's Institute for Leisure Behavior, pp. 63-77.

2. A few years ago, after much deliberation, we added a fourth player into the mix. We settled on a "Border Collie," Jack Harper from the University of Manitoba in Winnipeg. Jack is agreeable enough and he is a gourmet cook. He is also a boyhood chum of Neil Young of Crosby, Stills, Nash, and Young. While we benefit immensely from Jack's friendship and Epicurean talents, he has yet to introduce us to Neil Young.

Chapter 17: Fakahatchee Strand

1. Dustin, D., Wolff, R. (1998). 50 Years of Stewardship: The Ongoing Struggle to Preserve Everglades National Park. *Parks & Recreation*, Vol. 33, No. 2, February, pp. 80-84.

2. See Dustin, D., Barbar, R. (1998). Grand Staircase-Escalante National Monument: The Politics of Environmental Preservation. *Parks & Recreation*, Vol. 33, No. 8, August, pp. 52-57.

3. See Dustin, D. (1999). The Gift. In *Clyde Butcher: Nature's Places of Spiritual Sanctuary*. Ochopee, FL: Window of the Eye, Inc., p. 13.

4. Butcher, C., Butcher, N. (1999). *Clyde Butcher: Nature's Places of Spiritual Sanctuary*. Ochopee, FL: Window of the Eye, Inc., p. 12.

5. Ibid., p. 82.

6. Ibid, p. 27.

7. Ibid., pp. 40-41

8. Shroder, T., Barry, J. (1995). *Seeing the Light/Wilderness and Salvation: A Photographer's Tale*. New York, NY: Random House.

9. Butcher, C., Butcher, N. (1999).

10. Orleans, S. (1998). *The Orchid Thief*. New York, NY: Random House, p. 34.

11. Schroder, T., Barry, J. (1995). pp. 39-40.

Chapter 18: Wasting Away in Boca Grande

1. I met Ingrid Schneider in 1991 at the National Recreation and Park Association (NRPA) Congress in Baltimore, Maryland. Ingrid was among the first master's students in recreation, park, and leisure studies to be honored as a "future scholar" and given a monetary award to attend the NRPA convention. Soon thereafter, she earned a doctorate at Clemson University and began her academic career at Arizona State University. Ingrid is now an Associate Professor and Director of The University of Minnesota's Tourism Center.

Chapter 19: Confessions of a Technological Resistance Fighter

1. Postman, N. (1993). The Loving Resistance Fighter. In *Technopoly.* New York, NY: Vintage Books, pp. 181-199.

2. Postman, N. (1986). *Amusing Ourselves to Death: Public Discourse in the Age of Show Business.* New York, NY: Penguin Books, p. 90.

3. Ibid., p. 6.

4. Robinson, J., Godbey, G. (1997). *Time for Life: The Surprising Ways Americans Use Their Time.* University Park, PA: The Pennsylvania State University Press.

5. Huxley, A. (1969). *Brave New World.* New York, NY: Harper & Row.

6. Postman, N. (1986). p. vii.

Chapter 20: The Professor Who Mistook His Life for a Stat

1. Stokowski, P. (1999). Trophy Hunting in the Shadow of the Castle Keep. *Journal of Leisure Research*, Vol. 31, No. 2, Second Quarter, pp. 189-191.

2. Driver, B. (1970). *Elements of Outdoor Recreation Planning.* Ann Arbor, MI: University Microfilms.

3. Bronowski, J. (1959). *Science and Human Values*. New York, NY: Harper.

4. See Marano, H. (1999). The Power of Play. *Psychology Today*. July/August, pp. 36-40, 68-69.

5. Gleick, J. (1999). *Faster: The Acceleration of Just About Everything*. New York, NY: Pantheon Books.

6. See Nevada Barr's Anna Pigeon mysteries set in national parks throughout the country.

Chapter 22: Remembering Manzanar

1. See Dustin, D. (2002/2003). "Baseball Saved Us": Recreation as Refuge in a World War II Japanese American Prison Camp. *Leisure/Loisir: A Journal of the Canadian Association of Leisure Studies*, Vol. 27, Nos. 1-2, pp. 103-113, for a more detailed account of the role recreation played in the lives of Manzanar's internees.

Chapter 25: Free Spirit

1. In July 2005, I participated in the 33rd edition of RAGBRAI. The route was a more northerly one, and it was considered the fifth easiest in RAGBRAI history. Karla Henderson came off the disabled list, and we added three new members to the "Crazy Goofs." Karla's sister, Sue, joined us, as did our two good friends, Deb Bialeschki and Tom Goodale. I was lulled into training complacency by the prospect of an easy route, and painful cramping in my quadriceps highlighted the first day of the ride. That night in Sheldon, we endured an intense thunderstorm with torrential rain, lightning, and wind gusts of 60 to 70 miles per hour. The second day was capped off by tornado warnings and a night sleeping in the hallways of Estherville High School. As I said, each day of RAGBRAI brings a freshness of its own. Oh, yes, there's one more thing. Five hundred miles later, when the ride ended in Guttenberg, while everyone else was dipping their bicycles' front tires into the Mississippi River, I rode my Crestwood Free Spirit straight to police headquarters and implored the dispatcher on duty to find a good home for it. I guess you could say I finally came to my senses.

Chapter 26: Mapping the Geography of Hope

1. Driver, B. (1988). You Can Go Home Again. In Dustin, D. (Ed.) *Wilderness in America: Personal Perspectives.* San Diego, CA: San Diego State University's Institute for Leisure Behavior, pp. 55-63.

2. See Chapter 8 of Oelschlaeger, M. (1991). *The Idea of Wilderness: From Prehistory to the Age of Ecology* New Haven, CT: Yale University Press.

3. Rockefeller, S., Elder, J. [Eds.] (1992). *Spirit and Nature: Why the Environment Is a Religious Issue: An Interfaith Dialogue.* Boston, MA: Beacon Press.

4. Kaplan, R., Kaplan, S. (1989). *The Experience of Nature: A Psychological Perspective.* Cambridge: Cambridge University Press.

5. Nash, R. (1989). *The Rights of Nature: A History of Environmental Ethics.* Madison, WI: University of Wisconsin Press.

6. See Chapter 8 of Oelschlaeger, M. (1991).

7. Driver, B., Dustin, D., Baltic, T., Elsner, G., Peterson, G. [Eds.] (1996). *Nature and the Human Spirit: Toward an Expanded Land Management Ethic.* State College, PA: Venture Publishing, Inc.

8. Schumacher, E. (1977). *A Guide for the Perplexed.* New York, NY: Harper & Row.

9. Benson, J. (1996). *Wallace Stegner: His Life and Work.* New York, NY: Viking.

10. Cowan, J. (1996). *A Mapmaker's Dream.* Boston, MA: Shambhala Publications, Inc.

11. Bloom, A. (1987). *The Closing of the American Mind.* New York, NY: Simon & Schuster.

12. Nash, R. (1982). *Wilderness and the American Mind.* 3rd Edition. New Haven, CT: Yale University Press.

13. Patterson, M., Watson, A., Williams, D., Roggenbuck, J. (1998). An Hermeneutic Approach to Studying the Nature of Wilderness Experiences. *Journal of Leisure Research*, Vol. 30, No. 4, pp. 423-452.

Chapter 27: Were You Ever Out in the Great Alone?

1. Olson, S. (1958). "The Whistle." In *Listening Point*. Minneapolis, MN: The University of Minnesota Press, p. 147.

2. Olson, S. (1958). *Listening Point*. Minneapolis, MN: The University of Minnesota Press.

3. Ibid., p. 153.

4. McKibben, W. (1989). *The End of Nature*. New York, NY: Random House, Inc.

5. McKibben, W. (2003). *Enough: Staying Human in an Engineered Age*. New York, NY: Henry Holt and Company.

6. Berry, W. (2003). From a letter to Bill McKibben.

7. Ibid.

8. Whipple, T. (1943). *Study Out the Land*. Berkeley, CA: University of California Press, p. 65.

9. Benson, J. (1996). *Wallace Stegner: His Life and Work*. New York, NY: Viking.

10. McKibben, W. (2003). p. 70.

11. Diamond, J. (2005). *Collapse: How Societies Choose to Fail or Succeed*. New York, NY: Viking.

12. McKibben, (2003). p. 216.

13. Ibid., p. 217.

14. Ibid.

15. Nash, R. (2002). Power of the Wild. *New Scientist*, Vol.173, No. 2336, March, pp. 42-45.

16. Leopold, A. (1949). *A Sand County Almanac*. New York, NY: Oxford University Press.

17. Nash, R. (2001). *Wilderness and the American Mind*. 4th Edition. New Haven, CT: The Yale University Press.

18. McAvoy, L., Dustin, D. (1980). The Right to Risk in Wilderness. *Journal of Forestry*, Vol. 79, No. 3, March, pp. 150-152.

19. Leitch, W. (1978). Backpacking in 2078. *The Sierra Club Bulletin*, Vol. 3, No. 1, pp. 25-27.

20. Dustin, D., McAvoy, L. (2000). Of What Avail Are Forty Freedoms? The Significance of Wilderness in the 21st Century. *International Journal of Wilderness*, Vol. 6, No. 2, p. 25.

21. Ibid., p. 26.

22. Service, R. (1907). The Shooting of Dan McGrew. In *The Best of Robert Service*. New York, NY: Dodd, Mead & Company.

Chapter 28: Like Light Passing Through a Prism

1. Significant portions of this essay are taken verbatim from an essay by H. G. Wells published in *Living Philosophies: A Series of Intimate Credos*, a book edited by Albert Einstein in 1931. To a considerable extent, it is as if H. G. Wells were talking.

2. See Mannell, R. (1984). Personality in Leisure Theory: The Self as Entertainment Construct. *Society and Leisure*, Vol. 7, pp. 229-240.

3. See Henderson, K. (1991). *Dimensions of Choice: A Qualitative Approach to Recreation, Parks, and Leisure Research*. State College, PA: Venture Publishing, Inc.

4. See Chapter 6 of Wells, H. (1931). In *Living Philosophies: A Series of Intimate Credos*. New York, NY: Simon and Schuster, Inc., pp. 79-92.

Chapter 29: Gardening as a Subversive Activity

1. From Sagan, C. (1977). *The Dragons of Eden: Speculation on the Evolution of Human Intelligence.* New York, NY: Random House.

2. Ornstein, R., Ehrlich, P. (1989). *New World New Mind: Moving Toward Conscious Evolution.* New York, NY: Doubleday.

3. Ibid., p. 91.

4. Ibid., p. 45.

5. Hardin, G. (1985). *Filters Against Folly: How to Survive Despite Economists, Ecologists, and the Merely Eloquent.* New York, NY: Viking.

6. Slater, P. (1970). *The Pursuit of Loneliness—American Culture at the Breaking Point.* Boston, MA: Beacon Press.

7. Berry, W. (1970). *A Continuous Harmony.* San Diego, CA: Harcourt Brace Jovanovich, Publishers.

8. Ibid., p. 82.

9. Ibid., p. 80.

10. Ibid., p. 82.

About the Author

Daniel L. Dustin is Professor and Chair of the Department of Parks, Recreation and Tourism in the College of Health at the University of Utah. He served previously as Frost Professor and Chair of the Department of Health, Physical Education and Recreation at Florida International University in Miami and as Professor and Chair of the Department of Recreation, Parks and Tourism at San Diego State University. Dr. Dustin's academic interests center on environmental stewardship and the moral and ethical bases for leisure and recreation activity preferences and behaviors. A past president of the Society of Park and Recreation Educators (SPRE) and the Academy of Leisure Sciences, he is a recipient of the National Recreation and Park Association's Literary Award. In 1994 he was named an "honorary lifetime member" of the California Park Rangers Association for his contributions to the literature of outdoor recreation planning and policy, and in 2001 he received the SPRE Distinguished Colleague Award for a lifetime of achievement. *Wilderness in America: Personal Perspectives*; *Beyond Promotion and Tenure: On Being a Professor*; *For the Good of the Order: Administering Academic Programs in Higher Education*; *Stewards of Access/Custodians of Choice: A Philosophical Foundation for the Park and Recreation Profession*; and *Nature and the Human Spirit: Toward an Expanded Land Management Ethic* are among his other works as a contributing author and editor. In addition to his administrative duties, Dr. Dustin teaches a variety of courses in recreation, park, and leisure studies. In his free time, he enjoys backpacking, fly-fishing, and bicycling.